DIE HERRSCHAFT DER MINDERWERTIGEN/
THE RULE OF THE INFERIOUR

Edgar Julius Jung

Edited, Translated
and with an Introduction by
Alexander Jacob

Volume II

Part II (People, Society, State, Laws) Chapters VII-XVI
Part IV (Economics)
Part VI (Foreign Policy) Chapters V, VIII-X, XII

Studies in German Thought and History
Volume 15b

The Edwin Mellen Press
Lewiston/Queenston/Lampeter

Library of Congress Cataloging-in-Publication Data

Jung, Edgar J. (Edgar Julius), 1894-1934.
   [Herrschaft der Minderwertigen, ihr Zerfall und ihre Ablösung.
English]
   The Rule of the inferiour / Edgar Julius Jung ; edited, translated
and with an introduction by Alexander Jacob.
       p.   cm. -- (Studies in German thought and history ; v.
15a-15b)
   Includes bibliographical references and index.
   ISBN 0-7734-9054-X (v. 1). -- ISBN 0-7734-9056-6 (v. 2)
   1. State, The. 2. National socialism. I. Jacob, A. (Alexander)
II. Title. III. Series.
JC263.J813 1994
320.1'01--dc20   94-26054
                                              CIP

This is volume 15b in the continuing series
Studies in German Thought and History
Volume 15b ISBN 0-7734-9056-6
SGTH Series ISBN 0-88946-351-4

A CIP catalog record for this book is available from the British Library.

Copyright © 1995 The Edwin Mellen Press

The Edwin Mellen Press   The Edwin Mellen Press
Box 450   Box 67
Lewiston, New York   Queenston, Ontario
USA 14092-0450   CANADA L0S 1L0

The Edwin Mellen Press, Ltd.
Lampeter, Dyfed, Wales
UNITED KINGDOM SA48 7DY

Printed in the United States of America

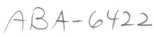

CONTENTS

Volume I

Volume II

THE RULE OF THE INFERIOUR

ITS DISINTEGRATION AND REMOVAL
THROUGH A NEW REICH

(continued)

Note on the Translation

I have in my translation omitted the sub-headings within each chapter which Jung provides as marginal notes to his text. Likewise, the 'Contents' to the present edition do not contain an enumeration of these sub-headings, as the 'Contents' provided in the original edition do. Throughout my edition, my annotations to the text are presented in box-brackets to distinguish them from Jung's own.

Part Two

People, Society, State, Laws (continued)
Chs. VII-XVI

VII

The legal philosophical foundations
of Liberalism and democracy

Before the transition from the observation of society to the description of the political life of the present, it seems required to throw a brief glance at the legal philosophical foundations on which individualism has built up the present-day state.

The essential result of the political philosophical investigation already lies at hand: that the present-day state does without the social substructure. The shattering of society and the presumption of the state are the real characteristics of the state sphere, and all renewal has therefore to begin with the building up of society and the dismantling of the state. This knowledge must be placed in front of the legal philosophical treatise because it alone guarantees the possibility of seeing Liberalism and democracy in a clear light. So long as Liberalism and democracy, without the great connection with the social scientific, are judged from only the present-day state, so long must every judgement remain inadequate.

It is now maintained that there is a non-individualistic Liberalism as well as an organic democracy. Switzerland is always pointed to as evidence of the latter opinion and at the same time it is stressed that this original German state formation contradicts the saying that democracy is something western and un-German. This objection is not sound; it proves rather the spirit of this book which lets the 'people' struggle against the masses, personality against equality. Genuine democracy, i.e., the rule of the *volonté générale* conceived of only metaphysically, is the highest state ideal; it cannot be thought of apart from the organic world-picture. In this sense, democracy is perfected Conservatism. If the rule of the people, to be sure, is conceived of as a mechanical majority system, then an exposition of democracy begins which has declared war on this book to the knife. The democracy of Switzerland is even based on the fact of its narrow space and, therewith, on the native experience, on the other hand on the rootedness in the soil and the vitality of the society. It must be repeated that democracy without a social life of its own is an impossibility.

Now there is supposed to be, however, a non-individualistic Liberalism. Of this opinion is L. von Wiese[1], and, in addition, even representatives of the organic social- and state conception are summoned as chief witnesses. Thus Lagarde[2] thinks that Liberal is not really synonymous with friend of freedom. He complains of Liberalism that it denies Nature and history, and exhausts itself in educational superstitions. It "murders, even if without intending it, conscience and the capicities of grasping life as a whole and kills thereby the personality". Lagarde believes at the same time in a genuine German individualism. The agreement revealing itself here between Lagarde and the author does not prevent the indication of differences of conceptual connotation. Even this book always emphasizes that individualism leads to collectivism, to the masses, and destroys personality. Only, it does not distinguish between genuine and false individualism, precisely so little as it recognizes a genuine and a false Liberalism. The over-

[1] "Liberalismus und Demokratie in ihren Zusammenhängen und Gegensätzen", *Zeitschrift für Politik*, Bd.9.
[2] [Paul de Lagarde], *Deutsche Schriften*, I, ["Der graue Internationale", *Deutsche Schriften*, Göttingen, 1886, p.400].

estimation of the individual cannot even be moderated at any chosen point, as many Liberals wish. World-views demand relentless logicality, and history is always logical. One who transforms moral freedom - and that is that often sworn upon "genuine German individualism" - into a political one thereby unstoppably traverses the way to anarchy. One who would like to leap out of time-conditioned lack of freedom and therefore demands the blasting of decrepit houses, may not make social freedom an eternally valid principle and the revolution to a lasting condition. Thus Liberalism plainly becomes a hostile principle for all who wish to end the lasting revolution of the West. No glossings over are allowed any more, no talk of a moderate, a misunderstood, an original, or a renewed Liberalism. Oswald Spengler[3] speaks, therefore, with bitterness of Liberalism which is a matter for ninnies. Möller van den Bruck[4] passes the devastating judgement: "In Liberalism the nations perish". This legal philosophical truth must be expressed, without damage being done in any way to the efforts of politicians who call themselves Liberal; quite apart from the fact that the latter mostly do not know what the Liberalism innoculated into them and considered highly by them really is.

Liberalism is the idea of political progress, realized in the freedom and the culture of the individual man. For that reason already a contradiction in itself, because a shift of striving for moral freedom into the political this-world is present. For, all followers of Liberalism are agreed on this that the individual is the highest value, that the microcosmic life stands in the central point of all feeling and thought, that therefore macrocosmic feeling is at best derived and transmitted from individual. All other values, therefore even the community, are necessarily subordinated to the higher worth of the individual. Legal and state order only have significance for the individualist: to grant and maintain for the

---

[3] *Preußentum und Sozialismus*, [Kap.II, "Sozialismus als Lebensform", Kap.III, "Engländer und Preußen"].

[4] *Das dritte Reich*, München, Ringverlag, [Kap.III: "Liberal", Sec.XI].

individual that amount of freedom in which he can feel morally fulfilled. The conceptual connotation of individualism customary in Liberal circles is deliberately chosen here. That it is based on false presuppositions has already been declared. For, the moral fulfilment of the individual is not at all dependent on the political form of his environment, thus, on external powers in general; but the highest morality of the individual lies, then, precisely in his self-sacrifice for the sake of higher values. - Individualism exhibits only two directions, on whose relation to each another much has been contested. In the sense of party, it is differentiated into left- and right Liberalism. Only one difference of the shading should be characterised therewith, whose removal was always striven for in the Liberal camp and demanded even today. Through closer investigation, however, oppositions of a not unessential sort strike one: Thus the left-Liberals believe in the rule of the majority, the right Liberals in the constitional form of the state. The difference between democracy and monarchy plays thereby only a catchword role. There are however monarchical democrats (England and Norway). Even so different is the attitude to the question: state administration or self-administration. The democratic wing tends to the former, the Liberal to the latter. Finally, the attitude to the idea of the nation is different: democracy shows a preference for cosmopolitanism, Liberalism for imperialism (the twin sons of individualism already come into view above). Legal philosophically, these differences are easily explicable. They are conceived at best by the sentence of Radbruch,[5] that democracy ascribes to the individual man only a finite worth, Liberalism, however, an infinite one. For democracy, the worth of the individual is multiplicable and thereby conditioned by the absolutism of the majority, whereas the infinite individual worth of Liberalism is even by conceptual necessity unsurpassable on account of the value-content of such a great majority. Liberalism, therefore, pays homage to the division of powers doctrine of

---

[5] [Gustav Radbruch (1878-1949)] *Grundzüge der Rechtsphilosophie*, Leipzig, Verlag Quelle & Meyer, [1914].

Montesquieu, whose aim it is to play out the two candidates to absolutism, the monarch and the majority, against each other, in favour of the unharmed right to freedom of the individual as the *tertius gaudens*.[6] Democracy discards, with Rousseau, the division of powers because it strives to combat the absolutism of the majority therewith. The Liberal freedom is predominantly freedom from the state, the democratic freedom predominantly participation in the state; the freedom from the state is, for Liberalism, undisturbed pre-state freedom, for democracy freedom granted by the state. Therefore Liberalism ends logically in anarchy, while the most radical form of democracy is Socialism.

In the legal philosophical doctrine, therefore, the two camps of individualism appear very far removed from each other. In the world of political actualities, however, they approach each other significantly. We can ignore the investigation whether the party groupings in Germany coincide in any way with the legal philosophical camps outlined here. Apparently, this is not the case because, behind the party ideologies, economic goals are hidden. In fact, however, the democratic orientation of individualism has totally triumphed. Not only in the realisation of its political idea, but also purely intellectually through the impact with which it transferred this into the entire public life. But this victory requires explanation. The question must therefore be further raised and answered whether finally the victory of democracy is not the natural result of individualism; whether therefore individualism must not always end in democracy and the right Liberalism aspire for an unattainable goal.

Already the French Revolution developed democracy as a hasty result. Constitutionalism remained only a transitional phase. Montesquieu's division of powers soon came to an end. Equality triumphed over freedom, and in this sentence lies contained the logical reason why Liberalism must never be followed by freedom but by the absolutism of the majority. Individualism develops by

---

[6] [the third beneficiary].

natural necessity the doctrine of equality. Where it did not penetrate (in England), that was only because the shattering of society was not fully accomplished. The untouched pre-state freedom of Radbruch is in fact untouched social life. Where, however, the demand for equality attains victory, the latter is destroyed. The Liberalism then preaching freedom from the state may imagine such only through the means of the state delegation. Thus it comes about that even right Liberalism in Germany is, in general, disposed to a united state and rejects the federalistic system, the form of true independence.

Even the fate of the constitutionalism founded by Bismarck was predetermined to and had to lead to democracy. The great Chancellor suspected this danger and spoke once of the fact that Socialism would be less dangerous than the "poison" of Liberalism. To be sure, he could not foresee at that time that Socialism would abandon the relatively conservative paths of a Lasalle and a worker's party, in order to become an appendage and a storming-party of the capitalistic left Liberal metropolitan press. In constitutionalism, state leader and popular representation are found in a swaying balance, in a condition which tends in the steady position of rest to one or the other side. So long, that is, as state represents the principle of all-powerfulness, so long will every power standing in competition strive for this all-powerfulness. The supervising parliament demands participation, and participation the sole possession of power. That is a process which is understandable. Thus the division of powers protecting the individual, the minority, gets lost. The true political freedom of the individual would be founded in a legal circle which lies outside the reach of the state. "If the French Revolution[7] had not provided the sham concept of human rights but of corporate body rights resting in reality", then the basic idea of Montesquieu would perhaps have been rescuable. But individualism must logically reject community rights and shatter the ranked society. Consequently, there remains no other way to the

---

[7] Heinz Brauweiler, *Berufstand und Staat[: Betrachtungen über eine neuständische Verfassung des deutschen Staates]*, Berlin, Ringverlag, [1925].

guarantee of the rights of the individual but the conquest of the all-powerful state. For, it alone can still create, through self-limitation of the absolute rule of the majority (in the form of basic rights) certain circles of individual human freedom. The freedom that was politically present already collapsed into the "police state", which is to be thought of legal philosophically as individualistic. Consequently, freedom from the state existed only for those who took possession of the state and made it serviceable to their goals. That is the way of democracy. One who does not participate in the state power is helplessly ruined.

Thus the result is: in the individualistic state, that legal philosophically founded ideal of the infinite worth of the individual, is not to be realized. Individualism forbids to itself the carrying out of its idea. That Liberal realm of ideas bears the law of sociological illogicality in itself. For, the natural necessity of social life together does not allow the aspired-for unrestricted freedom. Once again, the law that inner freedom can be accompanied only by external limitation and external freedom by inner limitation, finds a confirmation; the two alongside each other are irreconcilable.

Thus the triumphal procession of democracy was unstoppable. Mass democracy remains even the form of logically developed individualism. Liberalism is put down national politically: in a world-view way it has triumphed. This ascertainment has nothing to do with the observation of political parties. It would be false to equate the spirit of a certain party with the spirit of the present-day individualistic society. It would also be topsy-turvy to judge the world-view of men according to their party membership. "For they do not know what they do". It is the already described individualistic man who, disregarding his party membership, has either striven for or made possible the present-day state. Striven for, insofar as he belongs to the small, democratic group which sees in the western state the fulfilment of its wishes, and wants to be able to receive it in this form and struggles against every change. The others - and those are the predominant majority - indeed reject it (in spite of the "ground of facts"), and yet they have made it possible because they themselves were enslaved to individualistic thought and therefore did not raise the inner force to set against that small group who deliberately developed and realised their ideal a similarly logical realm of ideas. The intellectual-spiritual objectivity of a certain age (insofar as there is a spirit of the age) also takes care to draw under its influence the groups who represent programatically another orientation than the one ruling at the moment. The Liberal men live today in all parties; there is none who is free of Liberal thought. One, therefore, who would like to revitalise Liberalism wants to carry coals to Newcastle. Indeed, in a deeper sense, the party itself is nothing else but the form of association for Liberal men.

VIII

The true face of the party

The individualistic and the Liberal man are one. The concept of individualism means only the philosophical root of that which in politics is called Liberalism. The original representative of Liberalism is the liberal-minded city man, characterised by the educational ideas of humanism. He represents money as opposed to landed property. He places the demand for freedom against binding, the this-worldly belief against the other-worldly religion, the utilitarian state against the divinely felt order.

Through the parliament, the Liberal man exerts mastery over the state. In the age of early parliamentarianism, the Christian world-view operated, to be sure, not with mediaeval power, but still in a life-forming manner. The longing for social justice still flowed from religious depths; society was still, if not organized according to orders, still led according to notables. It still possessed a common foundation of value. There was a ruling stratum whose leadership was socially recognized and therefore also tacitly tolerated in the political life. The early parliaments therefore reveal - even in oppositions of creed and many others - a uniform world-view direction. The reciprocity in this popular representation is more of a pragmatic nature (Hellpach); the goal of dedicated and useful state leadership common; the debate is the means of becoming clear on the best way to the commonweal. The parliament is essentially a component of the state itself and tolerates, accordingly, in its ranks no hostility to the state. Parliamentary parties which deny the state are a contradiction in themselves, and where they emerge are signs of disintegration and the twilight of the parliament. The decisive role falls in the case of early parliamentarianism not on the party, but on the faction. Around leading personalities of the parliament, random battle-communities form themselves in which entry and exit are the order of the day. The change of party (faction) is not yet considered, as it is today, as a lack of strength of character. "Thus this political form is characterised as a 'transitional' political life- style of a period of imperfect rationalism. - and even social-historically the parliamentary system with its "parties" of notables lies between the ages: between the pitiable end of the old society of orders and the weak beginning of the new class society" (Marr).[8]

With urbanization, the rise of mass parties changes the picture. The emphasis moves from the faction to the party, from the faction leader to the party leadership. The parliament becomes an agreement machine on arrangements which the party "big-wigs" have made in the quiet small chamber. For the purpose of mass propaganda, the party ideology is hardened, the utilitarian standpoint shamefully concealed. And yet the individualistic forces which press towards mastery over the state and in the state are more utility-conscious than ever. The longing of the people for genuine leadership however demands the masking of the utilitarian instinct. On the other hand, parties will frequently appeal openly to the utilitarian instinct of the masses. Thus arises the present-day condition that the "world-view parties" frantically strive for the programme at the same time as the economic parties gain in following. Party and class stand still in an undecided

---

[8] [Heinz Marr (1876-1940), author of *Klasse und Partei in der modernen Demokratie*, Frankfurt am Main: Englert und Schlosser, 1925; *Proletarisches Verlangen: ein Beitrag zur Psychologie der Massen*, Jena: E. Diederichs, 1921].

battle against each other. The small intellectual theoretical-work of the world-view parties is now not directed by the intention of finding out the truth. This way could, otherwise, lead to a vantage point which reveals one's own party on the false way. The revival of the party ideology is rather attempted only in order to rescue the party from collapse: in order not to lose the voters who are employed for the attainment of the utilitarian goals. One cannot yet, even from any internal or external reasons, decide for pure class politics. The way from the party to the class is however inevitable: with the increase of materialistic thought, the Liberal man boldly and courageously throws away the cloak of a moral world- view from himself and announces, even freed from every "shame", utility as the essential core of all social life.

If the parties are reservoirs of similar interests, it is not maintained thereby that these interests are the same as those of the voter. This occurs approximately only in a class party which characterises itself openly as a workers', middle-class, or peasants' party. As a rule they lead a secret existence and misuse the voter for themselves by appealing to his feelings. In fact, the party is a private union for the exploitation of society. While all true statescraft and state philosophy works for the purpose of forming the state independent of interests and financial powers, the essence of mechanistic democracy is precisely the opposite effort. Where no organic, soil-bound community, no organization corresponding to the real social life, is present any longer, the task of organizing the detached individuals artificially for political ends falls to those who have in their hands the means of power for such organisatory activity. Inorganic masses are always ruled by money. "Crowds of men who come together only for voting, are in general not capable of representation" (Constantin Frantz). The state power thus passes into the hands of the possessor of money. The party becomes a "private undertaking for the collection of votes".[9] The greater the means of propaganda, the higher the number

---

[9] Arthur Mahraun, *Das Jungdeutsche Manifest[: Volk gegen Kast und Geldsicherung des Friedens durch Neubau der Staaten]* , Berlin, Jungdeutscher Verlag, 1927, [V. Abschnitt, 'Die parteiistische

of votes. The *Young German Manifesto* rightly points to the fact that hostile states which employ corresponding financial means and find appropriate obscurantists are in the position to exert a corresponding influence on any state through the parliament. In fact, the French have attempted this procedure in the election in the Saar area, and even Russia misuses German Communists for Russian nationalistic purposes.

The collection of votes happens in the same way in which the businessman seeks purchasers for a ware: through advertisement. The one who cries loudest wins; one who deals most lovingly with the lowest instincts captures their owner. The party disposes of the press, whips, and other means of propaganda. With their help, the public, that is, the voter, is made receptive for the viewpoints with which the interest groups standing behind the party intend to capture the ballot of the voter. The party programme thus plays the role of decoy. The true aims of the party are hidden and do not have anything to do with the voter. However, after a successful election, the entire competence of the party press is employed to bridge over the gap between election promises and the later, practical, politics of the party. If this succeeds as a rule, the voter must rejoice in complete intellectual enslavement. The voter is concerned only with questions which lie close to his own heart. He is almost always an apolitical man, mostly without expert knowledge and seldom endowed with a feeling of responsibility for the whole. He is insufficiently instructed on the condition of public affairs. In the final analysis, he demands support. Consequently, he takes up the world-views of the press regularly accessible to him and believes, after a certain time, that this opinion has not flowed into him from his paper, that rather he himself has conceived it. This is the first self-deception which he gives himself up to. In the age of the rule of the understanding, he succumbs to understanding-oriented persuasion so much the

Demokratie', p.64. Arthur Mahraun (1890-1950), a conservative anti-parliamentarian thinker, founded the Young German Order "to mould the 'esprit de corps' of the battling army in a civil form". The *Young German Manifesto* was designed to create a social state of the people which should be built up on the Führer- and community-principle].

more easily since no intellectual restraints spur him to criticism. Now comes the election. The same group of men who have worked on the voter with their press compete for the mandate. Persuasion alone would not lead here to the goal: still another influence must be effected on the emotional world of the voter. This occurs in the following manner. The election candidate explains cheerfully that he feels himself to be only the representative of his voters, who would have to make the decision on the fate of the state as a self-determining people. He therefore lets himself bring forward his opinions and ask them for a comment. What is brought forward is naturally the realm of ideas which was already for a long time suggested to the voter through the press. He sees to his astonishment or to his joy that the election candidate fully shares his, the voter's, view. Flattered to the utmost in his vanity, he grants enthusiastic agreement - to the man of his trust. That is the second self-deception which the voter falls victim to. Thus the age of the rule of the understanding which has seized the inner certainty of the man deceives him with the help of the tendency to self-deception which has grown overpowering. The individual has indeed become free, but spiritually enslaved. He boasts of his liberation from God and falls to the seducer of the people as well as to the money in his hands.

Certainly, there are also parties which, lacking financial means, compete through voluntary sacrifice of party members. Does this say anything against the money-ruled system of the party? This circumstance is rather only a proof of the fact that a significant number of pitiable captives believe in the "ideal" of the party. But which party leader reckoned with the stupidity of the voter! Not only of the voter of other parties - a Social Democratic leader maintained on the party day in Heidelberg in 1925 that the election success of the German Nationalists was based on the lack of understanding of the masses - but also of those of his own. By and large, thus, the possession of means of propaganda decides on the success of the party. What would a party be without the press and without the conference activity! One can talk the masses into buying a remedy for corns which possesses a production value of five pennies for a pound. Why should they not fall for high-sounding phrases and enticing promises, behind which empty-heads and liars stand?

The list system completes the enslavement of the masses and the triumph of the party leader. Usually the election plan is offered for approval to the money-providing groups or even to those which dispose of a certain number of votes by virtue of the propaganda apparatus, which they can set into activity as the leader of a union. The prepared list is then forced on the voter. He may sacrifice a free Sunday in order to confirm the election already carried out by the interest groups. Obviously, one also sets the new "man of the people" before his voter; he then pours the flood of his flattery speech over the harmless sacrifice. Finally, the people have elected their "representative", who can be euphemistically called, here and there, also a leader. The appointment already undertaken by the party is followed by the bye-election.

The true leader however grows from the social life, from the developed binding with those led by him. He is their leader in the daily life and not in a parliamentary committee, in the pursuit of his private business, or in an otherwise gay parliamentary life which he leades in the capital. If the representative has become a professional parliamentarian, and the insurance of the seat for life has reached the parliamentary list, then he can afford the complete withdrawal from the people who have "elected" him. He now knows the rank and file by whom parliament is conducted. He is, so to speak, the "stock exchange man" of the "high house". His own profit or those of his party become a goal in itself for him, the destruction of the neighbouring party gives him thrills of joy which brighten his care-ridden life. - Now, precisely modern democracy is praised as the means to the selection of a leader. The experiences made, however, prove the opposite. Political science has always ascertained this: among many others, also Kelsen,[10]

---

[10] "Vom Wesen und Wert der Demokratie", *Archiv für Sozialwissenschaft*, Bd.47 [1920-21, pp.50-85; cf. p.63n. below].

James Bryce,[11] and Karl Schmitt.[12] Voices of this sort are frequent, but, naturally, they resound unheard. For, parties are concerned only of their advantage and not of the state's.

The rulers of the parties are mostly mediocre, in no way unclever, but petty bourgeois, very seldom heads disposed in a statesmanly way. They are professional "dealers" (Georg Steinhausen)[13] or, as Jakob Burckhardt calls them, "strivers who consume all modern states to the last mark". In the large parties the demagogue triumphs, in the small the intriguer. The one who has in his hands connections with the money-providers, the strings to certain power groups, the apparatus of the party bureaucrats, rules the party. For, the dependence of the party on party bureaucracy is becoming increasingly stronger. The party bureaucrat holds the few friends of the regular party circle together who must, as the yeast, raise up the big loaf of bread which is baked during the election. The power of social democracy is based for the most part on the tightly organised party bureaucracy, on the enormously ramified fodder-trough economics which is carried out in the party. Party today means, for thousands of men, dwelling, clothing, and food for oneself and for one's family. They combat basically neither for the state nor for the party, but for their own pathetic existence.

Thus it becomes increasingly more apparent that the innermost essence of the party is determined by the system of representation. Just as the commercial representative, less pledged inwardly to his profession than to his gift of the gab, penetrates into the ranks of the consumers, so the political representative between the people and the government. Representation of interests is the magic catchword of a commercial age. A straight line leads from the business "leaders", and from

[11] [James, Viscount Bryce], *Modern Democracies*, Vol.III [London: Macmillan, 1921, 2 vols, especially Part III, Ch.LXXVI: 'Leadership in democracies'].

[12] *Hochland*, June issue, 1926.

[13] [Georg Steinhausen (1866-1933), cultural and social historian, author of *Der Kaufmann in der deutschen Vergangenheit*, Leipzig, 1899, *Die deutsche Stände in Einzeldarstellungen*, Jena, 1924, *Der politische Niedergang Deutschlands in seinen tieferen Ursachen*, Osterwieck am Harz, 1927].

the general secretaries, to the lawyer, the born party man, and the representative. Even as a statesman, Poincaré[14] remained a lawyer and a syndic. These sort of men live on representation, they represent to the end of their life everything which one entrusts to them; only not their own conviction which they have already a long time ago lost, or change by the day. The true statesman however is not a representative, in this sense, not even a representative, of his own people. He knows no division between himself and his people: he and his people are one.

The representative lives on persuasion, in the political life on demagogy. One who flatters the mass instincts - vanity - has won. No limit is therefore drawn to competition. The unscrupulous demogogy wins the victory therein. There is no limit at the bottom. Ever filthier characteristics of the human soul are discovered which are usable for business. The means of "selection of a leader" is agility of eloquence. Supposing that there were men suited for state leadership, outstanding, and selfless, but without the gift of the gab: then, as things stand today, they would be excluded from the political life. The emptiest prattler strikes down the most intellectual head; the inferiour can unsaddle with unscrupulous jangling of words the one who does not want to follow on such a path. The gift of the gab is indeed a temptation rather than a grace. The demagogue is spiritually bound to no creative activity. He earns, like the business representative, his money with the wares for which precisely he travels. He is intoxicated with himself when he hears himself prattle. What and for whom is to him a matter of indifference. Working for a party means to him injuring other parties. No lie is too low, no slander too common, no opinion too stupid, in order to serve this exalted goal. The more unscrupulously he agitates, the more the party praises him for his "loyalty". On his 60th birthday, the party executive committee organises for him a wet evening of homage, where, under alcoholic tears of emotion, his selfless dedication to the

[14] [Raymond Poincaré (1860-1934), President of the Third Republic during the first World War, trained as a lawyer at the University of Paris].

party is praised. The people however feels the filth of the election battle as obvious. Christian ethics and German character are forgotten. The loathsome flattery of the masses is the essence of all democracies going down. Spengler says on this: "The right to self-determination of the masses is a polite form of speech; in fact, with every universal-inorganic right to vote, the original sense of the election has in generally very soon ceased. The more basically the developed organisations of the orders and the professions are politically dissolved, and the more formless, the more helpless, the voting masses become, the more unconditionally are they delivered to the new powers, the party leaderships, which dictate their will to the crowd with all the means of intellectual pressure, fight out the battle for the rule among themselves with methods of which the crowd finally neither perceives nor understands anything, and which raise the public opinion merely as a self-forged weapon against one another. - We know the beginnings from the Athens of 400 B.C., the end in the frightful measures in the Rome of Caesar and Cicero. It is as everywhere: the elections have turned, from an appointment of state representatives, into a battle between party candidates. But therewith the arena is formed in which money enters and indeed since the time of Zama with enormous increase of dimensions. - But it is, nevertheless, in a deeper sense, false to speak of corruption. It is not the degeneration of morality, it is morality itself, that of mature democracy, which assumes such forms with ominous necessity. - Within a dictatorship of money, however, the work of money cannot be characterized as a decay".[15]

Even Heinz Marr speaks of the patronage party which has entered in place of the party of notables. In the democracy of notables, the political formation of the will was carried out from the bottom to the top, from the free country to the free representative. Today, the political formation of the will proceeds from the top to the bottom: from the party oligarchy which is there first of all, down to all

---

[15] [Spengler, *Der Untergang des Abendlandes*, Kap.IV, 'Der Staat', Abschnitt C: 'Philosophie der Politik'].

the others, finally however to the unorganised, unfree party masses. They are held together by the army of beneficiaries. Patronage is a system of compromises, merely politics of compromise, for the purpose of binding the voting masses and their small leadership to the party. Spengler reports on this point from the case of Rome: "Pompei was *patronus* of half the world, from the peasant of Picenum to the kings of the East; he represented and protected everything; that was his political capital which he could make use of against the interest-free loan of Crassus and the "gilding" of all the ambitious by the conqueror of Gaul. - Meals were served to the voters according to the district, free places were allotted for gladiatorial games, or even, as in the case of Milo, money dispatched directly to the house. Cicero calls that observing the morals of the ancestors. The election capital assumed American dimensions and amounted, in the meantime, to hundreds of millions of sesterces".[16] The German democratic philistine swollen by ideals will become indignant at such a description and maintain the purity of the German political life. But, apart from the fact that the Germans - seen from the standpoint of the democrat - stand only at the beginning of this development, cases are known to the author from the last parliamentary election in which election assemblies were organized in the form of tea-receptions. The Roman breakfast has thus set a precedent.

The patronage of modern democracies is much more developed in another, apparently harmless form: not only is enormous private wealth collected and employed for the party work as in Rome, but public monies are simply used for this purpose. This happens in the way of the bureaucratic economy, of the food-trough insurance. Numberless new positions were created in the nation, provinces, and municipalities only in order to endow proven party followers with hotly desired state incomes. Promotions were undertaken only in order to settle the debt of the party to especially competent election heroes. Semi-public institutions, like

[16] [*Ibid.*]

social insurance, take up thousands of rest-requiring class warriors, promising bourgeois comfort and monthly payments. Large private economic concerns, like consumer co-operatives and newspaper establishments, open their doors to the one seeking a position only when he produces his membership book at the gate. Quite openly the party chiefs invite one to enter the party; not only their party, but just the party. One who is without a party sits between all stools. There is formed against him, immediately, a coalition of suspicious persons. To young bureaucratic candidates who believed that they could preserve their independence it is suggested from the highest position that they join a government party, if they wish to have prospects for advancement. Thus the party becomes, in spite of its inner weakness, a powerful force, since it disposes of not only the mostly empty party treasury, but also the all-too full state purse, filled by an economics which has turned into a plunderer.

For, the inner strength of the parties is very small. Heinz Marr divides the voters into party members, hangers-on of the party, and into non-voters. The followers make up hardly seven out of a hundred people entitled to vote. They are split up further into active and passive followers; the former form the famous regular circle of party friends,[17] the latter have the membership book of the party in their writing desk, without worrying about it. Nevertheless, the relatively small number of party fanatics suffices to destroy the inner unity of the people. If they are world-view politicians, and they thus have ideals related to the state, they are, by nature, intolerant; the more intolerant the more distant the world-views are to one another. If the development of the party to a class has already been accomplished, the common third, the state is, in general, missing. Then the class interest of the one combats, raw and naked, that of the other. In the western countries (especially in England and North America), the party has preserved its pragmatic manner. It is a purely functional object, the form in which a leader

---

[17] [Parteistammtisch, literally, reserved table for regular Party members].

orders his troops and the means whereby the people declare their trust or mistrust in this leadership. In a freely mobile decision, therefore, the voting masses change from one party to the other. The danger of the party in Germany, however, consists in the fact that it conceals the interest and places world-view values in the service of bare utility. Or that - in the case of the class parties - the interest influences the "world view", without being remarked by the party affected. Thus, every party defends its utilitarian goal, even if be of the lowest sort, namely the share in the food-trough. This commonality of the party advantage leads directly to the intellectual blinding of the individual party follower. Since the utility of the party - actually, or only in the imagination - is also his own and, for that reason, with a threat to it, even one to his own existence appears, the party man loses all objectivity the moment an attack on the view represented by his party occurs. The party above everything! Every realistic politics is destroyed! The result is that the party leader today can conduct a politics which he perhaps years ago chastised most sharply. Summoning all the arts of misrepresentation, the leader is then maintained by the party clique for the reason that all-too many interests are attached to him. From falsely understood comradeship, even those who do not have any personal gains to expect follow his tortuous paths with proud steadfastness. Men who are in the civil life, so to speak, highly cultured, and are unconditionally capable of judgement, fall back to the intellectual level of school children when it is a question of their party. Men who are accustomed to settle their differences of opinion in restrained forms come to blows in public assemblies when their party is attacked. Thus the party becomes the grave of every intellectuality and morality.

Every statement not in accordance with the party is silenced by the press and the public. If the cleverest man may say the cleverest thoughts on German politics, one does not listen to him if he has no party book in his pocket. A person counting among the "party big-wigs" however possesses the tacit privilege of being able to express schoolboyish wisdom as the winged words of a great man.

One may read the catchwords in the ministerial speeches which are wont to fill up even the serious press in enormous letters. If a normal mortal would express such platitudes, the contempt of every student would be certain for him. Remember the infamous term of 'the national community'! This phrase, which is either self-evident or absurd, was glorified as an intellectual achievement: self-evident where the fact of a national community is simply naturally given; absurd where one understands by national community a peaceful distribution of ministerial seats.

An investigation into the original core of the party, the party association, the party local branch, makes still clearer the disaster of the party system. Here inferiority is the highest trump! It should not be maintained that the impulse towards participation in the party life is to be explained just by the search of cowardly husbands for excuses for all-too frequent visits to the bar. Serious sociologists[18] mention this circumstance. However, it stands firm that the intellectual level on which party associations move lies deep below the general intellectual level of the society. Thereby the curve of this development falls down stlll lower. The few men of intellect who entered into public life after the collapse of 1918 have withdrawn in fright. Their time is too good for worthless prattle, they live mostly in professions which they take very seriously and carry out with full power, or they spend their free time in self-chosen intellectual work. It is otherwise with those professional manual labourers who are not fulfilled with the profession and do not have the power for spiritual self-occupation. They appease their bad conscience in the "party work". Practically, this means that they transfer the entire importance which is lacking in their work to the regular circle of party friends and there hold unbearably empty speeches which gives them the satisfaction of an alleged achievement. It must be declared that bureaucrats with much freedom misuse the advantage of their secure existence very often in aiming

---

[18] Robert Michels, *Zur Soziologie des Parteiwesens*, Leipzig, Verlag Alred Kröner, 1925.

through party political activity at an advancement which would not be suited to their professional performances. Just as it is, in general, a nonsense to endow bureaucrats with the franchise. But precisely the post-war period has created a ruling role in the parties for the bureaucrat because, for him, time is not money in the same measure that it is for other professions which must earn a living every day anew.

The intellectual life of the people is today carried out parallel to the political. One who is occupied with the present-day sort of politics is already from the start considered as an unintellectual man. Not wrongly, in view of the coincidence of politics and the party. And, vice-versa, an intellectual man who comes into a party assembly and begins to talk is considered there as a fool. One who does not speak of tangible interests or does not babble in the flood of conventional patriotic or class-warfare forms of speech falls victim to the laughter of those who feel superiour out of stupidity. Every person entering the party newly meets a tacitly forming front which combats the new man as a burdensome competition. He is killed before he was ever alive.

The battles for the setting up of the election candidate, strengthened by the list franchise and the power of the party clique conditioned by it, rage in a quagmire of impropriety. Already long before the election, the game of intrigues begins. Every candidate is concerned to collect with numerous promises to friends and professional associates the necessary people who propose him for the election list at the sitting of the party executive committee. No allegation is low enough in order to remove the opponents from the way on such occasions. A man of intellect and distinction is destroyed helplessly in this battle, for no particular leadership nature is wanted to adapt oneself to such a circumstance. He cannot go about it with the customary weapons. He is used to the foil, not to the flail. With all condescension he cannot descend so low as is necessary for winning the favour of the decisive men. In addition, there is the self-interest of the different professional groups. Every one wants, if possible, to bring a representative to the list; supposing that the representation of professional interests in a parliament were worth desiring, the question however remains open whether a professional comrade is also always suited to this. It is still thinkable that an intellectually high-standing man, without consideration of his profession, due to general education and basic training, could better deputize for other professions than the guild comrade. Such an objective consideration however plays no role nowadays. If it is a question of do or die, then the one wins who can say, or has the nonchalance to lie: "I have this or that professional union behind me in the election". The one who could say: "I have great ability and the feeling of responsibility in me" (such men never declare such a thing) disappears into the trapdoor if ever he had, in general, emerged from it.

Every reasonable party man also knows all that. From time to time, therefore, every party gives itself the well-known jolt to a renewal. Memoranda are written, one lets an outsider bring forward new ideas and a rousing appeal is made to the youth. Then however dullness triumphs once again, and all remains as before. Nothing more reactionary than the parties. In themselves, they are all reactionary, in their programme none of them want to be it. Even in cases of public breakdowns, no redress takes place: a representative may have demonstrated his entire incompetence, the recourse to a much better substitute should stand in the realm of possibility; but in the new election the current representative of the people raises the obvious demand for a re-election. In the anxiety of appearing ungrateful, for fear that common confidences - mostly of a bad sort - could be exposed, from cowardliness with regard to the scorn of the neighbouring party, the party remains standing by the current representative. That is the progress of modern democracy. If a politician has succeeded, quite exceptionally, in entering the parliament at the age of thirty, then he has the ambition to die therein at the age of eighty. He would like to cite his maiden parliamentary speech even in his "funeral oration". The age passes over nothing so tracelessly as over the head of a representative. This cowardly dishonorability of the party however shows itself in its brilliance in the election of a female election candidate. A really significant woman, who can perhaps help the idea of motherhood to a breakthrough in legislation, unfortunately stands seldom for election, because she is occupied with the rearing of her children and finds her fulfilment therein. There remains, therefore, only the female association-steward with her marvellous troops of female voters. Mostly the following process is played out: if it appears inevitable to make a draught of fish from the female votes, a certain election circle is condemned by the party to set up and elect "the woman". Then the women's associations become active. Everybody wants to have the most followers, and from a flood of slanders emerges as the election candidate the woman with the best nerves. All serious politicians therefore joke about, and mock among themselves, the female representative. None, however, has the courage to express the truth aloud. Thus appears then "the female representative of the people" as the fifth wheel on the wagon, worthy of her male counterpart, described in a masterly and prophetic way by Balzac.

If the party thus seems at the lower level already questionable, it cannot, at the top, which is called upon to make state politics, assume a heroic shape. One may just carefully read the speeches of precisely those party leaders who approve the party system as the last keystone of wisdom. One will always find that their thoughts are not borne in the spirit of saying the best to the point, and of serving the state, but of putting down the previous speakers of the opposite party as much as possible and of contradicting their opinions. With questions of the fate of the people a catch-ball of eloquence is played. Every foreign policy becomes internal policy. Where the contradiction of the opponent does not succeed any longer, it is at least maintained that he has stolen his wisdom. Naturally, from the party of the speaker. If anywhere in the working and professional life the men who must work together communicated with one another in such a senseless and destructive manner as those to whom the welfare of the state is entrusted do, no loaf of bread and no article of clothing would be produced in Germany any longer. For, all powers would be exhausted in the strife regarding the "how". An upright Democrat, Conrad Hausmann, writes on 5th October, 1918, in his diary:[19] "The parliament has not developed to the great turning point. It does not have the men who find the style for this beginning of its period of rule; for this reason it is questionable whether this rule can be maintained". The apostles of Weimar speak of the education of the people to democracy, enthuse about the great leaders whom this school will once bring about. They forget that the parliament of notables unites in itself free leading men, that, however, the parliament belongs to the mass rule of unscrupulous demagogues, that it does not tolerate any heads any longer. Genuine parliamentarianism may have occupied noble minds; the party rule knows still only philistines striving for success. Therefore the intellectual level of the parliament will unrelentingly go down. Where inferiority rules no heroes can sit in the popular representation.

Here enters the evaluation of the social-anthropological investigations which Kretschmer[20] and Lubosch[21] have initiated. According to that, alongside the classification of a community according to racial types, there runs one according to constitutional types which influences the conditions under which the life of society is developed. Lubosch distinguishes four or five such constitutional types (geniuses, heroes, common bourgeois, philistines, and diplomats) who as special characters influence history through their predetermined conduct. "The hero and genius are always solitary and non-recurring; common bourgeois and philistines are, on the other hand, many and frequently recurring and are therefore real character types". The genius and hero embody the creative, spiritual and the formative powers, petty bourgeois and philistines are the material for shaping,

---

[19] Cited from Georg Steinhausen, *Der politische Niedergang Deutschlands*, Osterwieck, Verlag Zickfeldt, 1927.

[20] [Ernst Kretschmer (1888-1964), author of *Körperbau und Charakter: Untersuchungen zum Konstitutionsproblem und zur Lehre von den Temperamenten*, Berlin: J. Springer, 1921; *Rasse und Geist*, Leipzig: J.A. Bart, 1932].

[21] [Wilhelm Lubosch], "Der Spießbürger und der Philister, ein Vortrag", *Süddeutsche Monatshefte*, Heft 12, 1928, [= Bd.24,ii (1927), pp.435-43].

therefore uncreative.

The petty bourgeois is not something merely ridiculous, as he is mostly represented. Ridiculous is only the attempt to educate him into a state citizen of free responsibility and highest self-determination, to see him as the lever of history. In truth, he is a loyal and useful member of society, distinguished by healthy morality, persistent adherence to tradition, diligent work performance, abilities as educator of his children. He is the human material, the matter, from which the society completes itself, and the leaders form their following. The petty bourgeois are the hangers-on of the parties, they are born people of the masses, as much summoned to be the protector of the spirit of the people (the people in arms) as they are capable of becoming a soulless metropolitan mass which imitates every absurd fashion. Their core however is healthy, their existence useful; it becomes dangerous only when the petty bourgeois attains positions which powerful leader natures should fill. This is partially the case in the parties. Petty bourgeois, only usable as voting masses, today raise the claim to leadership or are placed at the head, in order to play out the weakling beloved on all sides against uncomfortable genuine leaders. The "man of the people" of party political stamp, inflated and uncreative, witty and sufficiently fed, smiles at the man of spirit and responsibility, at his "ideals" and "world alienation".

Worse, however, is the philistine, the eternal contrast to the youth who still believes in the wholeness of life. He knows all better and has an answer to everything. "He is very clever, very industrious, on the level of technology, but without the notion that true science is a whole". Thus does Lubosch characterise the servant Wagner as a scientific philistine and sets next to him the philistine of art: Beckmesser, the idle, clumsy, simple-minded, city writer ready to combat the genius.[22] In the philistine, instead of daring, there enters the consideration of utility; the certainty of his opinions corresponds to his short-sighted one-sidedness.

---

[22] [Wagner, the servant of Faust in Goethe's *Faust*, and Beckmesser, the small-minded town clerk in Richard Wagner's *Die Meistersinger von Nürnberg*].

He is a blinded man of the understanding; he comes into the world already as a privy councillor of the E.T.A. Hoffmann stamp . He is the born success hunter, but shuns every employment. "Only there where the life instinct has been crippled or artificially suppressed, and where selection accordingly is lacking, does the possibility exist that the philistine, the one hunting for his own gain, the utilitarian, the man without problems, attains power. - It seems as if it is the fault of this human type if anywhere a great moment has found a petty generation" (Lubosch).

It seems also as if the parties were the means which common bourgeois and philistines, but especially the latter, manipulate to eliminate the genius and the hero.

One believes now that one can improve the party system by the removal of the splinter parties, raising the voting age, abolition of the list system, etc. Certainly, all these ways would be, if performed resolutely, suited to the removal of the crudest aberrations. Especially if relative franchise is departed from and an approximation to the basic democratic idea of the rule of the majority resulted. Typically, however, Liberalism in Germany goes so far as to want to give up the protection of the minority at any price. Thereby the immediate result of the introduction of the democractic-parliamentary system would have been really a clear admission of the rule of the majority. Otherwise, in general, it does not indeed come to the formation of a majority bearing the state. There arises then a taking into consideration of minorities which must degenerate into disintegrating party-divisions. Tocqueville describes the difference between large and small parties in the following way: "Large political parties are concerned more with maintaining the principles than their consequences. The personal interests which always co-determine the political passions are then quite hidden behind the veil of the public interest, even the leaders assume these great gestures. The small parties are, on an average, the opposite. Since they do not feel that they have arisen through and are maintained by great problems, their character takes the stamp of an irresponsible egoism which reveals itself in every action of theirs". But whether the parties are large or small, they remain in their inner being captivated by the rule of interests. Reform can therefore delay the collapse, but never prevent it. A renewal of the franchise is, however, not to be expected, every change of the franchise encounters hard resistances. For, all representatives are naturally beneficiaries of the present-day system. They cannot agree to their political self-destruction. That is a heroism which thrives on other soil than parliamentarianism.

It is always said that a more just franchise than the existing one is unthinkable. Against that, many demand the raising of the voting age. As welcome as it would be, it does not change much in the inner untruthfulness of the entire voting system. The individual equal to all is today the foundation of political education of the will: the franchise is valid in equal range for the drunkard who quaffs a quart and the world-famous scholar, the convict, to whom the civil rights are not unknown, the high-standing man, the wage-earner of the war and the warrior of the front, the twenty year old gigolo and the sixty-year old tutor of six good children. Such a franchise can never be surpassed in injustice. Every new formation which deviates from this equality means therefore a step towards health. To be sure, only a small one. For, voting is today the expression of a mechanistic adding up, is the rule by force of the irresponsible, is everything but a democracy. However, the party lives on voting, the soulless machine which makes life lifeless, kills spirit and soul, and bears the inferiour to the top. Nothing deserves a quick downfall so much as the party. One who eradicates it with fire and sword performs a holy work.

IX

The party state

As anonymous as the financial capital are the masses. Money, masses, and the press are the three great anonymities of the collapsing individualistic age. The modern party is a mass party. It rules over and through the masses, that nameless something for which everybody and yet nobody takes responsibility. It acts and determines, but no individual wants to be responsible. It has its own soul, basically different from the soul of the individual. It destroys the thought capacities of the individual who, after every action of the masses, with himself belonging to it, asks in fright how he could take part in an act which went against his own conviction and his own will. Nothing is so ruled by lower instincts and vague feelings as the masses. Nothing dehumanises man so much as the crowding of men. The ordering power of the reason is nowhere more eliminated as in the madness of the masses. The American people wanted no war: its press brought it in the shortest time to enthusiastically support the crusade against the "Huns", and to throw the war-service avoiders who had maintained their reason into prison. After ten years of peace - in view of the total historical scientific explanation of the question of war-guilt - the broad masses still believe in the criminal will of Germany in kindling the world war. Horrible lack of freedom lies on the masses as a scourging force. Mass madness is the true characterisation of that condition which the man of the Enlightenment, always euphemising, calls the free self-determination of the people.

Modern democracy is the rule of the masses, exerted through the parties. The all-powerful state, whose foundation-stone the unrestrainedly ruling princes laid, has changed its masters. If the monarch was at least responsible to his conscience and his heriditarily succeeding descendants, this responsibility is destroyed with the passing of power to the masses. In place of personality, enters the nameless power in the hand of the one who can lead the masses openly or secretly. The favour of the masses and money, mostly not only closely united but in themselves one, take up the rule.

When the absolute king was replaced by the absolute people by the French Revolution, there came about one of the first laws which the new possessors of power produced, a property qualification for franchise similar to the earlier Prussian three class francise. Here the idea which attained mastery in the French Revolution was revealed in bare nakedness: financial capital, the economic form of individualism, pressed towards the conquest of the state. Landed property was broken up in its mastery. The forms of employment of force changed. In place of the external subjection of the people entered spiritual serfdom. The nebulous promises of equality, brotherhood and freedom had their reason-destroying, intoxicating effect. The great flattery of the street begins. "Pure democracy[23] lies in a constant self-worship. The lightest attack injures it already and one must therefore incessantly praise it. The unbelieving finally find no organ any longer in order to express their thoughts, and so democracy can aim at a better result than the Inquisition in Spain. In every form of government, one will meet the lower character and flattery next to power, in the democratic republic and in the absolute monarchy. Instead of talk of His Majesty and Sire, one speaks incessantly of the

---

[23] Tocqueville, *Dém.* Vol.III, cited after Göring [*Tocqueville und die Democratie*, München: R. Oldenbourg, 1928].

natural illumination of Milady Democracy. Without further ado, even the new ruler possesses all the virtues, without having striven for them or, in general, wanting them. Allegories are no longer required to convey the truth; that means simply: we know that we speak to a people too high above all human weaknesses not to remain masters of ourselves. The flatterers of Louis XIV could not have done it better. - The people never have the time and the possibility to give themselves fully to the study of the men to be elected. They must decide quickly and adhere to the most salient points. Therefore, charlatans of all sorts know so well the secret of pleasing it, whereas very often its true friends fail".

The ruling power of money is subject to no limitation in democracy. Democracy has chosen and created money as the form of its tyranny. The metropolitan masses of all levels, who can think only in terms of money, feel it as natural to be ruled by money too. The economic form of the high capitalistic age is, however, business. The true man of money produces no values any longer, but acts with values already present. Business, however, comes from negotiation; already in the economic life, persuasion is a means of business. The best negotiator bears home the resounding success. If the intellectual business community conquers the power in the state, it transfers the experiences of its economics also to the political life, to politics. The commercial politician, the one with the better art of persuasion, the one endowed with the greater craftiness and the broader conscience, becomes the leader. Just as every business transaction is a balance on the mean, by which the stronger wins the advantage, so every political transaction becomes the result of business activity. Nothing is made correctly or purposefully; everything only in such a way that the competing interests come to a tolerable rest.

The will of the true state aims at the fulfilment of the social aim: welfare and the maintenance of the society. The social aim, however, is not synonymous with the sum of interests of all the members of a society. This would be Rousseau's *volonté générale*. If it were the highest law of society, then war -

because it contradicts its striving for self-maintenance - would have to be, in general, denied. But since society encompasses not only one's environment, but also the after-world, the true social interests can demand the denial of the *volonté de tous*, the will of all, in order to affirm war. Society, however, must, under circumstances, demand the destruction of the living generation, in order to rescue its continuance and its future. But even the sum of interests of all the members of the present living society is not to be conveyed on the path of a counting together. This experience would only lead to the goal if all were equally in the position of perceiving their own advantage as well. But exactly as the advantage of young children must naturally be preserved by the parents - even against the will of the dependent - so also the interest of the masses by the leader, mostly against the insight and the will of the ones led. The most serious failure of thought of the defender of universal franchise lies in the false supposition that every enfranchised person possesses the capacity to recognize what is best for him. A further source of error of modern democracy is contained in the circumstance that the will of the majority represents a further weakening of the *volonté de tous*. Only a part of the present-day living society stands under the will of the state. Even this part is, however, not the majority. For, the non-voters are lost in the formation of the will of the state just as the followers of splinter parties are. Finally, however, within the parties, an outvoting of the inferiour once again takes place, so that even in logical carrying through of the mechanistic poll the will of the people never appears as a final result, but always only the wish of a minority. - But even the so-called majority government is not to be equated with the will of the majority. For it makes its decisions in the way of negotiation: of compromise. One can therefore outline the present-day will of the state in the following manner: it is the components of individual advantages, represented through compromises of the interest groups forming the majority. How infinitely far this pathetic result is removed from the real will of the state, from the *volonté générale*, requires, according to this exposition, no emphasis. For, the true social interest is, in general, not perceivable through the determination of the wishes of the masses.

Money has established its rule on the most tortuous paths in numerous forms. The most perfect, however, is that over the press and propaganda. It would be false to suppose that only the so-called capital, thus the entrepreneurial side of German economics, has learnt to manipulate the power of the press. It is exactly the reverse. At the beginning of the Liberal age, the press was in no way thought of as an instrument of interests, it also did not lie in its nature to carry out the enslavement of the masses; it lived indeed still in the innocent idea of serving the illumination of the people. It was Socialism precisely which built up the press as a instrument of rule in the grand style. The so-called capitalistic camp followed only much later - through its opposition - after the opponents' model. Thus the trades-union press is also, apparently even in scope, the strongest instrument of power of its kind. Only with total democratisation does the press become a complete slave holder. - How much the party is dependent on money was demonstrated above. Thus every party too is composed of representatives of professions and interests. It has its experts for every profession, for every business and for every economic power group. Where the class character of the party, purely economic thought, does not yet emerge (as in the case of the workers's party, the middle class party, the revaluation party, etc.), the great professional and economic associations with their demands and their enticing cheques stand behind the former world-view parties. A sort of economic parallel government is formed, strenuously concealed by the high- sounding national and world-view expressions with which every representative of interests settles his little complaint of economic need. All voters, regardless of party, though in different degrees, are in this way held under the sway of money, because the appeal to the material instinct must precisely lead to the dehumanisation of the masses. The longing for material possession was inoculated into them as the chief characteristic and in this way the power of resisting enticing promises, or indeed offered advantages taken away from them. The more paradisiacal the deceptive illusion, the more painless the spiritual enslavement. Number and raw force are the only weapons which remain, under the circumstances, to the non-propertied circles of the people. If one silences them with the catchwords of fraternity, of world peace, and with cultural talk, one disarms them and alienates them from the idea of using force against dominant financial rule. If a leader of the masses sees through this entire bustle, the possibility still remains of letting the dangerous champion of the "disenfranchised" participate in the enjoyment of money-possession: either through direct bribery or through support of an economic sort, or through the offer of a state income, that is: enrolment in the bureaucracy. The "hostility to capital" of the leader thus becomes the means of force against capital, which must open its safe in this way at least to the leaders of the opposite side.

The opinion that democracy is the rule of money could be countered by the fact of the expansion of Socialistic thought processes, of the existence of large Socialistic parties. Here the question raises itself, whether the most influential champion of Socialism, Karl Marx, was actually anti-capitalistically disposed or whether his battle against capital was only a means to the goal. Thereby conscious deception should not be objected against him. But why, in general, did Marx become a Socialist? He himself has always bluntly rejected a moral foundation of Socialism.[24] His correspondence with Engels betrays a "frightful coldness of feeling with regard to the workers, the coarse people, as they are mostly contemptuously called". In fact, Marx was revolutionary in the bourgeois sense. He was a Jacobin who battled against the Holy Alliance. He, the Jacobin, borrowed freedom and equality from the intellectal arsenal of the French Revolution. When however he saw the bourgeois revolution of 1848 collapsing, he did not battle any longer directly for the establishment of the bourgeois rule, but turned to the proletariat. He thus appealed to the working masses for help, in

---

[24] Ottokar Lorenz, in the February issue, [Bd.25, i, (1927/] 1928), of the *Süddeutsche Monatshefte*, "Karl Marx als Schrittmacher des Kapitalismus", pp.314-33].

order to replace the old order with the democratic bourgeois state, the form of the rule of money-possession.

Since then, wherever Socialism has battled politically, it stands on the side of money against the state. Thus it combated the monarchy, landed property, indigenous industry, the middle class and, finally, also the worker through the rejection of all social politics. Anything that just reminds one of the soil, blood, culture, religious binding, and in general of traditional values is undermined or rejected. Socialism became, under the influence of Karl Marx, degenerate Liberalism. Finally he was only the faithful mirror-image of materialistic, bourgeois thought: of course, aggresively; the bourgeoisie, on the other hand, defensively so. The idea of combatting capitalism as an intellectual condition, as the destroyer of the soul, did not come to Karl Marx, for whom there was matter, and no soul. He had the fanaticism of the scholar who used his scholarship as a means to a goal, for the creation of an ideology which denied every spirituality. His exaggerating way of thought made economics mere greed for profit. The hate of the worker was directed to the one who stood inwardly closest to them of all the capitalists: to the entrepreneur. The private capitalistic economic form, not to be removed as a way of production, since based on human nature, was established as an object of combat and, at the same time, intellectual capitalism protected and reared. The one who produced values was the enemy, the one who dealt with them and aimed at arbitrary profits the friend. Thus the pathetic picture came about that the German Socialistic worker stormed against creative economics and guarded the revenue-seeking capital with his body. The factory owner, concerned day and night for the welfare and the suffering of his enterprise, is considered as the mortal enemy of the worker. The financial power which directs the current of money uniquely to the law of gain and is thus the true beneficiary of the performance of the manual labourer as well as of the director of the enterprise, remains invisible in the background. The owner of the warehouse enterprise secures his display windows with contributions to the purses of Socialism. A

Viennese joke says that in the distinguished quarters the ruling houses vote Socialist, and the rear quarters Christian-Socialist or Great German. This saying characterises also the internal condition of present-day Germany. It proves that the German worker in 1918 did not make *his* revolution, but that of his true, but concealed, mortal enemy, the financial capital. Thus, even in 1918, then, the financial democracy triumphed over the idea of the workers' state. Fleeting efforts to apply the Soviet system to the construction of the German state instead of bourgeois party democracy were wrecked. Every idea of an organic state of work was lacking in the bourgeoisie. The working class, however, was more Liberal than Liberalism and helped to remove the small beginnings of a national German state. Perhaps this had to be so, because the taking over of the Soviet idea would have meant the Bolshevisation and, therewith, the Russification or indeed the Asiatisation of Germany. Of the disappeared splendour one high column which is really more than broken still gives evidence: the National Economic Council.

How does it come about now that precisely Socialism, allegedly so hostile to capital, became the chief support of plutocracy? Only because the German workers' movement had lost its original, spiritually-bound, basically German character.[25] In the battle between Marx on the one hand, and Lasalle and Weitling on the other, the former had won. The conservative German position of the latter was combatted almost as bitterly as the whole of capitalism. Marx wanted no culture and no developed binding, he hated the affirmative, creative man. Man should become part of the masses, who exhaust themselves in wage work and earthly blessedness. Richard Bie[26] describes this individualistic ideal which Communism then sought to realise in Russia in the following manner: "In and for itself this idea is not new, for it is the idea of the Inquisition, which Dostojewski has described in his *Grand Inquisitor*:[27] humanity should obey, and

---

[25] [cf. Oswald Spengler's *Preussentum und Socialismus*, where Spengler characterizes the spiritual ethos of the original German Socialism as "Prussianism"].

[26] *Revolution und Karl Marx*, Leipzig, Voigtländers Verlag, 1929.

[27] [Fyodor Dostoievski's 'Grand Inquisitor' first appeared as Ch.5 of Bk.V of his *Brothers Karamazov*

not trust any longer the messianic madness that stones can transform themselves
into bread and that faith moves mountains; on the contrary, humanity should
resign itself to itself and be happy, if only its bodily hunger is appeased. On this
point there is no difference between the Cardinal of the Inquisition and the
Tcheka.[28] Both are directed against the rebellious and reformational, the
scrupulous and the morally responsible, in short, the Protestant spirit in man". In
the language of this book, this means that Communism transformed the legal
religious side of religion into the dictatorial mass state as much as the protestant
side of Liberalism was falsified into humanitarianising anarchy.

Today, the German party Socialism is the marching-troop of the quietly
and dominantly ruling financial capital which it uses to bring the creative
agriculture and the value-producing entrepreneurship under its "control". The
German worker has become an obedient storming-party of money.

Apart from the basic philosophical mistake of historical materialism, Marx
has overlooked one thing in the erection of his doctrinal edifice: that, namely, for
the condition of society, money alone is not essential, but also the disposal of it.
In the age of high capitalism the one who has a monopoly on capital is not always
powerful, but the one who disposes of it is. Certainly, most of the possessors of
capital receive a certain revenue. It has however become increasingly smaller, so
small that, today, the profits of the great business societies lie far below the rate
of interest of loan capital. At the same time, in the joint-stock companies, the
emphasis has changed from the board of trustees to the board of directors. The
general directors become the all-powerful personages of capitalism. They have
become a sort of feudal undertakers who, to be sure, can be forced by a single
decision out of their position, but mostly maintain it by virtue of outstanding
performance and capacities. The so-called economic leaders of Germany are, for

(1880). It is a narrative composed by Ivan Karamazov and related by him to his brother Alyosha, and
deals with an imaginary confrontation between a sixteenth century Spanish Inquisitor and Jesus].
[28] [The Tcheka was an organisation set up in 1917 under the Soviet regime for the investigation of
counter-revolutionary activities].

the most part, basically not real capitalists but the most highly graded workers. This important change in the system of private economics could not naturally remain without a reaction on the efforts of Socialism. It changed its tactics in a way which must be recognized in its full scope because such a knowledge forms the key to the understanding of the present-day political life: if the Socialist movement in Germany had further pursued the path it had taken for a generation, it would logically have had to establish in 1918 the dictatorship of the proletariat and put Socialism into effect. In fact, there was also a strong orientation within Socialism which demanded the realisation of such plans. The majority, however, recognised that socialisation is an economic absurdity, whose continuance would have destined the German people to death by hunger. Already Engels feared in a letter from 1853,[29] that the party "drawn by the proletariat populace, bound by its own more or less falsely interpreted printed statements and plans, more or less passionately dragged to the fore, was required to make Communistic experiments and leaps, of which one knows best how untimely they are". Socialism thus really had to explain its collapse in 1918 and transform itself fully. It did not do that; for it had quickly recognised that its participation in the political life could bring no socialisation, but in its place something similar in effect, even if deviating from its own basic idea. If, indeed, the private capitalistic structure of economics could not be questioned, such a pressure could be exerted on private capital, by means of the all-powerful state, that it was "voluntarily" ready to give a series of beneficiaries financial profits. And indeed such who - economically considered - were not capitalists and had no legal claim to this usufruct. In other words: money is not only power, but power, too, is money. However, after party Socialism had become a power, first through the heightened significance of the party in general, then through the sharing in the state, there arose for this new power also new possibilities of converting itself into money. Since that time, significant means

---

[29] [Friedrich Engels, Letter dated 12 April, 1853, to Joseph Weydemeyer, in Karl Marx, Friedrich Engels, *Gesamtausgabe*, Berlin: Dietz Verlag, 1987, 3te Abteilung, *Briefwechsel*, Bd.6, p.153].

from financial capitalistic circles flowed to Socialism. The pressure which the party exerted directly on capital worked in a treasury-filling way. Much greater, however, is the path across the state, the provinces, the great autonomous bodies, and the municipalities which are indeed also totally parliamentarised. The share in capital revenues is, for the most part, carried out in the detour through the tax legislation and the employer's contributions. Obviously, all that happens in the alleged interests of the state. In fact, however, it is not a question of the state, but of class. Much may be made even of a corresponding manipulation of the credit concession; finally, even through participation of the public sector in the private economics. In this way, numerous possibilities are produced of making men who would never have attained the disposal of great capitals in a purely economic way administrators of enormous sums. Since, on the other hand, the free formation of capital is made harder, the dependence on the over-full public treasury must increase further. Thus the financial power, which the state in increasingly greater measure becomes, approaches closer the pure political power. Both increase themselves reciprocally. That the people disposing of large capitals do not let themselves come off too badly is well known. An exciting game! The workers are incited against the capital which supporting itself on them is however used for the leaders: for participation in the capitalistic system.

This situation can correctly, without further ado, be characterised as corrupt. The social scientists may however calmly speak of a financial rule. Obviously these conditions degenerate here and there into open corruption; there arises then a "Panama", which upto now has not been spared to any modern democracy. The objection that such things come about only in especially troubled times, as an exceptional phenomenon, is not sound. For, the exception appears to lie less in the moral field than in the intellectual. Only undertakings which are set going too clumsily lead to a scandal. Many times also such in which reinsurance has been neglected. This consists in the fact of letting the dangerous man share in every haul of fish. There forms itself then such a dense clique of beneficiaries that their exposure would mean a political crisis: the entire leading class would come under the wheels. One however knows too much of one another; often, one begins one's career by collecting incriminating material on all leading men which, at the given moment, works in a blackmailing manner through its mere existence. Above all things there is no independent authority existent any more which could raise complaints. State administration and even, later, the judges become servants of the holders of party-power. One who would like to annul this service - in accordance with his oath - loses his bread and reputation. Thus it becomes understandable that modern republics that are well under way do not experience any great scandals any longer. Indeed everybody knows that all that is rotten, but rebellion becomes too dangerous. The Hercules ready to clean out the stables of Augeas[30] is missing.

In addition, there is the personal politics of the parties - as the harmless circumlocution of the circumstance runs - the fact that the parties have become great patronage associations. Indeed, it is a question thereby of booty for small robber animals, but for that reason of such with which entire troops can be satisfied. In America, the entire army of bureaucrats changes along with the president. Thus the effort of collecting in the fat years reserves for the lean years. The professionalism of the German bureaucracy prevented for a long time a development in this direction. For that reason, however, Germany has become the model of a welfare democracy. Salaried class and retirement salary are the magic catchwords which bring ever new hundreds of thousands of people to the queuing at the state feeding-trough. The appeal for the substitution of the professional bureaucrats by elected ones, a basic democratic demand, thus becomes increasingly weaker. It only sounded from time to time in order to remove unpopular bureaucrats who did not wish to subject themselves to the ruling parties, in order to make places free for party faithfuls. This is called, in a fine term, the

---

[30] [one of the most odious tasks of Hercules, since the stables of Augeas containing 3000 oxen had not been cleaned for 30 years].

republicanisation of the state. All too often, deserving party veterans even press for the honouring of the change set out by the party leaders. And still the possibilities are too limited which are given to the parties for the rewarding of their faithfuls. One therefore turns to parliamentising even the higher bureaucrats and to occupying the ground of quiet businesses between the parties. The number of ministers and state secretaries out of service who wish to be brought "to the level of their profession" swells. New offices must be created for these high officials. The small people are satisfied if their position is raised to a salaried class. This "raising" has become one of the chief activities of the municipal parliament. Thus, since the public hand is still the most generous and the treasury into which it reaches the fullest, there occurs a not exactly reluctant dovetailing into the "capitalistic world-order". That this happens in political positions is so much more convenient: it seems non-capitalistic, the employer cannot dismiss without notice, and, besides, the appeal is maintained that one is a man who exhausts himself for the state and the party ideal in authoritative positions.

Even the career of the representatives offers rich opportunity for corruption. In the present-day parliaments encompassing a far overstretched circle of influence, the activity of the representative is such a time-consuming one that he must neglect his profession. If he does not achieve in some way one of the numerous state incomes or economic interest representations, the parliamentary career leads to his financial collapse. If the professional representative was an unemployed or otherwise a "small man", the representation allowance of the parliament means social rise. But the decisive life-style of former times is quickly forgotten. The representation allowance as the only strong income does not suffice any longer. Then the party must reach into its purse or draw upon the state treasury for help. For, the representative is a bureaucrat, and so his entire activity for the state consists in confirming the pay receipt on the first of the month. Never was the sacrifice for the fatherland made easier for a profession. Here too therefore the principle is maintained that power lends money. Obviously, that is not a corruption and therefore so much more beloved. A seventh of the German population lives today from the public hand. All bureaucrat-representatives operate consciously or unconsciously for the maintenance of this absurd situation. These are, however, as representatives, the employers of wage-earners: thus employer and employee in one person; except that others must bring the means which they grant themselves. Another sub-species of the popular representative is the representative who, concerned about the favour of his voters, would fulfil numerous personal petitions of the same by virtue of his influence. Beginning with the loan of millions of the state to the unfortunate end of a divorce trial, the voter's brain hatches petitions and memoranda which rob the poor representative of the people of his mid-day nap. This pronounced representative of interests can, however, keep up with the numberless wishes of his voters only if he is pledged, in return, to the government, and to the leading men in some form. Thus even here it boils down to a crowding of interests which endangers the capacity of free decision of the representative in decisive settlements. The whole thing reaches a peak in the total mixture of private economic, personal and state interests. Between parties there arises a group of dedicated persons who still perform only shadow-fights against one another to delight the hearts of the voters. In fact, they are very united, and only occasionally do they fight quiet but bitter battles for the participation in the great food-trough which is called power.

The bearers of high worth of the petty bourgeois democracy - indeed it is a question of such in Germany - are exposed to the danger of corruption in extraordinary measure. From the top down, therefore, corruption penetrates into increasingly wider circles, destroying moral restrictions. Precisely those who have attained their posts through the favour of the party are aware that with the passing over of their party into the opposition, the positions may be lost. One therefore takes precautions. If a bureaucrat or a petty bourgeois parliamentarian attains a post requiring expenditure, indeed that of the minister, his life-style is then suddenly raised many degrees. In a world of financial princes, he must represent, and his house tolerates, no petty bourgeois style unless in quite rare cases his superiority of mind and character lets external deficiencies be forgotten. Thus a higher life-style becomes a customary thing, as it corresponds to the circumstances of wealth. All at once, the bearer of high worth loses his office and should now return to petty bourgeois circumstances. That is naturally possible and will also, often, succeed through self-overcoming. Often, however, especially supported by the wife, the wish arises to "remain on top", at least in a purely social sense, even after the loss of the high position. In this conflict even a morally strong man can lose his stability. Almost all former ministers from proletariat circles therefore take care today to maintain a middle class life-style. With what means, God only knows.

Unsatisfiable is the hunger of those persons who are united in the tacit programme of insurance. Power provides money and money in turn provides power; that is a continuous raising of oneself up. All legal barriers fall apart under this attack. The parliament, so to speak the brain of this power-hungry system, wants to become the sole source of power by removal of every distribution of powers. Not only that the division of executive, legislative, and judiciary power is annulled; even the distribution of powers between the individual political organs is constantly contested. The anonymous clique of the party powers wishes to unite the uses of power of every sort in their hand. Thus every parliamentarianism works, by nature, centralisingly. Nobody exercises any control over the despots of the parliament. No binding can restrict the irresponsible in their decisions. The one-chamber system is the licence to legal self-will, but also the enticement to lasting encroachments of administration and justice. Between the parliament and the government there is no difference any more. The constant anxiety of the parliamentary powers is that a government might make itself independent of them. By preference, therefore, so-called weak men are set on the chancellory seats; all free powers which could influence the social or political life outside the parliament are suppressed. If such are formed on purely social soil, the parliamentary state plays equally constituted efforts against one another, thus destroying the possibility of a real accomplishment. The mortal enemies of the parliamentary democracy are the federations and leagues. Tocqueville characterises them as the only check against the rule of the self-will of the majority. The parliament seeks therefore, sometimes with friendly promises, sometimes with "protective laws", to kill the life of the federations. Once they promise influence in the parties, then they intimidate them, but never do they mean to act honorably by them.

The parliament would like to subject even the institution of the state, just as the knighthood, to its influence. This is the final goal of democratic-Liberal thought. Thus many parliamentarians are pleased in this way in the role of judge which they play out in investigatory committees. All processes of political and social life can be the object of the investigatory activity of such committees. Every policy can be examined before the proper justice. Now it is said that the activity of the investigatory committee is suited to demonstrate the unprincipled nature of the complaints against German judges. That, however, a sentence does not represent a final jugement any more if popular tribunals reexamine them is clear. Every examination means a disturbance of the idea of justice which, to be sure, comes to the awareness of only that person for whom justice is not only a political command but a morality growing from the soul of the people. Even administrative law courts, supposedly one of the proudest achievements of the modern state, lose, in view of the unconditional rule of the parliament, their final significance. For, where still does their significance lie, if these judges do not have any longer to balance rights against one another but must apply laws created by parliamentary arbitration, according to which they should pass their judgement?

A well known statesman once said that the content of the Wilhelminian politics may be traced back to the principle: "Only do not arouse the enemy". That the German foreign policy was, partially forced, but also due to blindness, conducted in this spirit provokes no wonder. But even the internal policy stands under the law of this statement: the readiness to the glossing over and suppression of weaknesses is surpassed only by the tendency to pay homage to these weaknesses. All wounds which bleed anywhere are therefore quickly bandaged and concealed. Whether they fester under the bandage and threaten the destruction of the entire body is a matter of indifference; the final healing one gladly leaves to one's descendants who also have to do something. The evil is never grasped at the root, only the external beautiful picture is the object of care. The most enthusiastic followers of this superficial therapeutics are the parties themselves. If one of the state-ruling clique lets himself become guilty of something, then no fuss may be made of that. Crimes which would have led a normal mortal to jails are hushed up, high treason proceedings struck down in cosy silence. The legal impunity of the popular representative becomes an actual one. Regardless of parties, they are all one on this point. Thus there arises gradually an idea which has been glorified in gutter novels: the model of the "lawless man".

These lawless men are, however, not heroic figures or brilliant intriguers who, for the sake of the great goal, could afford the freedom to listen to their own conscience alone. They are only the hostile parties courageous with regard to one another and, moreover, small schemers, philistines and petty bourgeois. For, democracy tends to support itself on the rule of the lower classes, if not indeed of the masses, but at least to keep the higher classes from the top. "Envy is customary as a result of democracy" (Tocqueville).[31] The French political philosopher goes so far as to maintain that the natural instinct of democracy demands the exclusion of all significant personalities. The entire democratic state, and the "society" attached to it, are directed by this feeling of envy. Nothing makes one more beloved than the introduction of envious taxations. Every financial politics, however, which is determined by the passions of the majority leads to a collapse. - The legal machine works indefatigably and superficially, for

[31] [*Democratie en Amérique*, Part I, Ch.XIII].

hardly is a government at the helm, than envy already sweeps it away once again. Now indeed, as the case of North America shows, every democracy does not need to be parliamentary; it is however more Liberal, and corresponds much more to the individualistic lack of restraint, to avoid every constitutional institution and to repeat the game of change of governments as often as one wants. A government independent of parliament could not, in the end, cater to the numerous personal wishes compliantly enough. Only the parliamentary system offers a guarantee for weak ministers and on the grounds that everybody at one time comes up against it. Thence the absurd picture that a new minister, hardly instructed on where the rooms related to his portfolio are, already disappears into the trap-door. He hardly begins ruling. Mostly he does nothing but administer badly. Many a party leader draws the conclusion therefrom of making use of the party leadership and a ministerial office at the same time. He feels himself securer in his position in this way because a party leader is to be thrown down only by the simultaneous withdrawal of the party from the coalition. This leads, in turn, once again to sticking to the office. For, such a minister can afford the most impossible stocks so long as his party is used for the coalition. He governs practically without political responsibility. Mostly, however, he lets himself perform nothing at all but the making of colourless speeches. Thereby he does not run any danger and can skillfully conceal his lack of ideas or indeed his deficient capacities. For, if the majority of the representatives are already not burdened with any expert knowledge, then no superhuman performance should be expected of their leader. Overall, where one hopes for performance, one demands expert suitability. One does not let one's shoes be soled by a tailor, one does not buy one's bread at the carpenter's. Governing is the only business which in Germany is made dependent on no prerequirement. (Thereby it should not be said that politics can be "learnt"). Already the representative is governed by the spirit of this paradox: the popular representative should make laws and has, before he came into parliament, learnt no law. Thereby the flood of submissions swells, the production of laws is the only one which has been increasing unstoppably since the revolution. Already before the war, as a consequence of the smaller election circles and the outstanding position of Bismarck, the office of a parliamentary representative represented the highest level of the dairy-farm of associations, the most respected masters of handicrafts and the school professors sat together and quarreled for months on the question whether new mountain batteries should be granted for South America or whether the new torpedo boots should have fifty tons more or less of water-displacement. It never occurred to one of the respected men, to an expert of the bourgeois professional life, to dabble in handicraft. But the special atmosphere of the parliament brought along with it the fact that the regular circle of party friends would be empowered to authoritative judgements in the field of foreign policy and of military armament. But at that time the petty bourgeois still ruled, who is always better than the philistine. Now, the latter has reached the highest rung of the ladder. His dilettantism is surpassed only by his own imagination. The monotonously babbling flood of his unintelligent speech expands over all matters. Why does one have "experts" in the committees whose wisdom is imitated? Why do those unfortunate products of the doctoral machine, which all year long throws out new academic proletariat with eight-semester-long 'National Economics' into the hard world of money-earning, sit in hundreds in the party secretariats? They provide expert work on every matter, easily comprehensible and everywhere utilizable. Thus dilettantism becomes the charateristic of parliamentary government. No wonder! For, where prattling becomes a means of success, the gift of speech strikes all objectivity dead.

But governing must be undertaken, and there arises the question who does that. For, in spite of all changes and all lack of objectivity, the apparatus of authority runs on. The merit in this respect belongs unrestrictedly to the German bureaucrats. Let it be thankfully acknowledged that, in comparison to the older republics, Germany possesses the best and the purest bureaucratic body. Will that remain so and for how long? Strong efforts which lie in the direction of the

western democracy work against it. Already today, the bureaucracy is strongly
pervaded by "bureaucrats by virtue of their party" and not by virtue of education
or competence. Obviously, even a party can raise a capable man to the suited post.
Every caste, even that of the bureaucrats, needs fresh blood and outsiders. But the
party uses its influence, indeed not for the insertion of outsiders into the
bureaucratic career; rather, for the support of the most steadfast and the loudest
party criers. Thus the basic moral idea of service, once alive through the personal
binding of the bureaucracy to the princes, had to suffer strongly. Today there rules
contempt for the economics of the orders of the ruling houses. But was it not
more moral to faithfully perform one's duty for 25 years in the hope of being
distinguished by an order whose monetary worth perhaps amounted to five marks,
than to see in the bureaucratic profession nothing but a trade like any other? Even
if for the time being the cry for a higher salaried class sounds somewhat
restrained, the bureaucrat has however suffered damage in his political ethos. The
basic character of serving and the idea of human worth derived from it are on the
point of disappearing. State revenues and irrevocability today rule the thought of
all those who press towards the bureaucratic career. The lower and the middle
bureaucrats want to be elevated, the public employees to designate the
achievement of the bureaucratic character as the goal of their striving. They
always speak of the state, but mean often only themselves. They do not have the
feeling of being there for the people, but that the people must let the gracious
bureaucratic sun radiate over themselves. They do not see the service, but only the
power, of their position, and want to see this already brought to external
expression. Every bureaucrat wants to be a regent in little, there should be no
more lower bureaucrats, only higher ones. Earlier there were in chancellories
numerous middle and lower bureaucrats whose business it was to write. Today
they feel above that, and demand stenographers. Gottfried Keller was indeed also
a counsel secretary, and was not ashamed of this "official designation". But the
battle of those bureaucrats against the designation "writer" is more than amusing:

it is a sad sign of lack of inner worth, human and professional. It signifies that their self-consciousness does not arise in them out of fulfilment of duty, but that they seek external support in an exaggerated bureaucratic designation. They are spiritually unfree men who want to shamefully conceal their feeling of inferiority. The most beloved substitute title for writer has become that of inspector. One only asks oneself where the unnumbered army troops are which have to "inspect"; or does this title feign a superiour power that is indeed not present? Thus there reign, then, higher inspectors and councillors. Quite presumptuous persons, however, want to become presidents and thereby call the uniqueness of the Reich presidentship into question. The author sees the time coming when official permission merely to bear one's family name is granted as the highest distinction. All that is called the rule of the free people.

But even in a bureaucracy the feeling of envy triumphs. The "high" wages of the higher bureaucrats are always pointed to. "A sum suited for the rich already seems enviable and wasteful to the people. They naturally think only of their own needs and are correspondingly interested especially in the smaller and lower bureaucrat, who corresponds to their social level" (Tocqueville).[32] The majority of the people abandon the necessary concept of determining the livelihood of the upper classes. They want to drag everything down to themselves, no one should be better off than the masses themselves. In turn, the lower and the middle bureaucrat use the higher income of the upper to commence with efforts for the equalisation of their own income to the former. The emptiest egalitarianism and shameless welfare economy celebrate their triumphal procession.

With increasing quantity, however, quality must fall. That is law to which even the bureaucracy is subject. The enormous army of the German bureaucrats is a machine by and large working clumsily. Mobility is lost to them in the same measure that their weight increases. Against the welfare impulse of the party

[32] [*Ibid.*]

masses and the trade unions there is the abundance of tasks which the public
bodies have seized for themselves. The false conception of the state works itself
out in a way that the time is not far ahead when the number of those who wish
to live on tax receipts is greater than that of those who pay them. "A sixth of the
population is freed of the battle for existence and no man can bear the fact that
the battle for existence is taken away at the age of 25".[33] The bureaucratic
character is lent at random, purely economically active men (railway, post,
electricity-, gas-, and water-insurance, city construction, etc.) are called
bureaucrats, and a special position designed under quite different presuppositions
is granted to them. The idea that the insulting of a streetcar conductor is punished
more harshly than that of a high-standing man of private employment already has
a grotesque effect.

This Mammon admnistration - the mirror-image of the Mammon state -
rules. It kills all freedom, it is concerned with everything and, yet again, about
nothing. It torments, but never helps. If the administrative technique be ever so
perfect - at the moment it is very backward - it can never replace the citizens'
spirit of self-administration. One reads in Stein[34] how he storms against the
bureaucratic state, one follows the battle of Bismarck against the bureaucracy.
Stein calls the numberless army of bureaucrats a "true scourge of God for
Germany". What falls into their hands is petrified and hardened. Even if the
individual bureaucrat may be a very distinguished man and an excellent worker.
The official channels hold him fast on the "assembly line" and grants nothing but
the fitting of the famous 'screw'. Mostly however, for the sake of this screw, an
exchange of writings must take place, because it is not there; and until it enters
the line has passed by. If Stein and Bismarck had lived today they would hardly

---

[33] Spengler, *Neubau des [deutschen] Reiches*, München: C.H. Beck, 1924, Kap.2: 'Staatsdienst und
Persönlichkeit', p.33].
[34] [Heinrich, Freiherr vom und zum Stein (1757-1831), the Prussian statesman who was influential in
the reorganisation of the bureaucracy].

change their judgement, rather they would sharpen it. It is not directed against the bureaucrats as men but against the fact that a professional caste has become a general go-between of public businesses. That is already bad! But it becomes more dangerous when, thanks to the weakness of parliamentary government, the high bureaucrats consider themselves as the real power-holders. How far this conceit of power goes, posterity knows from Bismarck, who never succeeded at all in removing Holstein[35] from the foreign office. Today the highest bureaucrats indeed make their promotions and advancements among themselves; the will of the parliamentary minister plays therein a very subordinate role. The bad saying that the German Reich is ruled today by 300 ministerial directors and state secretaries whose favorite occupation is the departmental strife has a kernel of truth: it indicates the anarchy of the present situation. These higher bureaucrats work now under quite special conditions: free of political responsibility, they actually influence politics in an extraordinary manner. Throughout the continuous change of parliamentary superiours, they are the only experts. For that reason, the most ambitious amongst them also want to rule. They know how to skilfully obtain, at the right time, the busy minister's signature for their plans. On the other hand, a feeling of uncertainty overcomes them. For they have to reckon with diverse superiors and ones in opposition to one another. Consequently, they obtain a certain colourlessness and develop a flexibility which, more than tactics, is communicated to their life. The famous middle line becomes their guiding principle. Their work principle is *"noli tangere"*. The last exit from all difficulties however is *laisser faire, laisser aller.* Hard situations which demand powers of decision are hardly developed in these men. That the higher bureaucracy worked during the revolution like a machine was less a virtue than a weakness. The orders were locked up in the drawer, some painful speeches exchanged on the oath of loyalty, and the protection of the monarchy explained with a shrug of the

---

[35] [Friedrich von Holstein (1837-1909) played a key role in shaping German foreign policy especially after the fall of Bismarck. He was forced to resign in 1906].

shoulders as an impossibility. The military bureaucracy, in contrast to the troop officer, was not essentially differently disposed; this too must be mentioned for the sake of justice. Since the collapse, there were in Germany enough critical moments; but seldom did the German bureaucrat decisively attack, brave as he considered himself. Mostly the driving force came from others and had to be achieved in opposition to him. All German border battles, after the end of the war, whose favorable outcome is to be traced back to free self-moving forces, were won against the bureaucracy. From everything there becomes evident a deficient understanding of national necessities, incapacity for great measures, lack of preparedness for action. Only this way of thought explains the deplorable manner in which bureaucrats, regardless of party membership and of persuasion, acted against the numerous circles which sacrificed themselves for the German national culture in the colonies, at the borders, and abroad. A turbid chapter of German democracy, over which a rare unanimity reigns. The genuine bureaucrat indeed bows only to the authority which threatens his position; to that which approaches him pleadingly he shows his superiority, even if it may be established a thousand times that the latter has performed the most valuable service to the state. Thus, for this bureaucrat, it is a crime to want to serve one's people differently than in a bureaucratic position or as a party duck. Woe to the people who are delivered to the councillors; they are threatened at the earliest by revolution and external political collapse. For, their spiritual powers, without which they cannot exist, are suppressed by these tyrants.

The all-powerfulness of the bureaucracy threatens most strongly the foreign policy which precisely cannot be carried out without that great character which is, in general, lacking in the bureaucracy. The bureaucrat is an administrator. The maintenance of the internal political situation lies closer to him than the carrying out of a great external political programme. The bureaucrat is not a historically and sociologically disposed man, but a formally thinking one. The career of the higher bureaucrat is not accomplished in the world but in the chancellory. The juridical training is, in its exclusiveness, likewise not suited to make thinking in broad connections customary. The bureaucrat knows no responsibility before history, but only before his superiors. Modest but secure relations are more exciting for him than ventures for the nation. Where it is a question of the existence or non-existence of peoples, the bureaucracy fails as leadership. It is not used to venturing and, therefore, wins nothing. The maintenance of the "*status quo*" becomes the purpose and goal of all politics which bureaucrats conduct. The historical act falls out of circulation.

Thus then the foreign policy of modern democracy is badly set out. The bureaucrat is not suited to external political leadership, the parliamentary minister, because he is too short-lived, cannot develop any external political activity, for which reason great aims are lost. Accident and mass passions play increasingly the role of historical providence. In politics, one obeys more the feelings than the superiour reason. Nothing is more childish than the view of our literary mob-worshippers that the rule of the street guarantees peace. The common people and the masses "guarantee" nothing but the unexpected outbreak of unrestricted passions. Tocqueville reports that the avoidance of a war with England was due only to the unshakeable will of Washington.[36] The public opinion would have stormily demanded the declaration of war. During the world war, resisting governments were simply forced to a declaration of war against Germany by the street folk who were worked on by the Entente propaganda. Nothing is more war-like than mass democracy, and no state has spilt more blood than France after the French Revolution. On the other hand, however, there exists for unrestricted democracy the danger that it would lose its war as easily as it stumbles into war-like developments. The democracies which do not save themselves through transitional dictatorship indeed do not carry on war to the end. "For, the people feel much more than they deliberate; they do not have a clear idea of the future

[36] *Ibid.*

and the danger exists that, in the evils of the moment, they forget the much greater ones of a downfall".[37] This statement of Tocqueville prophesied the fate of the German people in the world war.

Not only was the bureaucracy lacking in will to action, but almost every beneficiary of the modern republic. A trait of reaction pervades the progressives. It goes so far as to deny the principles of parliamentarianism itself. With what bitterness, for example, do the parties of the Centre battle to eliminate the large side-wing parties in order to exercise a quiet rule of force, and to shut off every fresh draught of air. Precisely the appeals of Liberalism for the assembly betray an "unliberal" character. They aim at the lasting rule of the Centre and the perpetuation of its beneficiaries. Indeed, the majority, not the minority, are misused and violated with regard to the usual basic Liberal-democratic idea. It is customarily objected against a comparative observation of German relations with those of the model parliamentary country, England, that in Germany there are world-view parties and, therefore, matters stand otherwise here. The system therefore which served as a model for the downfall was not at all aspired to in its good side. For a time one could believe that the German development went in the direction of the two-party system. This hope may be considered as buried. It is apparent that the social foundation of the English people is different and that state-forms without such are empty edifices without content. Thus the rule of the inferiour indeed comes about in the way of the dictatorship of the minority: really the most amazing perversity that is thinkable. Here the objection could take ground that this development already means the rise of genuine leadership, of a leadership which deliberately abandons the foundation of the majority, and, based only on itself, strives for universal recognition.

But the 'Rule of the Centre'[38] in fact does not at all lose in numbers, it

---

[37] [*Ibid.*].

[38] Julius Paul Köhler, [*Die Hindenburg-Linie und die Herrschaft der Mitte*] Leipzig, Xenienverlag, [1928].

only obtains the majority surreptitiously through skilled playing out of the side-wing parties against one another. Therefore one cannot already speak of leadership in that high sense, apart from the basic considerations made above, because the will of acting against the masses is lacking in this system. The individual party leader may possess a personal ethics, and be capable of no immoral action: the social ethics, that of the preparedness for responsibility, is missing. For, to that belongs the courage to swim against the current. The rule of the Centre however is built on weakness. Only lasting pliability on all sides, only inner balance, borne by the striving to do justice even to the most inferiour claims, holds this leader at the top. They are even less than those "neutral greats" which, according to Carl Schmitt, the politicians of the Centre approximately develop.

The authority which the present day-state demands is, in fact, forced obedience, in no way facilitated by inner willingness. For, authority may not be judged according to the degree in which the individual freedom is chained, but according to the measure in which voluntary subjection to it takes place. Authority in this sense is a moral-social concept and not a purely political one. In the old army, whose discipline was built on the much disparaged "slavish submission", ruled much more inner willingness than the present-day state citizen brings with respect to the "self-elected" government. There indeed the idea of voluntary service rooted in the feeling lived. In the present-day state only the fear of punishment still holds the "subject" in check. That is not surprising, where every man knows that business and state leadership are connected to each other in their innermost essence, that party and state coincide with each other. Authority arises always from the distance which the leader may socially maintain from the people led. Above all things, however, even from that which the state leaders preserve from the interest groups. The feeling and the certainty, that one who is raised above all interests claims it, causes attention to the leader. Since, however, the popular consciousness today is moved rightly in the opposite idea, true feeling of authority cannot in general grow. This even the power-holders of the German republic feel now. They have therefore invented a peculiar sort of government system: with regard to one's own political friends one is Liberal to the core, one lets them say, write, and do what they want, if the direction of their utterances of opinion only goes against the people of different persuasion. Thus it comes about that often, instead of the "protection of the republic", the disintegration of the state is propagated. For, the individualistic apostles have not yet recognized that even the republic is a state which must be affirmed. The other side however, which is in and for itself disposed only in a state-enthusiastic way, is persecuted on account of its aversion to the present-day party democracy. The few affirmers of the state and republic thus fall into the rear assembly and form a mistrusted minority. But one who does not consider the present-day condition of society and state as the final conclusion of wisdom is bitterly combatted by the new power-holders. To the left, libertinage; to the right, the whip: that is the "authority" of the modern German democracy. The unjustly disparaged Metternich - for he had at least the idea of a political picture of Europe - would blush with envy if he observed the refined methods with which Liberalism follows in his tracks. The democratic despots are, to be sure, not so generous with confinement as the first half of the 19th century. Perhaps they like to open the doors of the prison in a welcoming manner to the resistors. But that happens only in quite rough cases. Mostly they are satisfied with the surely operating means of bringing the "state criminal" down from his position and reputation. The means to the personal denigration of those who do not greet the "victory of the people all along the line" with enthusiasm are extremely petty and fussed over. What is performed just in the realm of flag decrees in the last decade offers a frightful picture of the lack of freedom and the neglect of the soul of the people. The subject should be made docile with unrelenting pressure. The predictions of a Balzac, a Tocqueville, a Kant, a Montesquieu, a Chamberlain, who all warned of spiritual enslavement and the rule of force of mass democracy have been movingly confirmed. The German democracy has not raised the banner of political freedom. It has either disgracefully betrayed it or manipulated it a way which lets the dregs rise up to the top. The age of democratic absolutism is over. If it is not removed, then the German people are threatened by the democratic Inquisition.

All that occurs, however, under the flag of progress. If man, however, should approximate ever more to the divine being, and moral fulfilment - the only justified, eternal human effort for progress - then it must, according to the presentation so far, be true that our age stands not under the sign of this progress, but under that of retrogression. There is no higher development without the rise of the chosen ones who have overcome the all-too-human in themselves to the highest possible degree. There is no rise of the masses to genuine culture without the impressive model of the true leader. At all times it was the duty of the superiour to drag the dull along with them; indeed, it must be said: even under the use of force. Humanity requires discipline, that is an eternal law of social life. What would have become of the West if the legions of Caesar, the great rulers of the earlier Middle Ages had not lent their sword to culture? What would have become of the individual man if there were not an education which carried out even with strictness the suppression of lower instincts in man to the degree which makes the achieved higher condition a joyful custom? The Liberal educational ideal of education without discipline could arise only in heads alienated from reality which glimpsed in that insight the only hindrance of immoral ways of conduct. Experience teaches that the removal of discipline would have as a consequence the battle of all against all. This effective means of education has today almost disappeared. Somewhere there still stir in modern society interests which would feel themselves hurt if the training rod were wielded by the state. The state in perfection is always an educational state. Not in the ridiculous sense that the teachers becomes state officials but in the spirit of Plato. Where the highest force gives up the protection of the educational task, the masses sink ever deeper, obeying the law of gravity, and drag those who should be leaders with them. In the end, even the true great leader-natures are suffocated and destroyed.

Thus the face of Western mankind becomes increasingly harder, their soul increasingly poorer. But the civilised man swaggers proudly and babbles of the progress of the human race, because he needs to climb no more steps, because he can tear through the country in the upholstery of his automobile and because he can receive stock-exchange reports through the wireless. Where however does the German man remain, who educates and sets his stamp on him, if the state abandons its high task and leaves to a thoughtless freedom of speech and writing the spiritual disintegration of the people become unprincipled? External freedom can be vouchsafed in some measure if those endowed with it wish the same thing from similar moral determination. But to vouchsafe external freedom to a people, besides, who consist of millions of spiritually different and unequal individuals means to give rise to the battle of all against all. Either spiritual freedom or social. Both at the same time lead to national cultural and political self-destruction. Here even economic success does not help much. The Germans call the English a nation of shopkeepers: questionable, whether they are not on the point of becoming as shopkeeperish as the latter. The English businessman did not proceed so much for the sake of the revenue as for masterly conquest. If, however, the businessman lacks the political support in his people, he is forced, not to battle for the world market, but to obtain it by stealth. Commercialism thereby begins to rule in the inner being of a people. The new German, genuinely philistine, separation from economics which is supposed to rescue the German people from destruction belongs here. They are on the point of subjecting themselves so basically to the spirit of the age, which is commercial, as never a people did. Does this mean that the German people will make the manner and method of the Jewish people their own, with the result that - from a broad perspective - they would once again be forcibly repressed?

Thus does the formation of masses and the lack of true rule operate destructively on the national cultural character. No one, however, wants to admit this. The historical writers and social critics abandon their warning task and do not support themselves against the triumphal procession of inferiority. Either because they feared state retributory measures, or because they themselves are captivated by the "spirit of the age". Where the masses rule, even the historical philosopher falls victim to the illusion that the masses make history. He does not see any more the driving forces, undervalues the power of personality, and considers at least every resistance as utopian. In fact, however, the masses are not there to shape destiny but to be determined. Where this does not happen any longer, state and culture decay and the peoples degenerate.

X

From the decayed society to the vital community

No community without a common feeling of worth. This principle already presented in the first part of the book is the key to the understanding of the social and political decay as it has been represented in the last chapter. Every feeling of worth however is basically a belief, and its uniformity therefore secured most strongly by vital religiosity. In the ages strong in belief, society and state receive the law founding them from religious revelation. The ruling body is felt as established by God and, in turn, the leading stratum feels itself obliged to the community. Rule is, at the same time, service with regard to the divine order. Between the top and the bottom flow alternating streams, and it is a matter of less importance whether the community life is at one time built and influenced stronger from the top, at another time more from the bottom; decisive remains the common feeling of reposing in the same wholeness willed by God. Whether the state is ruled by a single person who derives his ruling vocation from divine grace or by a plurality of persons who give themselves a ranked form in their consciousness of being children of God, is in no way decisive; for, all laws come from God. Thus, even the hierarchical structure of the Catholic Church is an admirable union of democratic and monarchic ideas: every priest can - and indeed through election - attain the seat of Peter. This aristocracy, however, is formed from above by appointment. The power of the Pope is absolutely unlimited.

The opposition between democracy from below and the rule by force from above obtains its modern significance only the moment that the community of values whose political will-content should be presented by the state disintegrates. When the Christian cultural community began to crumble, and the Catholic natural law was replaced by the rational law, there were, temporarily, still limited communities of value represented by the national cultural circle. The national feeling provided to society and state the community-forming power. It removed the opposition of will present in every multiplicity of men in the national community of values. This itself was at that time uncontested, it coincided with Classicism, in which the humanistic educational ideal sought to redeem with its all-encompassing worldliness the universalism of the Church. Society and people still formed at that time a whole, full of inner uniformity of worth; a parliamentary democracy arising at that time could lead to a healthy formation of the state will. Majority decision within an equally oriented community of values is significant. This national community of culture and worth is - as already set out above - characterized by the society of notables. It is the historical transition from the social organization of orders of the Middle Ages to the dispersed mass society of the present.

With the fading away of Classical Idealism, the last world- picture striving for a wholistic world-view disappeared. Society disintegrated, the national community of values - robbed of its ethical-cultural content - became questionable. Nationalism became feeling, became a direction like many others which now arose for the first time. For, the national idea may assert itself only where it arises from racial spiritual worthiness, and thus is, in the broadest sense of the word, cultural, and does not represent only one of many possibilities which are given to the universalistic impulse of man, when he seeks, aberrantly and branching off, for himself an object of emotional reverence. In place of the true God, then, enter idols which could be called as well nation as class, economics as Communism, civilisation as humanity. - Every sense of the whole, of unconditional existence, of a historical 'ought' is lost. With Hegel began that reverse belief in the historical existence which had to end with the complete emptying of all values. One believed still only in the legitimacy of Nature and of social life, no longer in living men, in moral content and eternal values. With the scientific belief rises that age of legal positivism whose present-day representative, Kelsen,[39] logically fully equates law and state to each other. Every state is for him a constitutional state and every politically created law justice. The value content of state and law plays no role for this legal philosophical school any longer. Democracy is for it an impersonal rule of law, and it imagines the ideal democracy as leaderless. Value and reality have no more *raison d'être* in this world of abstractions which has become absurd. The idea of the whole is transferred simply to the letter of the law, the revenge of the metaphysical instinct is revealed in an idea of the state fully alienated from reality. Hermann Heller[40] is of the same view when he thinks, "metaphysically this humanity lived and lives on an overpowering belief in science and history, on the inverted religion of a this-worldly paradise, whose legal truths of redemption science has to discover and history to realize".

This life-killing legal formalism in fact rules, as is demonstrated in the description of the modern party state. It remains as the only exit of a society, which abandons value content and uniformity of will. Mechanical collectivism must necessarily set up the rules for life together which prevent anarchy, because a spiritually living idea of worth penetrating the community order is lacking. Where this is the case, where the society and state-forming population cannot

---

[39] *Vom Wert und Wesen der Demokratie*, 1929 [Hans Kelsen (1881-1973), Viennese jurist who made major contributions to the formulation of constitutional law in Austria].

[40] *Europa und der Faschismus*, Berlin and Leipzig, Walter de Gruyter & Co., 1929, [Kap.1, 'Die politische Krise Europas', in *Gesammelte Schriften*, Leiden: A.W. Sijtjhoff, 1971, Bd.II, p.474. Heller (1891-1933) was a jurist and Social Democratic politician. In opposition to Kelsen's theory of political norms, Heller's conception of the state is as a reality based on human activity].

develop any more organic will, only two ways remain for the development of the
will: the modern democracy and the sole rule of an individual. Both - that must
be emphasized - do not arise from living law. Both are forms of rule by force
which creates only formal legal principles. They are differentiated from each other
only by the different constitution of the existing bearers of rule. In the party
democracy, the majority, which is - as was already set out -really no rule, rules
unrestrictedly; in a dictatorship, a single person, presupposing that it is not only
a method of government but is rooted in a constitution. Both forms of the state
are, in the sense of the organic idea of the law, states of injustice. For, both live
so long from force that they do not succeed either in justifying the rule of the
majority as the product of an organic whole, or in establishing the dictatorial
political will organically. Italian Fascism makes attempts in the latter direction,
wherefore a final conclusion on it is not yet possible. It stands otherwise with the
party democracy. It already has its "organic" age, early parliamentarianism, behind
it. To attain a new community of values through the class parties is an historical
and logical impossibility. The way to the true national state never leads through
party rule and the ballot-box.

It can be objected now that the injustice of the rule of the majority is
smaller than that of sole rule; democracy, however, balances the oppositions and
forms a uniform plurality of will-orientations. With regard to that there remains
to be emphasised indeed that, measured against an unconditional law, an injustice
never becomes smaller when it affects fewer men; still less can the social and
ethical value of a minority be greater than that of a majority. Besides, there is the
consideration that in democracy the will of the majority does not really rule, but
"the mind thinks, money leads" (Spengler). The "philosopher of the downfall" is
therefore right when he conjures up Caesarism, which frees the people from the
rule of money, as the moral redeemer, to which a belief of the author in the
coming age of Caesarism should in no way - as will be expounded later - be
connected. Correct, to be sure, is an objection which the humanitarian, weak-

nerved, money- worshipping bourgeoisie can raise in favour of democracy: that it is easier to rule against a minority than against the entire people. This convenient excuse, arising from an unheroic intellectual constitution, is however not always sound. Often, dictatorships are conducted with a stronger agreement of the ruled than "free" democracies. It is only a matter of whether the act of agreement takes place before or after the action of the government. The bourgeois statute-book differentiates between consent (antecedent agreement) and approbation (subsequent agreement). If one disregards the political legal forms, it is precisely as democratic to work with the approbation of the ruled as with their consent. Basically, indeed, genuine democracy, which must be daily confirmed anew, is supported only on approbation. In mass democracies, where the decision of the people is an almost unusable means, one cannot speak of a consent of the people in the actions of the ruling persons; indeed, not even in the establishment of the government, which is mostly beyond its will. It even fully contradicts the idea of self-rule to permit governmental actions in advance. Thus there remained as the essential expression of genuine democracy only the right of recalling the ruling persons. Mistakes of the leaders are, accordingly, not eliminated in democracy, but the erring person is only removed when the misfortune has occurred. Theoretically, one could therefore represent all government actions of democracy as a chain of mistakes which have led to the deposition of the incompetent. Then only the fact that the "sinners" are called once again to leading posts, as is the case in almost all democracies, remains as worth noting. Seldom does the parliament basically take account of a statesman; mostly, only when he reveals himself to be a man and has attempted to be more than a will-less representative of the people. The people themselves, however, in their social feelings healthier than political philosophers and understanding-obsessed doctrinaire persons, willingly tolerate at their head strong leaders who know how to maintain themselves. They "approve" their actions mostly more enthusiastically than the ruling activity of the majority. Carl Schmitt[41] is therefore in no way wrong when he affirms Caesarism as the form of democracy which could be even more democratic than the modern party rule. He sees thereby, to be sure, the system of democracy less formal-legally than, rather, politically. But, in the end, a state-form is living life and not a dead letter of the law.

Nevertheless there remains as the most effective objection against dictatorship, and for democracy, the opinion that rule by forces stands against constitutional state. Completely false naturally is the opposition of constitutional state and power state. According to the arguments of the first part on force and power, it is clear that the opposite of a power state would in fact be the powerless state. Ernst Krieck[42] correctly designates this artifically created opposition as an absurdity. This concept can at first be interpreted in such a way that the state does not wish any justice, but is based on the self-will of a class or an individual. Such a state is hardly possible in the age of civilisation. No leader can, in the long run, do without a minimum of agreement of those led. Doubtlessly all modern dictatorships are borne by a smaller or larger wave of agreement. - It is however imaginable for the world-view represented in this book that an individual represent the true law in a higher measure than the whole, at least in a society which is broken up and emptied of every value-content. If therefore a value-free or, indeed, worthless rule of philistines or of petty bourgeois exists, if fellahistation (Spengler) threatens, if the leadership abandons manliness and brings about through its powerlessness the downfall of the society, then the arrogation of power of the leader can be morally justified "by its own right", even if no voice encourages him to it except that of his own conscience. Such considerations however lie mostly far from the champions of the so-called constitutional state.

---

[41] *Verfassungslehre*, [Berlin: Duncker und Humblot] 1928, [p.237].

[42] *Der Staat des deutschen Menschen*, Berlin: Verlag Junker & Dünnhaupt, [1927; Ernst Krieck (1882-1947) was an educational scientist and cultural politician whose antidemocratic views led him to associations with, first, the neoconservative circles and, later, the Nazi movement, serving the latter for a while as its official educational propagandist].

For them, this concept is restricted to the formal legal foundation of the present rule; indeed, the fanatical democrat goes so far as to designate every constitution not built on the universal franchise as contrary to law: the convinced Weimarians do not shrink back from opposing the Reich of Bismark as a "power state" against the present-day "Reich of law". Only the claim to self-rule, which is attached to every individual man from birth, is considered as law. Only the structure from below, from the individual to the state, corresponds to the individual legal, human legal conception. Freedom and equality are the two conditions without which the individualist cannot imagine any constitutional state. From whence he derives this norm, however, remains questionable. To derive freedom and equality from natural law is a doubtful undertaking. Already Haller[43] points to the fact that the natural is the relation of dependence of the weaker on the superiour power of the stronger. In the last chapter, too, it was sufficiently explained that in the democracy of equality and freedom the stronger similarly prevails, but, to be sure, not the morally stronger.

Freedom and equality had a certain sense as law-forming norms so long as there was a substantial idea of moral reasonableness, social justice, thus at the beginning of the 19th century. When the idea of metaphysical content however was lost, one understood by constitutional state "every state in which the capacity for action of the ruling people is restricted by some laws" (Hermann Heller). The ideal of the constitutional state is thus to be understood historically only as a reversion to feudal rule. The self-will of the ruling people had to be made impossible through laws which the ruled concluded. All organs of the state should be subject to laws. Heller correctly points to the fact that this rule of law emerges from itself as soon as it is understood impersonally and no longer as the rule of

---

[43] [Karl Ludwig von Haller (1768-1854), Swiss German statesman and publicist, who dedicated his life to the destruction of the work of the French Revolution. His chief work is the *Restauration der Staatswissenschaft oder Theorie des natürlichen Zustandes der Chimäre des künstlich-bürgerlichen engegengesetzt*, 6 vols. (1816-34), where he maintained the inevitability of inequality among men and the superiority of the conception of the state as a slowly grown, God-willed organism].

the will of the people. For, only men can rule, and democracy is only possible "as a hierarchy of ruling acts of will which, motivated by legal principles and legal decrees, individualise these norms for their part temporally, locally and personally. Political rule of the law is a rule of the will acting within the scope of laws, it is standardized power or it is nothing at all".

Where the interests, spanned by no community of value, battle for bare rule (class battle), where no organic way to a standardisation of the will exists, no true state power can be developed, and a lasting opposition arises: on the one hand, between the existing laws which, made mechanically, forfeit a response in a political community of value, and the people. It does not understand law any more. On the other hand, between the laws and the rulers, who should do justice to the demands of the state, but are restricted by all-too strong legal bindings. The "constitutional state" thus becomes the enemy of all: the people whom it should protect feel themselves suppressed, the rulers find it a hindrance to state political expressions of will. Thereby the basic law of the state, the constitution, is devalued in every relation and the way to force is free. Thus, even then, modern democracy, distancing itself increasingly more from the Liberal demands, has practically annulled the division of powers, and ignored the basic state laws - and founded the unbounded rule by force of the majority. The legal positivism of Kelsen, which equates law and state, is the capping stone of this development. A constitutional state without a supporting community of law is just impossible and the mechanically calculated will of the majority can never replace the community of political worth.

Therewith the historical death-sentence on modern democracy has been passed. It is only a question of whether it is removed by a rule of force which does not bear in itself the elements of disintegration and the weaknesses of the majority rule, or whether the development of a new community of political worth and therewith of an organic state will be drawn into the realm of the possible. The rule of force of an individual is, if an intelligent personality exerts it to counter the rule of force of the majority, to be preferred to the rule of force of the majority, provided that it can maintain itself without a civil war. Dictatorship is a governmental method imaginable constitutionally even in democracies, it is however not a state form. If Fascism had removed the king, it would well have been, in spite of the great Fascist Council, in a quandary on the question of the succession of the dictator. Mussolini indeed did not develop, when he appropriated the state power for himself, any essentially comprehensive programme other than the declaration that the Fascists wanted to rule Italy. But once come into power, he was incessantly concerned to make the Fascist constitutional state from dictatorial governmental methods, to establish new bases of value, and to fill the people from top downwards with a new political idea. He wants what the historical legal school and Romanticism in Germany wanted: to bestow on Italy an organic state.

The chief objection against this effort now runs that a revolution can always found only a new rule of force, but that conservative and organic thought are opposed to the revolutionary. For, Conservatism is the belief in development that is like natural growth. A Conservative thinker like Georg Quabbe[44] thinks that in democracy the renewer is never forced to break the formal law, since even a small group of the people have it in their power to convince the majority and therewith to receive the state leadership into their hands. This belief in the insight of the masses is perhaps as unconservative as the overvaluation of tolerance of the democratic power-holders. With both these presuppositions one cannot think of a political victory of new ideas. For, there is nothing more tenacious than democracy because it is built on intellectually incapicated masses and on the support of all the beneficiaries. Quabbe reports even then that there were many great revolutionaries of doubtlessly Conservative stamp, from Gregory VII to Richelieu. He could also have mentioned Bismarck. On the other hand, he admits

---

[44] *Tar a Ri*, Berlin, Verlag für Politik und Wirtschaft, 1927.

that a conflict between formal rights and the inner conviction of right of the people is possible, that the victory of the democratic form of government does not secure the lasting agreement of both. The tender plant of legal consciousness is hardly a product of the souls of that enormous crowd of ignorant people, fools and philistines who form the majority of every people. Even the most decided progressive must admit the possibility that ideas of unequivocal objectivity may develop in a part of the people without these ideas being able to transform themselves, on account of the resistance of the majority, into law, e.g. into constitutional law. If the minority attained its goal outside the constitutionally given way, one could justly say: the inner legal consciousness of the nation, represented by its best and most powerful people, has prevailed against the law which is in this case, namely on account of the resistance of the majority, not formally alterable.

The objection of Quabbe that this tempting thought process signifies the declaration of lasting revolution and is therefore impassable for the Conservatives is not convincing. To be Conservative means to want the natural life to which legal regulation belongs. But how, if this life is threatened by the force of a lifeless law? If a mechanical legal order damages the vital law of society, then the statement of Ihering[45] is always true, that force sacrifices law to rescue life. For, law is even for life and not vice-versa. If Edmund Burke warned the English of every "break with the past", therewith is not meant the break with a dead law. There is also a revolution of maintenance (Hofmannsthal) which wishes to heal the breaches with the past.

Thereby the use of force which occurs in the name of true law is affirmed. Herein lies the difference of the conception of the organic society from the doctrine of the circle of elites as the Italian sociologist Pareto[46] has developed

---

[45] [Rudolf von Ihering (1818-1892), eminent German jurist who stressed the social reality of all human life and the teleological significance of laws, author of *Der Kampf ums Recht* (1872), *Der Zweck im Recht* (1877-74), *Der Geist des römischen Rechts* (1852-65)].

[46] Even the fact that Pareto introduced the author in Lausanne to Social Science cannot change

it. He correctly sees the system of parliamentary democracy, which he, exactly like this book, calls plutocratic democracy, in that in which the ruling classes maintain themselves in power only through cunning, deception, and calculation. The "elite" of parliamentary democracy of the recent times is even not a selection of the best any longer, but one of the inferiour. The socially obliged do not rule but financial wealth. But always the minority rules, and it is only a matter of the selection standards and their basis of worth. "Between a war-like landed-propertied aristocracy and a plutocracy there is finally only the difference of methods and of evaluation, of life style and world-view: the fact of social rule is the same in both cases. A revolution can transvalue mankind and alter its level; it can never, however, cross the limits of the human, never remove the dynamic following from the differences of human power and situation and establish a heaven of equality and fraternity on earth. Where men live together, it follows, from the inequality of their type and function, that a top and a bottom, rule and service, is set up. The formal determination of such relations is the social law" (Ernst Krieck).

One must however differentiate between a genuine elite which feels itself socially obliged and a ungenuine which rules only by virtue of material force. A raw rule of force will never be able to count on the agreement of the ruled. It will also not be able to standardize the people in their will or, indeed, culturally from top to bottom - through an educational dictatorship. Even the protracted education to an idea of the nation as an all-encompassing basis of worth is impossible. One who strives for this forgets that precisely nationalism is a product of democracy. After this basis of worth has been shaken, it would be contradictory to want to establish it anew from above. State and right must be derived from an unconditional spiritual fundamental law, should a uniform state occur. The idea of the nation cannot do this, at least not any longer. Heller is right when he

anything in his opposed view. [Vilfredo Pareto (1848-1923) is reknowned for his sociological treatises, *Manuale di Economia*, Milano, 1906, and *Trattato di Sociologia generale*, Firenze, 1916. He was appointed chairman of political economy at Lausanne in 1894. Pareto's final social philosophy was based on a theory of elitism which favored political authoritarianism].

maintains of it that it says nothing about the concrete structure of the state, nothing about the definite positioning above and below within the state, wherefore nationalism too is always forced to borrowing from other circles of thought.

This knowledge means for the German nationalists of the old stamp a bitter drop in the cup of its national enthusiasm. One however who believes that he can rescue the German people and the German state through those thinking of a dictatorial nation sees only the morrow, not the day after, not to mention the distant future. One cannot build from top to bottom, if one wishes to establish a lasting structure. Such a state had to be inorganic, would be precisely as necessarily a centralistic dictatorship as Fascism upto now exercises it. For, today, it is still a corporative state without vital corporate bodies.

On the other hand, it would be misguided to leave everything to the structure from below to the top. In centralistic, unrestricted democracies, a growth from the base to the top is impossible. It is artificially held down, restrained or indeed destroyed. It is also not thought out organically to leave the development of a whole to the parts. The parts themselves must be nourished by the whole, balanced and brought into harmony, if they should fulfil their duties. Essentially organic is the reciprocal opposition and effect of the members on one another as well as between the members and the whole, and finally the self-determination and the freedom of development resulting from it, in the members and in the whole (Krieck). The nature of the living and the growing demands a movement in polarity.

A dictatorship from the top to the bottom cannot thus produce a universally binding world of values, without which organic life and therewith the future political community of will is unthinkable. It can at best be the highest expression and executor of the new life striving for form. The new vitality must come from life itself. The first part of the book, which set forth the development of a new feeling of the whole, obtains in this place its justification. We must refer to it generally. It tries not only to describe the new life-feeling but to conceive it in its essence and to develop its standards. That the rest of the present-day world-views, which seek to perpetuate the class oppositions and therewith the impossibility of a new community of worth, are not suited to unravelling these standards was explained. However, let a brief glance at the beginnings of a new conception of society, as they become visible in all possible situations, be permitted.

The powerful reaction against the purely understanding-related legal thought of the 19th century has set in, based on a philosophy which does not exhaust itself in dialectics but strives for the vision of the whole. One does not believe any more in laws, neither in natural scientific ones, whose doubtfulness was exhibited by leading natural scientists (Nernst and Dingler), nor in the legitimacy of social life. As Nietzsche became a champion of the new vitality for the entire Western cultural sphere, so the life philosophy of a Bergson influenced the French social sciences. The Syndicalist revolutionary Sorel, of great influence on Italian Fascism, teaches "the free creation of warriors morally convinced and inspired by myths, the trained power of heroic pessimists".[47] In the Socialist camp, a new direction defends itself as much against the life-killing materialism as a young Conservatism, in turn, loads itself with the revolutionary energies of a new vitality. Even Catholicism reveals currents which turn against the Liberalising humanitarianism in its own ranks. Common to these movements running through the peoples and their parties is a new life-feeling. It is heroic, pessimistic with regard to life, sober in the jugement of reality, and related to the society and not to the individual. This new man is basically political, anti-utilitarian, ready for action, moved by feeling, and tragic.

Certainly, this spiritual conception is closely related to that of Romanticism. But, because Romanticism could not break through to state-formation, those believing in the understanding are always ready to reproach the most recent movement of renewal with alienation from reality and failure. These

---

[47] Cited after Heller, *loc.cit.*, [p.486; cf. Georges Sorel's *Réflexions sur la Violence*, Paris, 1908]

complaints however are also philosophically grounded: you demand a new activity - so they say - but without direction and goal. Movement is to you a goal in itself, and valid form unimportant. You are powerless people filled with resentment, without being able to found new values. You teach life, but do not say what correct life is. You affirm religion, especially Catholicism, but are basically heathen. (A reproach which is especially made by Blüher)[48]. You are 'quasi-Catholics', not true believers (Heller). You want value without recognising more than its abstract concept. What is lacking in you is the tangible world of values, effective spiritually as well as sociologically. The rule of the best - thus thinks Heller - is a demand without content, so long as there is not present a universally binding idea of the good. Without the relations to an unconditional greatness, a living value-feeling which alone makes life-formation possible will never awake. But what is your unconditional value?

In order to counter these objections, the first part of this work would have to be presented anew, and indeed with special respect to the questions posed here. Their answer has therefore been already anticipated. Because these questions upto now remained still open, a purely philosophical foundation was given to this political book. Genuine feeling of the whole, in the last analysis religious, develops even the value-standards which fulfil a new social reality in a universally binding manner. It is, for example, false to consider heroism only as a feeling and not as as value- feeling; in the heroic feeling lies, rather, already another evaluation of life than in humanitarianism. The total experience brings to consciousness the difference of organic life from mechanistic organisation. The series of values obtained in the first part of this book conveyed a judgement on almost all questions of social formation. If the scope of this book were not limited and if it did not lie in the essence of organic thought to encounter value-decisions

---

[48] [Hans Blüher (1888-1955), author of *Elemente der deutschen Position: offener Brief an den Grafen Keyserling in deutscher und christlicher Sache*, Berlin: Ring Verlag, 1927; *Die Theorie der Religionen und ihres Untergangs*, Berlin-Tempelhof: B. Weise, 1912; *Der Geist der Weltrevolution*, Prien: Anthropos Verlag, 1920].

from case to case, there would be no question of political formation which could not be answered objectively. The new life-feeling is in the process of development; it is developed by men who, from different levels, partly burdened with the prejudices of the previous age, strive for new goals. A ready common dogmatism of value is therefore not to be expected at the stage of the rise of a new value-feeling. The critics demand a result in cases where the effects have just begun. That a convergence of the bearers of this new value-feeling, in spite of their origin from opposed camps, takes place is already a guarantee of the future commonality of the objective value concept. The universally binding practical world of values can today be at best surmised: an attempt such as this book makes. It is false to deprive the organic life-picture, even if it gives up religious dogmas - not religiosity plainly, which belongs to it - of the inherence of a conceivable world of values. The whole which Plato represented in his *Republic* and his *Symposium* provides the basic laws of vitality. Their forms are, to be sure, time-conditioned. An example of that: the Platonic community is purely "politically" ordered, because a division of the concept of the community has not yet taken place in Plato. Attempts towards the reestablishment of the wholeness of the community therefore would be unsuccessful, if they did not wish to take this division into consideration and simply leave to the modern state the protection of all community functions. It is only a question of historical and social scientific observation to investigate the present-day condition of the community life on the basis of how, under consideration of the once accomplished division, an approximate unity can be established. "The essence of man and of worth is based on the fact that he is a citizen of two worlds. The ideal beyond (higher reality) does not enter the this-world as a condition, but it is the eternal standard for the this-worldly reality and it operates constantly on it as the force of motion, of transformation and renewal. Never does the divine and ideal state emerge from it, but there grows from it the power of faith, to which, in the final instance, all great historical movements are to be traced, which preserves life from ossification and glaciation and steadily enables new formation and development. Paradises do not lie in the this-world, neither at the beginning nor at the end of history" (Ernst Krieck). It belongs, therefore, to the essence of the ideas developed here that they presuppose the development of a new community of values, and that they believe in the reversal of faith from the this-world to the higher reality, and, therewith, in the natural inner order of the human spirit. The deepest conviction of the author is thus that it is impossible, without that faith represented in the first part of this work which founds anew the community of values, to attain a genuine society and a true state. Otherwise, there remains only the perpetual revolution, the lasting civil war of social groups which already torments Kjellén.[49] Even he started in his great intellectual edifice from the knowledge that the one-sided individualistic conception of the state, which sees only the individual man, can as little bring a resolution as the Socialistic, which sees only the same happiness of the many; that these two are not state views in the real sense of the word, that both deny the essence of the state in their one-sided practice, and tear apart the organic connectedness. He wanted to see the preservation of society from lasting revolution in a state power which, as a balancing, independent judge, has the power to soften and to distribute pressure and counter-pressure. Similarly, Krieck sees two by-ways for the state: once, when the state is given up into the hands of the higher class, which has become free of social obligation, and disappears as an independent power, whence the enslavement of the lower classes results. And then, however, when the state undertakes to establish the material equality of possession, when it wishes to represent in itself the organisation of economic and social powers, when it thus dissolves the entire society into itself and, with regard to every freedom of powers and of development, becomes a tyrant (Marxism).

European mankind stands today at a cross-road. If it struggles through to

---

[49] *Der Staat als Lebensform*, [Leipzig: S. Hirzel Verlag], 1917. Kjellén's opposition of individualism and Socialism is repeated by this book insofar as Socialism is for the author the collective variety of individualism.

a new religiosity, a new ethics will arise from it and therewith a new value-foundation. And are the beginnings of such a new ethics not already recognizable? Does modern society not already turn away from a money-ruled age insofar as a new outline of the concept of property, the new evaluation of work and the idea of true social justice also glimmer from the confusion of an individualistic and often false social politics?

In addition to that, the question of the content-related value-foundation of a new community life can also be answered in a philosophically exhaustive manner. The individualism of modern democracy destroys with its doctrine of equality every value. The new vitality, the coming idea of the whole, the withdrawal from the this-worldly belief to the belief in the higher reality, will establish once again the sense of reality, from the lack of which the modern society ails.

This sense of reality which is present in every age of crisis and born of the doubt of the traditional, which has not preserved itself, will explain much of the fact that even state and law, as life-forms of living men, fall under the basic knowledge which a new natural science, in the sense of this book, has set up for everything living. It is the service of Karl Ernst Ranke[50], in the field of the natural sciences - and of their methods - of having put aside once again the reality-alienated, and purely objective way of observation which has been ruling here for the longest time, through the comprehensive view of the doctor who has seen, apart from cause and effect, even the aim, connection of part and whole, and indeed the danger of a merely dividing understanding for all living things. Ranke has shown in epistemologically critical presentations that all basic intellectual formations: perception, imagination, concept, lead to false results with regard to a living object, if they divide and partition this object in the manner and method of the atomising, equalising, way of thought of the Enlightenment which has been

---

[50] [Karl Ernst] Ranke, *Die Kategorien des Lebendigen[: eine Fortführung der Kant'schen Erkenntniskritik]*, München, Verlag C.H. Beck, 1928, [1er Teil, 2ter Kap., pp.109-25].

overcome. But what is more important is: it has been illustrated in this work that the process of all human formation, as the spiritual formation of living beings, as a living process itself, is really not a dividing (discursive) one, but that the healthy spiritual formation spontaneously establishes the connection with the whole in every division.

Even this knowledge taken from reality will not tolerate in future that the human apparatuses important for life, the state, be ruled by a way of observation of dividing equalisation which has been recognized as false and reality-alienated. Today, the statement of Taine[51] about the French Revolution is still valid: "It signified its imaginary edifice with its universal idea of man - with the most topsy-turvy, most stunted and wrong idea. Thence its false conclusions. It is the Classical spirit of simplification which made the Jacobin politics, the theory of the abstract man, of the modern state citizen, the conception at the same time anarchic and despotic of the independent people and of the all-powerful state, which gave the madness of equality, the levelling, the improvised and artificial constitution". With this doctrine of equality, every community which was indeed based not only on the claim to rule but on the performance of service had to perish. The concrete ethical law of social justice is, however, infinitely simple: every authorization must stand against the corresponding measure of obligation. Only higher community notables can establish the performances and, therewith, the rights; only they are empowered with the social ranking of the individual. The worth of the personality, today neglected and trampled underfoot, consists in the measure in which it mirrors the content of the community and participates in the formation and care of the whole. However, just as the individual is ranked and endowed with rights by the unions, classified into corporate bodies, so also stands the independent political power of the true state, powerfully, with regard to the organic classification of the people, securing the social justice.

---

[51] [Hippolyte Adolphe Taine (1828-1893)] *Correspondence*, III.

Therewith the essence of the organic conception of society and state has been outlined. It is a matter of indifference whether the people and the state represent an actual organism in the sense of the animal- and plant-world, or whether the organic hovers only as a model in its formation. Essentially, in the organic, the living unity of the whole is reflected by the parts, which in turn possess their own life; the simultaneous freedom and servitude of the parts, the reciprocal effect between them and the whole. The life of the whole, secured by the service of the parts, which preserves the parts from the force and the power of the whole. State power is, first of all, the protective crowning of the people-related whole.

The polarity of the organic conditions a reciprocal effect of top and bottom, which is, at the same time, tension and concentration. Against the doctrine of organism of an Othmar Spann, it is objected that it wants to build from top to bottom, and thus aspires to rule of force; that democracy is precisely the opposite, the rule from the bottom to the top. It is right in the fact that the mass democracy brings along with it an effect from the bottom to the top: namely, the dependence of the demagogical leaders on popular favour. The only bond which actually exists between the leaders and the led in democracy is woven of the sum of bad characteristics and lower instincts of the masses. That the people however rule themselves in a pyramidal structure is a witty fable. The previous chapters have unequivocally brought forward the evidence that mass rule is organised from the top and not from the bottom. It is also not correct that the responsibility of the rulers, as it is declared in the democratic constitutions, prevents absolutism. On the contrary! A rule of force which is built on the favour of the masses knows no responsibility. For, one who is responsible to the masses is, in fact, responsible to no one. If, therefore, it can be admitted that dictatorships without a structure from the bottom to the top would be actual rules of force - not considering the possible advantages of the rule of an individual - the fact remains that the present-day democracies are nothing else and organise likewise from the top to the bottom.

The complaint of many convinced democrats against us, that we are battling against the true rule of the people, is a thrust into the void. We represent, on the contrary, the idea of the true rule of the people against the dictatorship of money. We are those who wish to lead against the movement from the top to the bottom the countercurrent from the bottom to the top. It is we who wish to free the people from serfdom in that we change it back once again from a mass into a people. One who does not want this has not perceived the organic world-picture correctly, and remains perpetually stuck in Liberalism and, at best, aspires for an improved form of the rule of force. That the urbanised, unhistoried, uprooted masses however are there, that the one who wants organism must reckon with them, is a bitter fact which can never be forgotten, if a powerless return to tasteless Romanticism should not result. The entire emphasis of this work lies therefore in its knowledge that state reforms which do not prerequire the new structure of society remain a patchwork. The thought-edifice erected here stands and falls with the demand for social reconstruction.

The heads of the society in the sense of the world-views represented here are the small groups of socially superior men who feel themselves responsible for the whole, because they themselves bear the total experience in themselves. Only they are impelled by the confidence of the people and therefore do not require artificial uninterrupted declarations of trust. Seen thus, the modern election system is nothing but the expression of the deficient trust, of those who are led, in the leaders. If a people do not succeed any longer in bringing the truly superiour, those prepared for social responsibility, to the top, their turning into a mass, their fellahisation, is confirmed. If one observes how skilfully England refurbishes and supplements its social upper class through the working parties, what a consciousness of mastery these workers' leaders develop, and compare to it the resentment-filled petty bourgeois wretchedness of German mob-worshippers who call themselves the leaders of the people, the feeling of heavy discouragement could creep over the German observer. The Germans are already well on their way to sinking deep below the average of the already mediocre ruling class of the pre-war period.

It is therefore wrong to see the renewal of German life always from the point of view of the political. The present-day state plays for the true renewer only the role of a hindrance on the way to reform. It makes social reconstruction impossible as a result of its all-powerfulness and its false attitude. This, however, is the only condition under which a renewed rise of Germany is thinkable. It is therefore topsy-turvy to want to solve the question of the leaders while the structure of the society is to a certain degree planned from the political point of view. The Young German Manifesto, which of all the programme-related political groups accomplishes the most logical divergence from the false democracy of the west, has not entirely avoided this mistake in its structural part. Apart from the basic cell of the "organic state" planned there, and of the neighbourhood, which however could be effective only in a deurbanised people, the republic of the Young Germans is still based on the illusion of the equal and free state citizen. Perhaps the knowledge shines through the Young German Manifesto that one must first earn state citizenship, that it does not fall without any further ado to all those who have attained their majority - as democracy wishes. The further pursuit of this idea however leads first to the entire deviation from the purely political way of thought. It provides the insight that there is, from nature, no immediate relation between the individual and the state, that man perhaps becomes through his birth, inevitably, a member of the society, a citizen of his nation, that, however, the real embodiment of the state is first achieved in the social-ethically disposed leading stratum. The doubling of society and state is the only way to the overcoming of Liberalism, of the doctrine of equality, of the mechanised election system, and, therewith, of the rule of money. It is also the only possibility of countering the authorized striving for equality, of realizing the true democracy which is always reflected in social life, and to bring the personality to development and to leadership. It remains, finally, the only guarantee that a leading stratum is formed which binds with a feeling of mastery that constancy of the will which alone enables a people to contribute its share to the history of mankind.

Religion and culture are the two community circles which can develop powers for organic binding. In the chapter "The splitting-up of community", it was established why a whole in the Platonic sense, related to the purely political, is today impossible. From this present-day situation, it is important to draw the conclusion: the prevention of the mechanisation of the community through the limitation of the state to its own tasks.

One who objects to this guiding principle that it itself already presupposes a community of values without which a renewal is impossible, that this community of values is however not present and therefore the striving outlined here utopian, to him it may be replied: the world-view law which has been developed here has claim to unconditional timeless validity; even if it arises from the feeling of the whole, which is a human actuality, and therefore unchangeable. What this book has undertaken as its task is the sketching of the social forms which, under consideration of the historical development, correspond to the total experience. The mechanisation and the disintegration of western community forms would not have resulted if a stratum conscious of mastery, and socially obliged, had not preserved this total experience and transmitted it to the people through education. Where such a stratum however has lost the leadership, there rules mechanical majority-will which can never develop from itself the common foundation of value. It is as such already an expression of the loss of all commonality. The social form of life, however, demands the stamping of the society by the leader. The new foundation of value will thus arise only as the emanation of the striving of being maintained, led, and more highly developed from the bottom; as well as the result of the feeling of obligation of the leaders to shape and form the people spiritually and intellectually in the sense of true humanity from the top.

A chief cause of the return to the organic thought was seen in the purely spiritual experience. Often, however, a social transformation is bound to the change of world picture. Where cause and effect lie may remain undecided. It obviously contradicts the world-view represented here to see in the social biological the last causes of spiritual revolutions. Nevertheless, social currents are of the greatest influence on spiritual, and vice-versa. Upper social strata develop their life- and even their political style. The political style of the secularised bourgeoisie thinking in terms of money was democracy. Against the bourgeoisie storms the working class, in its feeling hostile to money, in spite of all the politics of envy, in spite of all the materialisation. This hostility to money, insofar as it is more than envy, insofar as it arises from the moral consciousness of the performance of work, can signify the beginning of a new social ethics. August Winnig[52] wishes to see in the growing working class the great human pelvis from which the leaders of a German generation rooted in the suprasensual could arise. For him, therefore, the correctly disposed Socialism is a movement of regrouping of the people. Much can be said of this conception. Thus there can be no doubt that the commercial-materialistic trait in the working class is weaker than in the present-day leaders of the party Socialism and of the so-called bourgeoisie, from which the leadership has intellectually arrived, liberalising and destroying the soul of the working class. On the other hand, Sombart[53] rejects this "milieu theory" as too one-sided and emphasises that the heroic trait is one of the blood, and the lack of a heroic conception of life among the bourgeoisie of the West, and especially of Germany, is to be traced to the mixture of blood with the Jewish commercial blood. Even if Sombart sees in the working class, therefore, more a "milieu" than an order, the two views can however be reconciled to each other: the rise of the proletarian powers takes place even from a stratum which in its

---

[52] *Das Reich als Republik*, Berlin: Verlag Cottasche Buchhandlung, 1928. [Winnig (1878-1956) was a politician and publicist who sympathised with the anti-democratic conservatives in his rejection of the "Jewish-inspired" proletarian "class warfare", and even welcomed the Nazi regime in the thirties].

[53] *Der Bourgeois*, München, Verlag Duncker und Humblot, [1920, esp. Kap.16; cf. Sombart's *Die Juden und das Wirtschaftsleben*, Leipzig: Duncker und Humblot, 1911].

entirety is less mixed, in its blood, with commercially disposed constituents. The share of the Jews in manual labour is diminishingly small. To this extent, Winnig's hopes of the spiritual powers of the working class can be completely shared. The question is only, whether it does not increasingly bourgeoisise itself intellectually. If it travels further on the intellectual tracks of Karl Marx, if it remains in the hands of declassed bourgeois leaders, then it becomes unserviceable for a coming rule of true spirtuality, just as the Communistic part of the working class does, so long as it subscribes to Russian Nihilism. The beginnings of a workers' politics which wants to proudly take up the responsibility for the German people before history, in order to establish in place of the rotten bourgeois state the true German state (not that of a class), are extremely weak. It almost seems as if the moral powers of construction among the war-generation of the bourgeoisie, so far as it feels itself consciously unbourgeois, were stronger. If they would go closer to the working class, then perhaps a great mobilisation could take place for the outbreak of a new age.

If the fundamental thing for the overcoming of the mechanised society has thus been said, the task of the author would be really fulfilled; arguments about the shaping forms of the organic society and of the true state could be omitted. The future development could be left confidently to the spontaneous operation of the new German man, whereby the logical acknowledgement of a new vitality would be accomplished. Where a new life-feeling rules all-pervasively, a new style also forms itself. For generations, Gothic cathedrals were built, the plans were subject to manifold changes. And yet there arose a predominantly uniform thing, because the fundamental spirit, the operative sense, went in one direction. So also here. It can be shown how the present looks, what has remained of organic life, and how it is to be developed anew. The new law however cannot be "written", a constitutional sketch which would have to be validated piece by piece cannot be put forward. It would be a task worthy of an Ihering to sketch the system of an organic law in the next decade; to create law itself remains left to the political powers, and to the new leadership. Perhaps the active life would find forms which even correct forecast and good reflection can hardly surmise. "The sailor on the night sea also knows that he does not sail to the stars, according to which he orients his voyage; but the eternal stars over him indicate to him the direction to be approached and reachable goals of reality which he does not see because they are covered by the darkness of the future. Ideologies are models for the forms of the will, for the establishment of humanity, not directly patterns for the life-forms: that is their meaning, and therein may their powerful significance of reality lie" (Krieck).

If nevertheless, in the chapters now following, it is attempted to indicate the forms of organic social and political life, it is only in order to demonstrate that even the practical politics stands daily before the decision whether it wishes to confirm the final disintegration or the awakening of new life.

XI

Organic society (community) and state

The fragmented, unsocial, urbanized, money-ruled society of civilisation characterizes the present. It is formless and therefore, like everything formless, subject to matter, in this case the power of money. But because the state cannot support itself on the organic powers of a ranked community, it becomes likewise a victim to the financial powers: thus the present-day society rules the state because political all-powerfulness and all-responsibility have disintegrated and shattered the community. The political all-powerfulness is transformed - a process of revenge - into state powerlessness.

As a saving way out of the chaos appears the doubling of people (socially ranked) and state. Thereby the original Liberal opposition between state and state citizen, the authorities and the subjects, should not be renewed. A social life which is autonomous as the real form of life and with regard to which the state, therefore, should, to a certain degree, stand neutral is also not demanded. The state as a neutral power would be that disastrous minimum concept of the state which corresponds to the Liberal concept of the night-watcher state. The social powers alone always remain only a partial development of the spirit of the people. Only the idea of the great state crowns the development and creates state nations in a

sense in which it was perhaps known to the Middle Ages, but was lost through the
doctrine of the national state, with the exception of England. Besides, the people
in the sense of this book are not the sum of state citizens, but the receptacle of
the essence of the people. The doubling is demanded in order to make the
developed powers of the soul of the people useful for the formation of the
community. Only when, next to the mechanical and mechanising state, an organic
source of power enters which guarantees new vitality does the striving for a new
order promise success. The knowledge of the juxtaposition of society and state is
thus necessary in order to found a new unity. Where mechanism still exists, the
encapsulated organic power must be separated from this: the soul, be it that of the
individual, be it that of the people, demands development, in order to produce new
life.

Another consideration, which Walter Heinrich[54] has set forth, leads to the
same result. "According to the organic conception, the society is an objective
spiritual being which is divided into more subsidiary zones, independent spiritual
life spheres of particular sort and activity. Such life spheres or orders are, for
example, art, science, religion, church, family, economics, state, etc. By virtue of
the fact that the individual man belongs to these life spheres or sections of the
society he leads a spiritual life. The state appears then as that order which lends
to every historically concrete society its organisatory content, its firm historical
form." Walter Heinrich sets forth further the statement that all life in society and
history strives for political forms and develops also the actual condition of being
a state. There were therefore, in the organic state, a great number of partial
"states". The state is constructed on publically autonomous, i.e. on areas of life
enclosed in themselves and endowed with their own life and sovereign rights. This
conception of the essence of the "state" coincides with the Platonic *politeia*.
Basically this concept of the state encompasses the community.

[54] Heft 4 of the *Europäische Revue*, Berlin, Kurt Vowinkel, 1929.

From legal philosophical considerations which are dealt with further below, Bott-Bodenhausen[55] arrives at a similar conception of the state: It is "not a being existing next to the remaining social existence, something outside economics, education, etc., but the symbol of all these expressions. The legitimate binding of the cultural life. Such a concept however is not synonymous any longer with the (pure) state. To the different content corresponds a different concept: that of the Reich. To it belongs a deep conception of the law in oppositon to the superficial conception (façade) of formativism. To the impulse of doing justice to and grasping the multiplicity of life, instead of overpowering it, corresponds the striving for ranking in functional law. Instead of the principal opposition of state-citizen and non-state-citizen, a graded difference is required here".

Therewith the uniformity of community life, including that of one's own state, is outlined. The real state is, however, the encompassing protective cover of the entire community life. "State in full development, the national state, means that condition which makes foreign policy or history and is the highest leading organisation as compared to all the remaining organised conditions. The state is a history-bearing highest order". Walter Heinrich therefore has developed the being of the state from the condition (*status*).[56] From his explanations too the conclusion drawn here is produced: that the being of the independent state, of the highest order, is to be developed once again in purity only if, indeed, independent levels subject to it, but freely living, are present. That means that the true state can exist only as the peak of a developed society. Where, however, no social ranking is present, there the state cannot be a highest order; it is in its full orderlessness something formless: organisation without a developed foundation and without a natural task. It is an arbitrary institution of force for the prevention

---

[55] [Manfred Bott-Bodenhausen, *Formatives und funktionales Recht in der gegenwärtigen Kulturkrisis*, Berlin-Grünewald, 1926].

[56] With Louis XIV's *l'état* (state and order) *c'est moi* the fate of ranking according to the orders was sealed.

of anarchy.

No genuine state without a developed foundation, without an ordered independent sphere of life, on which higher life can build itself for a time. A structure is an artificial construction from phantoms of the imagination, never something capable of life for a length of time. The real state then loses vital powers; for there are, indeed, no independently living parts which could powerfully found a total life. The state can also not embody any unity, for characteristic multiplicities are lacking whose achievements would have to be unified for the purpose of the total development.

The lever for the switching on of genuine social life lies today with the all-powerful state. The Fascistic state-centralism finds - if temporarily - a certain explanation in this condition. The state has appropriated to itself the realm of tasks of the "state-condition" in the wider sense, thus of social life. The precondition of all reform is thus the basic knowledge of what the true tasks of the state, of the "highest order", are, and what must be transferred to the society ruling itself. This question boils down to the investigation of which achievements of the human mind arise from the immediate source of social life and which could be fulfilled according to their nature only by the state in the narrower sense. Economics, science, art, church, education, family, the municipality, social insurance, etc. are rooted, according to their nature, not in the realm of the purely political life. They owe their existence not to formed legal decrees and ordinances, but to the basic spiritual powers of the human society. The laws, according to which economics is developed lie in the essence of the human satisfaction of needs itself. This can perhaps be politically influenced and directed. But the state can neither decree nor forbid economic needs, at most trim excrescences. This example may be mentioned for many things. Thus foreign policy remains as the chief task of the state: to battle for and preserve its spiritual and bodily living space. Its internal political goal is: to develop entire life-powers and to take care for their balance. No part may, overgrown, threaten the life of another part. The state has internally to watch over, lead, and rule something already present; or to make possible, in conflicts of interests, judicial decisions for the advantage of the whole. Everything else is the task of the society ruling itself.

If, however, these purely social tasks should be taken by a mechanising bureaucracy and transferred back to the autonomous society, the question arises where the organic, i.e. natural bearers of this social activity are. It was established that the corporate bodies summoned and developed for that purpose have been shattered by the modern state. The complete fragmentation of the present-day state has been described. The great question, before which every renewal movement is placed, remains, accordingly: where are the points of departure in the present-day society for organic life which would be capable of development, and which are not abandoned to the curse of being a new artificial organisation? The differention of what is artificial and what living is therefore of special importance. Living, in the sense of this book, are only the powers which arise somehow from spirituality, and are based on the experience of the whole. Artificial or mechanical are organisations which are not thought of in relation to living processes, and are based on the separated condition of the material instinct. One therefore who, in place of so-called political representative bodies, would like to build the state on economics remains totally imprisoned in the errors of the materialistic conception of history. For, economics should be subordinated to politics and not vice-versa.[57] The economic life is based to a certain degree on a reasonably conducted battle of interests. Only spiritual powers can overcome this natural contradictoriness of profit. Since, however, the profit of a multiplicity is never to be brought to a common denominator, economics remains useless for the embodiment of political life. One therefore who understands by a state of orders

---

[57] P.J. Proudhon, who is designated as a forerunner of French Syndicalism (Sorel) and of the Fascist doctrine, says: "La vraie liberté est celle dans laquelle les forces économiques réunies volontairement et par contrat se substituent à la domination exercée par l'élément politique". - "C'est le renversement complet du contrat social de Jean-Jacques Rousseau", cries A.O. Olivetti in the *Annuaire 1928* of the *Centre international d'études sur le fascisme*, from which this quote is taken.

or a society of orders something similar to the cooperative working of unions of economic interest aspires merely for the perpetuation of the class struggle, indeed its raising to a valid political principle. That this, however, would be the opposite of genuine community life is obvious.

It is the greatest mistake of the contemporary thought - and yet so significant for the present - that the structure of our - as the historical legal school says - co-operative life is always brought into relation to the state. One can affirm economic autonomy, but one does not yet for a long time need to make it the foundation of political organisation. Economics is an order, and the state is an order, and indeed a higher one. The leaders of economics cannot be the leaders of the state. Similarly does it stand with the idea of professional orders. How seldom is a distinction made between a professional society and a professional state. The state is just an order different from a profession.

The followers of the mechanical democracy can extraordinarily easily combat all plans of the organic state doctrine so long as the idea of orders exhausts itself in the formula that a parliament of professional representatives must remove the present-day political parliaments. However, the professional order is only one among many orders, indeed the most comprehensive and, among the German people - in a moral conception of work - especially deeply based, but not suited to represent the real order of the state. It is the order effective in social life. This is apparently the reason why most of the predictions of future social development place the professional order in the foreground.[58]

The professional life offers, in opposition to economics in the general sense, actually an organic starting point, but only insofar as it really deals with a "vocation" and not with a job opportunity or pure earning of money. The work activity must be affirmed inwardly by those working. Only a professional order

---

[58] Apart from Fascism in Italy, the Austrian Fascist party, the German National Socialism, and a strong direction within Catholicism, do this. In addition, there is a rich literature, especially Heinz Brauweiler, *loc.cit.*, Berdjajew, *loc.cit.*, then H. Herrfahrdt, *Das Problem der berufständischen Vertretung von der französischen Revolution bis zur Gegenwart*, Berlin 1921, and even Constantin Frantz 50 years ago.

which consists of such men can develop worth and honour. It is, however, extremely hard to establish where inner coalescence with the profession exists. Obviously, there are in every profession such people to whom the work is a matter of indifference and financial success the main thing. But, even among the individual professions, there exist differences; they demand sometimes more, sometimes less dedication, one is preeminently mechanical, the other demands the soul. Only according to the standard of spiritual rootedness can individual professional groups be arranged into self-enclosed orders. The only completely corporate bodily structure that there is is the compulsory guilds. The spirit of the corporate body lives most strongly in craftsmen. It is however significant that the champions of the idea of the handicrafts profession have not yet, upto now, succeeded in gaining acceptance with their demand for a corporate bodily structure. Liberalism can convert itself as little to it as its complementing, similarly individualistic, brother, Socialism. For it has learnt nothing of French Syndicalism in spite of its genuinely German internationality. It has remained Jacobin like the Berlin gutter press. Thus it came about that the "bourgeois" craftsman most vigorously seized the Soviet plan of 1919. - In the meanwhile, to the lawyers' chamber existing for a long time, has been added the doctors' chamber. In the agricultural chambers and the commerce chambers there are, similarly, starting points for healthy professional life. In Italy, the attempts at professional combination cannot yet be considered as settled.[59] A discussion of the legislation there is therefore unnecessary. Let only so much be remarked that there the autonomy is extremely weakly developed. There a perfect state centralisation rules.

In comparison, there are in Germany numberless associations of interests. Indeed, there is no profession, no economic group, which is not organised. But here finer differences must be introduced. The association of German engineers,

---

[59] The Syndicates are indeed there; but for the most part the connecting corporate bodies are still missing.

the association of teachers, the association of judges, etc. can indeed be designated as unions of orders. But the transition to the association of interests is often hardly perceptible. Especially hard, however, does the question become in the observation of the associations of workers and of unions. An employer can be professionally an engineer; he can however, in the first place, be disposed in an organisatory manner and therefore be the born entrepreneur or businessman. Finally, there exists the possibilty that an employer is nothing but a rich man who seeks investments for his capital. All three types fall under the present-day concept of the employer. This example shows that the employer is not easily to be conceived in the context of professional orders. The German national commercial clerks are doubtless a professional association. The battle for wages is not their main goal.

There are, however, also trades unions which exhaust their being in the representation of employee interests, to which the professional activity of the individual employee is as much a matter of indifference as their spiritual and intellectual education to a man fully conscious of his profession. The grouping of the employee into intellectual- and manual-worker similarly does not suffice for an organic combination, the bond is too weak. Already more presumable as a principle of classification is the professional activity of individual trades-union groups. But even it is not the combining power. What lends the trades-unions stability and power is the class opposition between the employers and the employees. A class can however never become a professional order, even if one is aware that the comradely holding together of things organised in a trades union way represents something similar to a spiritual union. Let it also be admitted that the trades-union organisation is dependent on the worth of the worker, a markedly German idea. Certainly he is determined to thwart ideas of individualistic society, to combat the commercial spirit and therewith the false conception of property. But holding together does not suffice for the foundation of a professional order. There is missing the natural, that which has grown. All too much are many a trades union attached to the Liberal battle attitude - historically fully understandable - against the Liberal society. Thus the trades-unions do not indeed serve the demands of the profession, but of the necessary protection of interests. They are, in the field of economics, the mechanical counterpart of the political parties which, moreover, - as was already explained - are on the point of falling along with the former. These useful associations often pervade the professions and even the production organism. They do not represent the rise and welfare of the economic undertakings but, in the first place, the material interests of certain workers' groups. Herein lies also the reason why the National Economic Council in its present-day form can neither die nor live. It is not an organic entity, but a bad mirror-image of political representation, of the Parliament. Except that the interests meet one another unconcealed in the National Economic Council. Besides, there is in the National Economic Council a representation of consumers, although it has never been heard of before that consumption is a professional activity.

A further weakness of the trades-unions is that they are based on voluntary enrolment and encounter one another in competition. The driving law of their activity consequently becomes trades-union competition, which must always end in demagogy. As regards this, in comparison to the large professional associations, there is already today no free election any longer, for, where legal pressure is missing, there enters either economic pressure or the pressure of the professional comrades. But just as the right of vote of Liberalism mostly shrinks back from the duty of the vote, its association legislation remains stuck at the right of coalition instead of going over to the duty of coalition. It should be begun here. Only where a social structure does not represent partial interests any more but consciously encompasses a group in its entirety can that spirit oriented to the whole develop itself without which all social life signifies a crime against unity. The membership in a professional corporate body must therefore become a legal duty.[60]

---

[60] The Fascist A.O. Olivetti, *loc.cit.*, says on this: "De même, au moyen-âge, personne ne pouvait rester en dehors des corporations d'artisans sans être un factieux ou un rebelle".

Most men of a working country can be incorporated into society on the basis of their professional activity. There remain perhaps, always, the dregs, on account of their asocial or unsocial disposition, excluded from the community. These dregs encompass not only the so-called ragged proletariat but also those men who do not feel their profession as ordered in the whole, but feel themselves as freebooters of society. Here belongs also that marked commercial class which differentiates itself from the traders by its complete lack of social responsibility. The social refuse of the capitalistic age are the speculators. That it could gain influence is a chief reason of the disintegration. Against this component of the popultion there are only protective and battle measures. It is otherwise with the working class in its entirety, which Rudolf Böhmer calls "the disinherited".[61] They must be appointed to their inheritance. How this can happen economically will be explained in the part of this book dealing with economics. Hand in hand with economic measures, however, must go the effort of freeing the working class psychologically from its social state of disinheritance. The worker must receive his "generosity" (Hellpach). What Wilhelm Heinrich Riehl wrote two generations ago is still valid: "Society has to fear the proletariat only so long as it wishes, with the same proletariat mind, to level out by itself all historical facts of the order and of matters related to the order".[62] In the age of national and international division of labour the working man has separated himself increasingly from his natural community, family and relations, house and municipality. All plans for social satisfaction should not overlook this process. The combination into professional orders should compensate for the harmful results of isolation through the division of labour. The leading of the individual back to the original community will not totally succeed, the division of labour cannot be

---

[61] [cf. Rudolf Böhmer's *Das Erbe der Enterbten*, München: J.F. Lehmann, 1928].

[62] [Wilhelm Heinrich Riehl (1823-97), *Naturgeschichte des Volkes als Grundlage einer deutschen Socialpolitik*, Teil II, 2te Abteilung, Kap.XIII (tr. D.J. Diephouse, *The Natural History of the German People*, Lewiston: Edwin Mellen Press, 1990, p.257)].

revoked. The law of human blood-relationship cannot be transferred to the economic field. For, economic activity indeed does not need to rule the entire human reason, but it will be always ruled by reason. Therefore the reverse way is exceptionally allowed: from the individual to the community; to be sure, even this community is predetermined on the basis of the equality of "vocation". The organic conception of the profession (vocation) corresponds in contrast to the mechanical (livelihood-earning activity) to that social doctrine of Stein that the plan of the whole is prior to its parts. Nevertheless, the single creating person remains the smallest working unity. To that extent indeed does equality of individuals rule in the economic field as every job has its worth; on the other hand, never equality of achievement, wherefore the denial of worth restricts every creative activity. It only remains, therefore, to reach, from the communality of activity, the commonality of those acting. That is the professional order. In it all who stand in the same profession have equal right. That is not a violation of reality like the demagogic demands for equality. Here the equal, universal franchise can, because natural, be taken as a basis of the election of professional representations. If at all, here, the call for freedom and equality has its justification.

The carrying out of this idea of professional orders brings in an essential change of intellectual attitude in the trades-unions and other professional associations: they turn from people making demands into people who are obliged. It is a difference between the union for the preservation of advantage and the professional association which, encompassing the entire profession, equally watches over the duties of the individual with regard to his profession and the rights of the individual on the basis of his performance. The honour of a profession is thus taken under the care of a corporate body. It is not in small measure restrained by the effort to see that the order has to be of use to the society and derive its true worth only from its significance for the latter.

In this relation of the order to the ordered whole consists, in general, the essence of the organic. When Bott-Bodenhausen, starting from the foundation of the coming "functional" law, opposes the future order of service to the late mediaeval professional order, it is hardly to be perceived where the difference should lie. A professional order which does not recognize the relation (function) with regard to the social and cultural whole is indeed not an order, but possibly a representation. The concept of the order already bears in itself that of gradation and ranking. The view that work has a double nature: the livelihood-earning activity and the serving activity, is self-evident for the organic conception of society. For, the life of the organism is nothing but a "functioning" of the relations in which the parts stand to one another and to the whole.

The professionally formed compulsory trades-union does not have to canvass for the favour of its members; it grows out of the danger of having to venture demagogically. Its work can therefore be more objective. It is incorporated into the future society as an association, its rights are constitutionally protected. For, the corporate bodies as such must become bearers of certain rights and contribute to the regulation of the community life. Quite definite spheres of rights, today reserved to the state, will pass over to them, filled by them with norms from their own rights.[63] A right of assembly-based autonomy is today already present in its beginnings. In addition, as a non-recurring act, there is the transference of national law to the autonomous bodies. The objection that developed law could never arise thus is countered by the consideration that, in this way, an original and natural legal situation is merely reestablished: a revolutionary development is conservatively interrupted. Large professional associations must be built on smaller unities. For, every election becomes inorganic, indeed senseless, where the voters do not stand in personal contact with the voted. The head of the professional order arises through indirect election, in that the lower representation always determines the next higher one through voting. Only indirect election is organic, direct

---

[63] Dr. Meusch classified professional tasks, in great number, in an excellent speech on the professional organisation, which he held on the Rheinlandish-Westphalian-Lippean Carpenters' Day, 1923.

election sensible only in the lowest and smallest unity.

The professional orders which to a certain degree correspond to the trades-union associations, indeed are developed often from them as from cells, cannot in any way break up the organism of economic production. However, the production of a people is the immediate goal to which the conception of an organic society, in opposition to the capitalistic one, aspires. A binding through of the professional orders is therefore necessary where they are linked together to the economic production process. Metal workers belong to the metal industrialist, agricultural workers to the farmer. A community of workers of the corresponding members of the production process is therefore indispensable and even possible, regardless of the opposed personal economic interests. Where is it written that the employer and the employee must necessarily be enemies? There is an entire series of economy-promoting efforts which are common. Besides that, organic thought demands not only the community of workers between employers and employees of the same production branch but the community of enterprise of the individual undertakings. "Business is an organic existence" (Bott-Bodenhausen). The community of enterprise therefore remains as the final goal of all social new order; in no way does it contradict the professional and trades-union organisation, if the two ideas are not brought into an artificial opposition to each other. More on this in the economic-political part.[64]

Professional orders, workers' communities, organic production communities together form the collective concept of economics. This economics must be brought together and receive a head. The present-day National Economic Council is not equal to this task. In its place enters the National Chamber of Orders as the head of economic autonomy, not as the organ of the state. For, the state is a political, but not an economic "order". All legislation of an economic and social nature could start from the National Chamber of Orders. Since in it all

---

[64] Even Fascism therefore attempts the binding through of the syndicates to corporations.

professional activities are represented on a democratic foundation, an infringement of state interests is not seriously to be expected. The pure division of the economy and the state, the clear professional organisation, make every amalgamation of interests impossible.

The social legislation moves to the field of autonomy. Therewith a natural situation is once again established. If an economic system, capitalism, practically dispossesses broad sections of the people, it is thus the natural task of the entire social economic powers to remove once again this "disinheritance", and to combat its consequences respectively. It is not fitting that economics follow only commercial points of view and harm society and people, but leave the reparation of the injuries to the state. Indeed, it is maintained with some justification that economics has drawn this task to itself and therefore made the infringement of the state necessary. That is basically correct but false in its conclusion. For, only a false conception of the state and a deficient insight into the process of capitalisation of economics could bring about such errors. Today, where the view on the essence of the state is beginning to change, and that on economics has already for a long time experienced a fundamental change, it can be expected from economics that it fulfil its social tasks in no way worse than the state. For, the knowledge has prevailed that by economics not only the sum of employers is to be understood, but also the sum of employees. The present-day collective concept, "economics", encompasses in truth two components: the livelihood-earning activity (private economic) and the service activity (social political). If the sum of all economic powers attains a vitally strong organisation, the power for social action will only grow. State, parliament, bureaucracy are shut off, and the self-responsibility of the social powers is awakened. In place of the present-day social politics of the parties, in which the demagogic needs and political ulterior motives make the simplest solutions artificially harder, enters the objectivity of economic and social thought. Politics itself would be immediately poisoned if the deliberation and decision of all social laws were derived from their realm. The right to work, the right to insurance, social welfare and the remaining numerous branches of the present-day social politics, would belong then to the autonomous legislation. The bureacratic activity would be superseded by honorary activity. In place of the learned bureaucrat enters the social politician who has grown up in the particular field.

The knowledge that it was false to build up the system of insurance in the main politically is a commonplace. The class warfare was thereby sharpened: economics served perhaps the healthy worker and the one capable of work, it left the insurance for the sick and the invalid worker to the state. Since this could not take care sufficiently of those incapable of work, the hate of the worker against the state had to be added to that against the entrepreneur. This was the soil on which the doctrine of the class state thrived. Even the calculation of the entrepreneurs was wrong. They forgot that the treasuries of the state could be filled only from their own pockets. Today, since one has progressed in the political economic and fiscal scientific way of observation, this self-deception is admitted. One knows that all tasks, no matter who undertakes them, are settled finally only from the sole source which brings forth real values: creative economics. The overburdening of all the loads of the social state of the German people on the economy would signify no increasing, rather a reducing of means to be raised. The detour over the state would be saved. The social insurance of the autonomous, ranked economics however would work more cheaply. But the main advantage of this plan consists in the spiritual conversion of the worker: he cannot any longer make the state responsible for his personal economic situation, and therewith the cause of his hostility to the state is removed. But even his opposition to the entrepreneur is softened. For he will not be able any more to combat an economy of which he is an incorporated and ranked member, which maintains him further in case of incapacity for work. The source from which he upto now created half-heartedly now becomes openly that of his welfare.

A pernicious consequence of the state insurance which manifested itself after the Versailles Treaty may be just briefly mentioned: the migration of Germans insured by the Reich from the separated areas. They followed their income claims. If insurance had been a matter of economic autonomy in a reasonable decentralisation, it would not have come to that much- lamented phenomenon: to the German culture of the separated areas which has become blood-less. In addition, the Reich would not have had to take up increased burdens in the case of a diminished economic base and the advantageous existence of the migrant German workers and employees who found shelter in the Reich only through need would have remained preserved.

To the state remains the economic police. Thereby its task has perhaps become smaller in range, but greater in significance. It obtains a free hand to a real economic policy: the leading in of production powers to the suited positions, satisfaction of healthy needs, the highest possible development of the forces of the people, the rendering of the popular nourishment independent of foreign countries, securing the foundations of nourishment. Genuine economic policy is, accordingly, striving for popular self-maintenance and is based closely on foreign policy. Such a great economic policy however is not conducted at the moment in Germany; but instead in America, Italy, and - even if with doubtful omens - in Russia. The Reich is today not at all capable of supporting the collapsing agriculture. Along with the economic police and the economic policy, there remains to the state jurisdiction. The judge enters and decides where any complaint regarding an infringement of interests is brought forward. Every special jurisdiction is, in the meantime, to be rejected. One may create a special right of autonomy of economics. The care of this right however may not be subject to one's own judges but to the independent judge and the one protected in this independence by the state.

There are, likewise, border areas between autonomy and state activity: first, the duty- and trade-agreement legislation which the state must wield so long as popular political points of view have a part in it. The balance of economic interests within the duty tariff can however be left quietly to the preparatory work of the autonomous economy. The same is true of the tax legislation. It is the most important sovereign right of the state. Thereby, however, it is not meant that the collection of taxes must be undertaken through an enormous bureaucracy which personally communicates with every single person subject to taxes. The allocation of taxes can be transferred to tax communities which would have to be built anew. There are, however, today, large economic bodies in which an allocation of taxes no longer takes place. The state negotiates the level of the tax amount with them and leaves the raising of it to them.

If the bone of contention of economics is distanced from the political life in this way, the state loses its present-day aspect as the playground of interests. In return, it gains in reputation, its supervisory role raises it above the conflict of interests and attributes to it the superiour position of arbiter.

A further order in the sense of the doctrine of the organic society is the culture-creating spheres. It is a contradiction to believe that the state can create culture. Spiritual creation is a grace of great creative natures who always grow in a healthy culture. The state can hardly offer more than a certain patronage, presupposing that it is entrusts the furtherance of culture to a strong personality. In the bureaucracy it becomes favoritism.

Art lives in individual great persons and in the circles which form themselves round these. If art becomes once again theurgical, spiritual communities would need to become leaders more often. The beginnings of such a development are present. These artistic-spiritual communities, freely incorporated and not to be confused with the trades-unions of painters, stage artists, music teachers, etc. are the crystallisation points of future autonomous bearers of culture. The same is true of science. The politicisation of the universities has led to the fact that - especially in the falsely termed field of humanities - the emphasis of the scientific life gradually glides over the "private scholars". State and bureaucracy have also given evidence of their life-destroying effect on the scientific field. America has, almost without a tradition, performed surprising scientific achievements. But only because here the university grew out of free social necessity, mostly independently of every political influence. No scientific body is so suited to autonomy as the universities, and no autonomy is at the moment so unscrupulously neglected as the universities.

Church and state belong together insofar as both are the conclusion of the necessary social form in which human life is accomplished. They both create rules of the life lived together: the Church in the intellectual-spiritual sense and the state more in the functional. This proximity of the two can become competitive due to a lack of clear demarcation, can bring about cultural battles. But only when the state presumes to establish for itself moral-religious forms which it can never produce, and when the Church, in turn, wishes to make a worldly rule out of the spiritual. The undertaken formal division of the Church and the state should therefore remove all possibilities of friction. If this occurs with the Liberal ulterior motive: that religion is a private matter, then there is present a split of human community life which must operate fatally. If, however, it occurs in the sense of a clear division of reciprocal tasks, then the opposite can grow out of it: an organic unity. With the usual objection that one must decide between religion and the Church, practically not much is to be commenced. The essence of the religion becoming socially effective consists even in the ecclesiastical (cultural religion). And every healthy church bears in itself already absolute religious value. One, therefore, who diverges from the nightwatcher state must also deny the "private character" of religion. Religion and the Church are socially compulsory, are a certain partial sphere of the community life, and possess, in the sense of Walter Heinrich, partial politicality; the Church is therefore endowed with public legal powers. It may never become a private association, but must always remain a public institution.

The chief effectiveness of the Church and, therewith, the point where the contacts with the state occur, lies in the field of education. The first bearer of education is the mother, then follow the older brothers and sisters, and finally the father, wherewith the family circle is closed. The further education into a moral man devolves naturally on the community which, out of the religious experience, develops the idea of unconditional morality; on the Church. The education into a moral man is the will and act of a quite definite world-view circle, which the state can never be termed as. The perfect Eros of the family, beginning with the blood bonds, wishes also the spiritual community with the children. The latter, for its part, conditions once again the commonality of religious possessions. Nothing therefore is more natural than that the parents give up the further education to the religious community to which they themselves belong confessionally. Later, when the religious-moral education is completed, the professional order takes over the work of education, which as naturally befits it; finally, it gives the pupil up to the state, which educates the mature man into a political and national citizen in the higher sense. It is natural cultural and political goals which the state represents in its education.

To one, on the other hand, who objects that the education into a "state citizen" comes off badly, and that intellectual particularism, renewed splitting of the people, would gain ground, it may be replied that today, when the idea of national education is carried out to the point of exaggeration, there is no independent educational will of the state which guarantees spiritual uniformity. It is, rather, certain world-view circles which, circumscribing the parties, come to an agreement with one another in the parliament on the content and the form of the school. There is no "worldly" educational ideal which would correspond to the demand for wholeness of the human mind. Educational wholeness is therefore today only to be aimed at through clear separation of the bearers of education and through clever bringing together of their educational work into an educational whole. Moreover, the state has, to be sure, to indirectly watch over the school police. Infringements of the individual educational circles may occur as little as the failure of educational conscience in individual cases. The natural educational right of the parents ceases just as that of the other communities where no obligation is recognized with regard to the whole. The role of the supervisor and the judge in the field of education ensures true autonomy to the state and makes political cultural battles impossible. Differently from today, where politics, the real national activity, is just falsified by the playing out of cultural oppositions.

With these plans it is not necessarily meant that the Church must itself become the bearer of the elementary schools. It suffices, if the municipality or a public-legal corporate body, the school association, take over the education instead of the state. But every school must be a "denominational school". It is impossible to train children into complete men without the acknowledgement of an unconditional. A so-called secular school is incapable of that. It offers facts wihtout knowledge. There is, therefore, no more dangerous false conclusion than that a national standard school, introduced into Germany, could provide the people with a new basis of value, could unify its spiritual-intellectual attitude. In this way, at most, a mechanised, impersonal, and therefore unprincipled human type is created. The Anglo-Saxons are characterised less by the enormous abundance of national school types, such as we have, but rather by the fact that education remains left to the organic spheres of life. The attention to the common whole comes of itself in the man who owes his education to a vital community. The Englishman has, in spite of the relaxed compulsory schooling, and in spite of the small expansion of the state schools, attained a life-style and a state-affirming attitude; to a certain degree, even the Anglo-Saxons in America. Through the fact that the educational course is prescribed from above and offered in the entire Reich in equal measure, the spiritual unity has not yet, by far, been secured. If it does not stream directly from the cultural wealth itself, especially from the spirit of the language, it is in a bad way.

If, however, every school should be an educational community, it must also be borne by a real community circle, not by a law or an army. Therefore it misses the mark to want to provide the working child from Hamburg with the same educational material as the upper Bavarian peasant child. Precisely the elementary shool system demands soil-bound adaptation. The smaller municipalities are more than a legal unity, they still form a spiritually-bound community. Here there is still the agreement between parental will and the decision of the municipal council. When the state school still stood in competition with the municipal school, sometimes the one, at other times the other, had precedence. Where, however, the municipal schools became nationalised, entered the ossification of the educational vitality. Precisely the nationalisation of the school system has prevented the appearance of a new spirit in education to which everybody gropes. An old popular educator once said: the renewal of the school is possible only under the elimination of all those participating in the school competitively and professionally. That may sound exaggerated. But it is certain that it is more readily possible to obtain new educational ideas from a community of parents oriented in a world-view way than from numberless "teachers' conferences". Of the same view also is Eduard Spranger:[65] "If we could be rescued as a state and a people by pedagogical speeches and congresses, we should have looked good long ago". Thereby it should not be ignored that, precisely in the younger stratum of teachers, renewing powers are awakening. But the strong instructive personality wishes for the improving of the school in itself. The present-day spirit of the age often confuses the order of the teacher with that of the school. Thus, for example, the nationalisation of the elementary schools in Bavaria is due more to the effort of making the elementary school teacher a state bureaucrat than to that of improving the elementary school.

It is true of the intermediate and high schools more than of the elementary schools that they must be borne by the cultural will of a quite definite, narrowly limited, circle. Thereby it may be still left open whether the school structure: elementary school - intermediate school - high school, is correct and does not owe

---

[65] *Die Verschulung Deutschlands*, Leipzig, Quelle & Meyer.

its existence to a false educational ideal. For, the present-day intermediate school has its justification only as a transition to the high school. It, therefore, should be a select school and not, as it does today, serve a factory-made production of certifications. While the public has a certain claim to the establishment of as many elementary schools as possible, as places of moral education, this is true in much smaller measure of the present-day places of higher education. For, these provide only greater knowledge, seldom a higher feeling of responsibility, increased morality. This can be contested only by one who thinks, with the Greek sophists, that virtue is scientifically learnable. If today the state establishes a new intermediate school, it is not a matter of education, but of the understandable wish of many parents to "let their children become something". It therefore fulfils a basically economic private interest. If, on the other hand, the establishment of a high school or a university is determined by the demand of a cultural community, the number of such places would sink in comparison to that today. With regard to this, men are trained in true central-points of culture who, capable of life-preserving accomplishments, penetrate the culture spiritually in a quite different measure than the present day "educated persons".

Crystallisation cores for cultural autonomous bodies are present everywhere. The concept of the school municipality is not alien to the public law, the education of parental councillors points to new forms. Large associations which are based on commonality of character place the schooling of their members in the central point of their work. Foundations and associations already today perform educational activity. The universities had at one time such a far-reaching autonomous right that there was an academic "citizen". Much is easily revivable and to be completed through new forms, if the state is restricted in its unsatisfiable greed to swallow everything. Whether the entire intellectual or educational life of the people, combined into a ranked structure, would maintain an autonomous head, similar to the chamber of professional orders of the Reich, can be left to the development which, of course, is to be striven for.

It was not to be avoided that we touched on, in connection with the question of social autonomy, matters in the economic, social and cultural fields which are dealt with further in the special parts. Here the main thing was only to show the ways to the making independent of this social activity and to its separation from the state.

XII

Blood and homeland as foundations of the community

The enucleation of the economic and cultural life from the field of the political led to the founding of the formation of the social will on spiritual rootedness. Now, men live not only in the community of creation and of spiritual worth, but also in the blood-related and territorial bonds. Social philosophers who are determined to go on the way of the purely social organisation of man to the final end indeed contest with relentless logicality the binding of man to family and soil. They say that, since the disappearance of the heriditary orders, the family has no public-legal significance any more. From this assessment Bott-Bodenhausen concludes that the perfect carrying out of the social organisation destroys the public significance of the family. He thereby traverses the tracks of Plato when he gives expression to the hope that the indisposable tradition which the family inherits today will make itself independent at one time and new legal creation will produce the legal scope in which it could be made effective. The Catholic Church has resolved this task for itself in its cloisters and orders. As much as Bott-Bodenhausen is to be agreed with in the opinion that man just as a merely existing being has no legal significance, but only as the representative of a worth, a work, a performance or an influence, so erroneous is the conclusion drawn therefrom that the family is an accidental community and not one of achievement and influence. For, apart from the fact that the family has still a great economic significance as the community of production (in the case of the peasant) and as a consumer community, that view overlooks the "social" achievement of propagation and of breeding. Certainly the Catholic Church has solved the question of education to a tradition. But the material of this education is provided not by the Church, but by the family. Celibacy indeed promotes the development of excellent educational personalities, but demands precisely the biological maintenance of the Church through an external community: the family. The procreation and education of children is perhaps the task lying closest to the spiritual centre of man, and the activity directed to it the most markedly social. "From the soul and not from the body are questions of life to be answered". This statement of Bott-Bodenhausen's is contradicted by his denial of the family which perhaps owes its biological existence to bodily union, but precisely in man rests on spirituality. Here Bott-Bodenhausen seems to shift too strongly from the field of spirituality to that of intellectuality and thereby to give up the power of the nature-boundedness, the organic whole. - More evident does this judgement become in his deviation from the soil accomplished through wonderful logic. He wishes to build the new state not on the territory, but, after economic and political cells are reduced to a functional legal system, on the enterprise. "The enterprise and not a country area is the economic centre". Consequently, he calls "Reich" not the combination of corporate bodies, but the sum of work-directions: "It is a matter of indifference whether the associates of the Reich are united on one soil, whether a ship bears them, or whether they are separated from their locality. Insofar as their dependence on one another belongs only to a totality of influence which embraces the entire man, the solidarity of the Reich is not destroyed". Here Bott-Bodenhausen seems to sin against his own basic principle ("Despair pants only where the attitude to the whole has been lost"). Does abstraction not triumph here? Is not every economy, every enterprise, every man soil-bound? But to stick to one's own language: is the relation to the soil not a spiritual one, is it not indeed a service? Have all cultures not fallen which voluntarily cut off the soil roots? Are soul, social form, economic form, not attached to the soil, and cultures not bound to territory? Genuine community is based on the homeland experience. One who is not rooted any more in the earth cannot develop any feeling of the whole. The experience of Nature transmits that of the universe. One who has no homeland any longer forfeits his soul.[66] So strong is the homeland instinct in man that it clings to the ugliest factory state, that it fills with melancholy the heart of a soldier who had to separate himself from his dug-out. The strengthening of this trait of the human soul must be the goal of all organic politics. From it grows the demand to bring man once again more strongly in binding with grown Nature, and to hold him far from the artificial stone-heaps of the metropolis. The leader conscious of his goal must check the nomadising of a people. So enticing therefore as that great intellectual edifice of Bott-Bodenhausen already is, because every opposition seems to be fused into a new unity, so steadfastly must the author[67] hold to the foundations of all organic life, because given by nature: to the blood and the soil.

On the cell of the people, the family, the necessary things were said in the chapter, "The twilight of the family";[68] the population political part[69] will correspondingly bring forth its character as "the kernel of the peoples". Obviously, the spiritual condition of the modern woman cannot be influenced by legal prescriptions, as little as the slackening will to the maintenance of the species. Here there remains only the task of believing in the great revaluation of all values which the first part of this book announced. But the social and legal forms must

---

[66] [cf. C.G. Jung's reminder of the virtue of retaining links with one's native soil: "he who is rooted in the soil endures", "Mind and Earth", in *The Collected Works of C.G. Jung*, Vol.X, Princeton, N.J., 1964, p.49].

[67] i.e. Jung.

[68] [Part II, Ch.5, in Vol.I of this edition].

[69] [Part V of the *Herrschaft*, not translated in this edition].

be suited to this new spirit. The family itself (not the married couple in mutual competition) should become the bearer of private and public right. The creation of a family property which protects and secures the progeny from need stands at the centre of all efforts. This is helped by the knowledge that the greatest social performance of a man is the nurturing of a certain number of healthy children. Society is correctly constructed only when its smallest unity is the family and not the individual; when all fiscal, heriditary, social, partially also economic, legislation, takes account of this basic unity and no longer the individual man. Property and heriditary right are, in the old Germanic sense, fief which society distributes. They cannot be attached to the one who himself robs the society, in that he harms its future through a denial of posterity. The statement of Hegel: "He is not a man who is not a father", must be transferred to the legal life insofar as property and heriditary right are related chiefly to the family. The rise of the entail, no matter how one thinks of it for reasons of land reform, operated in a family-destructive way. Similarly, much individualistic heriditary right which drives the farmers from the soil. Even the discretionary power of the parents with regard to the wealth for their successors must be strongly restricted. The number of cases increases, especially in view of the increasing average life-span, in which wealthy old people on whom the inheritance of wealth between 1870 and 1910 fell relatively easily "sit on their money" or use it and exclude the young people from the enjoyment of wealth, precisely in the hard time of family foundation. This lack of the sense of family works in a manner directly restrictive of birth, especially in an age which places the young people before an unequally harder life-battle than before. - The formulation of the question upto now, which of the married couple is authorized to make dispositions, is outmoded. In fact, it is a question of providing the family as an independent personality unalienable property rights. That the man therein represents the family in a property legal way is even as natural as the foreseen possibility of transferring this right in special cases to the woman.

A further task of supraindividualistic creation of right is to hinder the development of the marriage to a time-bound contract. For, marriage is the form which secures best the protection of the child. All care for the progeny should therefore not lead to the taking care of the extra-marital child to a degree which could stimulate the neglect of marriage contracts. On the other hand, however, the individual worth of marriage stops where motherhood no longer forms its essential point. Extra-marital motherhood remains at all times more valuable than unfruitfulness sealed by the registry office. That the custom increasingly neglects the idea of the mother emerges from numerous phenomena of daily life. Professional positions are offered, from the competition for which family fathers are excluded in advance. A society and a state which let such things occur are sick. Thus, before all eyes, crimes against the culture are committed which are not felt as such only because, for the individualistic moral law and the penal code, it is only a question of the protection of the individual. The dawning age of community-worth will judge such dealings more sharply than offences against property. New laws arise before the intellectual eye of the one who rests spiritually on the whole and does not overestimate the part.

Finally, extraordinarily far-reaching innovations in the system of taxes would have to be considered. The man punishes himself in his wealth who today marries and produces children. The tax legislation, however, hardly considers the family situation of the persons subject to taxes. Could one not formulate the standard tax-rate for a family father with three children and on this foundation build up surtaxes for childless and single persons? A reduction for larger families is understandable by itself. One who believes in social justice wants to apply other standards than those of the present. The property tax, above all, could work in a stabilising way in the sense of the new idea of the society. If the state encroaches on wealth for a necessary reason, the tax-rate should be staggered according to the number of children of the person subject to taxes. The fewer children, the higher the tax- rate. One who earns wealth in order to let it be of benefit to seven children has a higher right to property than one to whom it serves only as pleasure. Strict educational measures, corresponding to true morality, can, applied over a long time and persistently, change the attitude of broad masses to property.

The plan of transferring the modest election processes which still remain in the coming state to a new bearer of rights, the family, was already made from different quarters; in France, a corresponding legal outline was indeed already put forward for consideration. The right of the individual was left to him where he acted as an individual: in the working life, in the profession. If, however, the family is the cell of the people, then the popular will must also be constructed organically on it. To the individualist, this plan seems incomprehensible because it lies beyond his ideas of justice. But one who wishes to let the will of a people grow from the blood and the soil feels the family franchise as natural. The family as a legal personality receives the franchise, which the father as legal representative exercises. The predominant number of all men can be incorporated into the family, which indeed could be extended to the relatives. It seems reasonable to grant the few necessary "single persons" an individual franchise. The objection that this plan means an unbearable disadvantaging of the unmarried persons arises from an individualistic feeling of justice which in fact has always created injustice. The family franchise is at least more moral than the one valid today. For, one who brings forth the courage for the rearing of children and therewith has proven his will to sacrifice will also show more understanding of society than one who lives only for himself. The more responsibility one voluntarily takes up, the more right should be due to him in the formation of the common will. The number of votes of the family father must therefore be ranked according to the number of the family members. In this way, even the child obtains the franchise indirectly, only that it is exercised by the person who bears the responsibility for his life.

The tight space allows us no comprehensive narration of all the measures which are possible for the protection of the family. Luise Scheffen-Döring,

Grotjahn, von Gruber, Kaup, the race hygienists, the association of those with large families, and many others have made plans which encompass all fields of public life, from the dwelling, the house-building, to the tax legislation. In order to round out the picture, the author has brought forward examples of family political measures. Only one idea still has to be touched on at the conclusion of these considerations: Followers of the idea of the organic state, beginning from Plato to certain Socialistic orientations, advocate the education of the children outside the family. Basically, such plans must be rejected for the present, from which the city-state in Plato's sense lies far removed. Only in a community whose spiritual harmony is so strong that it can replace the intellectual bond between parents and children can the education of the progeny take place publically. There will always be such educational communities - convent schools, country boarding schools - which not only dispose of the spiritual forces to replace a parental house but indeed earn the preference in comparison with incapable parents. Basically, however, the spiritual Eros demands the educational bond between parents and children.[70] One may also never forget that the family represents a vital community, but the best place of educaton always only an artificial institution. In the family, the child is schooled by life; in a boarding school, by the course of instruction. Even if the same may be ever so liberal, it is seldom bound to life-processes, but mostly to utilitarian considerations. If the metropolitan disintegration of the family in the previous age were to continue, the one-child system would become the dominant rule, and to be sure the worth of the family education would thus be so reduced that - especially in the case of unreasonable parents - public education would obtain precedence.

From the kith and kin to the territorial community is a small step. The border where it passes over to the neighbourhood and the municipality is hardly perceptible. For this reason, the already mentioned plan of the Young German

[70] [see Part II, Ch.5 (Vol.I of this edition) for Jung's discussion of the various kinds of Eros].

Manifesto, of constructing the political autonomy on the neighbourhood as the basic cell, is organically thought out. Unfortunately, however, the industrialisation and urbanisation makes impossible the recourse to this organism. Before it is drawn into the circle of considerations the preliminary question must be posed, whether the urbanisation can be made retrogressive. The construction of an organic society is impossible with metropolitan masses, especially if the asphalt rules, and the farm soil however is laid waste. The process of urbanisation is represented thoroughly further below, in the population political part, and seems unstoppable. The immigration to the state is considered today as a sociological law, the depopulation of the country land as inevitable, the mass-formation as a future destiny.

Is this supposition correct? That it is universally believed proves the triumphal procession of the historical materialistic school of Feuerbach and Marx. This bourgeoisie of today, even if it acts still in such an "anti-Marxist" and "patriotic" manner, is contaminated by matter to the bones. It maintains that, if profit and money wished it, new cities must arise. It considers migration and social transformation as the product of sacred laws which dwell within the economic life. Man, the forming personality, the leader is forgotten. One who believes in the soul is a "Romantic". In the school, one learns of Heinrich the city builder; in life, one considers it as self-evident that the modern metropolises are built by speculators. From history, one knows that individual men (Hermann von Salza) or cloisters (Admont) systematically colonised broad land stretches, indeed entire provinces. Today, one shrinks back from regulating even the smallest population movement. The anxiety may thereby arise of not touching that sufficiently well known - oh, how senseless! - freedom of the individual. Thus does the German national constitution indeed contain the right to migrate as the basic right of every German. Here the law becomes a satire.

In the part of this book dealing with the economic life,[71] the question whether industrialisation and the commercialisation of the European economy will proceed unrestrictedly is answered negatively. It is indeed also clear that, with increasing industrialisation of the earth, the export of European industrial countries must go down. Depopulation or consideration of one's own land-power are the two possibilities which remain to the European countries. This economic pressure must operate fatally in the sense of depopulation, if the urbanisation has progressed so far that the development of one's own land-power is no longer possible. In view of the frantically increasing urbanisation, it is high time to attempt the prevention of this process, and to make the population movement the object of great leadership and systematic pressure (example: Mussolini).

Sacrosanct principles like that of freedom of movement must of course fall. A regulated "freedom of movement" for the development of aspiring forces will always be necessary. Social rise should not be undermined. But the freedom of movement of today is without sense. Peasant sons move to Berlin in order to fall victim to unemployment insurance, Poles take over the agricultural jobs to great gain. One who moves to the city should receive a permission to immigrate only with a demonstrated long-term employment. A further starting point for deurbanisation is offered - along with the weekend movement which however proclaims a modest "return to Nature" - by the technical development: the automobile draws city and country closer to each other. The person necessarily working in the city can live in the country or at least in a suburb. The younger generation thus finds once again a contact with Nature; in place of the street, the garden appears for the children, the flat is replaced by the own home. This process is important. For, culture begins with the own home, in the rented apartment it is bogged down. To this is added the uneconomicality of the metropolis. Its administration becomes increasingly more bureaucratic and expensive, its expense

---

[71] [Part III below].

for the transportation system beyond its means. Modern breakthroughs, the construction of streets and tunnels, or indeed the establishment of underground railways, consume sums with which one could easily lay out large country dwellings outside the city. A Faustian formative impulse seems actually to be at play here, otherwise the ease would not be understandable with which large monies are granted to transform the interior of the metropolis into developed traffic machines.

The concentration of enormous human masses in individual places is uneconomical in the highest measure. For, the conveyance costs of all goods are higher because the way from the production places to the consumer is too long. The increase of the participation of the professional groups, trade and transport, within the total economy, points to the fact that the German national economy is becoming increasingly more unproductive. For, it is obvious that an economy is so much healthier the smaller the expense for intermediate activity of all sorts. A correct relation between country and city thus exists when the cities scattered equally over the country are approximately equally large. The technical limitation of the means of transportation in the Middle Ages prevented the inorganic growth of cities. Today, this is different, and therefore the point of time not far when the transportation costs consume the national economic profit.

Numerous are the striking proofs which Rudolf Böhmer[72] brings forward for the uneconomality of the metropolises. His plan of countering urbanisation is as great as it is well-founded. Insofar as he starts from social-political considerations (freeing of the working class from the class situation), the "Economics" part of this book will return to it. Here only Böhmer's plan for deurbanisation itself should be mentioned. It gives evidence of creative daring to finally hold against the unfruitfulness of the 19th century, which in general did not conduct any population policy (apart from border-political settlement), the idea of

[72] [Rudolf Böhmer, *Das Erbe der Enterbten*, München: J.F. Lehmann, 1928].

a systematic resettlement of the entire people. By appealing to practical experiences which Ford made in the establishment of his factories and his workers' dwellings, Böhmer combats the industrial gigantic enterprise which works too expensively and, as a result of the division of labour, can be easily disintegrated; he demonstrates that the metropolis makes industrial production more expensive, that our railway enterprise and railway construction through the gigantic cities is forced to enormous expense, that the metropolis is technically backward, that it means a danger in the case of war, and finally works as the "graveyard of the nation". He suggests nothing more and nothing less than the demolition of the metropolises and their reduction to a healthy size. The pseudo-wise worshippers of the spirit of the age will smile superciliously. Let it be said to them that a nation has only the choice of demolishing its metropolises themselves in time, or insofar as it is still living, to view their collapse. History shows many large cities which within a century were laid waste. Besides, in the age of technology, Böhmer's plan is not at all something impossible. He wishes to settle the men emigrating from the metropolises in small cities systematically distributed over the country and as systematically laid out, with on an average 12,000 inhabitants. To be sure, it is a question thereby of a pure garden-city with a circular area of about 3 kilometers diameter. The entire city consists, apart from factories, etc., of flat-construction homes, each of which is directed to agricultural-horticultural part-time occupation. Through basic horticultural cultivation, small livestock and poultry maintenance, the possibility should be offered of obtaining half of the life support of every family from one's own land. The enormous costs of developed canalisation, metropolitan street construction, traffic regulation, expensive administration, etc., will disappear, since such a communal system can be clearly and purposefully laid out and is even easy to administer honorarily.

It is not the place here to go into the plans of Böhmer, which in general are aptly founded - one can be of another view in points of detail. The encouraging thing is that he has sketched the plan of a modern, great and goal-conscious habitation- and land-reform. One can even agree with him that the costs of such a habitation would be sufficiently balanced by the promotion of German political economy and the power of the people. In any case, the present-day exhaustion of economic power and that of the people is much more expensive than the most comprehensive and daring plan for a complete transformation. The great unemployment and the increasing land depreciation demonstrate irrefutably the incompetence of the present-day social politics.

From the metropolitanised foundation, then, true political autonomy is possible, whereas the present-day incorporative politics of the metropolises goes ever further away from the genuine autonomy in the sense of Stein and all the thinkers of the organic state. Certainly, one can make allowances for the modern communication and the large territorial settlement policy by transference of these tasks to larger associations. It was, however, never necessary to swallow the many country muncipalities whose genuine autonomy falls away only in order to be replaced by a metropolitan, more expensive, mechanical bureaucracy. Autonomy as the expression of true freedom, as the meaning of genuine democracy, can only grow from small territorial, organically living structures. The metropolitan autonomy has today become a tower of Babel. The parliamentarianism of the states was transferred with all its evil consequences to the cities. Party-economics and favoritism circulate poisonous blood. The right to autonomy degenerates in caring for the party friends still more unrestrictedly than the state does. Gigantic numbers appear in the metropolitan budgets, the army of bureaucrats grows immeasurably. Oskar Aust[73] brings forward disturbing examples of the debt economics of the metropolises. The cases accumulate in which municipalities stand before the settlement of their payments. Here it becomes clear that an autonomy without self-responsibility is at hand. For, the necessary monies are indeed raised by way of financial balance and only partly through the

---

[73] *Die Reform der öffentlichen Verwaltung in Deutschland*, Berlin, Askanischer Verlag, 1928.

muncipalities themselves. But then in such a way that the non-propertied persons impose taxes on the propertied. The economicality of the matter is not questioned; without consideration of the consequences, property is blackmailed in order to maintain with the means obtained in this way a questionable ostentation, a splendid stadium or an expensive theatre which offers the common bourgeois literary filth. This development knows no boundaries and encroaches even on the small municipalities. Aust illustrates the budgets of two small municipalities: in the case of one the expense rose from around 20,000 marks in 1913 to 130,000 marks in 1925, in the other from 8000 marks to 38,000 marks; thereby, in the last case, it is a matter of only personal expenses. The bureaucratising goes so far in many German provinces that entire small provincial municipalities are maintained in order to appoint salaried mayors. Even around 1900 there were large cities in the Reich which were ruled honorarily and thereby fared very well. Stein would laugh if one wished to combat him with regard to the standpoint that the municipal parliament is an organ of genuine autonomy. A parliament is as little an expression of the will of the municipal citizens as the bureaucracy. The present-day municipal franchise leads only to the fact that every party votes without inner participation in the municipal concerns. Naturalization is therefore to be made more difficult. For, public spirit does not arise by itself from immigration into any municipality. Where, however, it is present, party programmes do not determine the municipal elections any longer, but questions of the local welfare.

To the state's all-powerfulness corresponds the municipal all-powerfulness, to the state bureaucracy, the municipal. They are of one mind and live beyond every idea of genuine autonomy which alone guarantees democracy and freedom. Genuine autonomy in Stein's sense is honorary. It is based on the citizens' consciousness of responsibility for his municipality.

The inflation of the municipal official apparatus has the same causes as the increasing all-powerfulness of the state: the citizen's self-help became increasingly weaker. Society, itself disorganized and split up, wishes to see all life-expressions regulated by the authorities, like the traffic by the constable. The moral code of the society is replaced by the police ordinance. However, where a people do not develop any impelling morality any more, even the source of genuine law is clogged. No life-style can arise out of such fallow ground. If, on the other hand, the municipal autonomy is debureaucratised, and the municipal all-powerfulness trimmed, only then is the space once again present for the development of a social moral code. The community will then take up creative self-help against vermin, to which it is today unresistingly exposed or against which it begs for the always insufficient help of the authorities. A new self-consciousness will penetrate the soil-rooted man and make him capable of the achievement of genuine freedom, which today is only an empty word and disguises political enslavement. The press expressly created for this purpose becomes superfluous. For, where personalities live, the pressure of ruling the masses in a demagogic way becomes superfluous. The power of money, effective only among the spiritually uprooted, is broken by the resistance of blood and soil. The press can then turn into that which its best people have always demanded: a true educational instrument which receives its intellectual guiding principles solely from leaders conscious of responsibility.

The unchained creative powers of self-responsible men will lend to society its stamp. The will to sacrifice for cultural goals will grow. One may think of what performances quite small cultural communities in a lower stage of technology and in relative poverty have brought forth in the Middle Ages. In spite of the fiscal power of millions, Germans today disintegrate that cathedral which some thousand men have built from the impulse to lend to their community consciousness a shaping form. The Transylvanian Saxons who, for over 800 years, stood under the hardest conditions of life, often under alien rule, have succeeded in remaining equal culturally to the motherland. The financial burden of the national budget for culture is there higher than in the Reich. It is, however, willingly borne because no political insurance lets the sacrificing forces of the people be impaired. Even England and Holland are salutary examples here. The school freedom is there the foundation of the educational system; the cultural will of the people, however, is strong enough to conduct pupils to schools. A cultural life standing on its own feet also cares for healthy physical education. Precisely here did the state intent on education sin the most: it offered almost nothing. And yet the need for it in the German people was so strong that it created its own forms of physical recreation. That is proved by the upswing which the rambler- and sports-associations have assumed.

The territorially organised community rooted in the soil offers to the inborn communal sense of the German the possibility of successful activity, and thereby raises him. The public spirit which upto now dissipated his impulse to activity in the regular circle of party friends fertilizes once again the work-area suited to it: the small territorial autonomy. Newly developing consciousness of orders and genuine public spirit form together the foundation on which a characteristic life-style can be developed. The worth of the individual will finally exterminate that ridiculous imitative impulse which has accompanied all ages of social downfall as the sign of lack of inner freedom. The rich man who exemplarily impressed his stamp on the modern society is sent back to the position belonging to him. There always was and must be wealth. In the hands of the best, it becomes the blessing of culture. But the rich man is not, by virtue of his wealth, at the same time a leader. This basic sociological knowledge must provide the universally valid value-standard, should the leadership of the best become once again possible. Only then does a life-style also arise which is not based on senseless increase of need but remains in modest, but cultivated forms. The distance between the strata, necessary and even demanded in the context of the striving for equality, is then based no longer on the wealthier endowment of the higher strata with external means, but on their more highly determined spiritual life, on their stronger sense of service. The establishment of this natural distance leads to true social satisfaction. For only then is every person content to create in his own place.

If the political cell of a people, the municipality, is healthy and filled with a life of the sort described above, then the political structure is, upto the acme in the state, no longer the object of mechanical construction, but the result of natural growth. The municipalities are united into circles, the latter into regions, the last finally into provinces, on the relation of which to the Reich there is more to be spoken of in its own chapter. With the higher administrative unities, however, this chapter does not need to concern itself, since it deals with social and not with the political structure. The municipality as the small territorial association is the mediator between society and state. If, however, the basic idea of this book is applied to the relation of higher administrative unities to lower ones, then a chief guiding principle can be set up: the higher administrative unity should be balanced by the lower ones: weak ones must be supported, strong ones brought closer to the former. The organic idea demands equal development of all parts and, therewith, the uninterrupted life current which flows through the whole. To be conscious of the whole is the task of the higher administrative unities. They should refrain from every ruling into the affairs of the lower ones. In turn, the amalgamation of their own municipal affairs with the transferred sphere of influence (state administration) is harmful. Where the state has to exercise real sovereign rights it should do this through its own officials. Where, however, marked autonomous tasks are to be resolved, the honorarily active mayor has basically to act and not the bureaucrat. Therewith the necessity of setting up full-time autonomous bodies for many tasks is not overlooked.

The present-day crowding of autonomy and political sovereignty of administration, and the large professional bureaucratic bodies conditioned by it in autonomous administrations, produce the danger that a sort of urban territorial principality arises from a democratic foundation. Thereby the state sovereignty itself is endangered. The opposition of the city and the state is too immediate. No circumstance elucidates the disparity between the present-day autonomy and the state more clearly than the following consideration: the inhabitants of Berlin allegedly administer themselves by themselves. The head of this autonomy is the mayor. The city of Berlin is therefore the lowest autonomous body which the citizen of Berlin knows. Perhaps there is a district administration in Berlin; it is however lifeless, an opposition and a juxtaposition, but not an organic structure. Moreover, Berlin has more inhabitants than Switzerland. The autonomous body of the population of Berlin is therefore greater than a sovereign state of medium size and international outlook. In this example the difference between genuine and false democracy becomes evident. One may compare only the structure of the city administration of Berlin with that of Switzerland and any additional statement becomes superflous. The scope of the administrative unity has natural limits even towards the top: the voters must know the voted personally. The person standing at the top of the self-administration must supervise personally not only the entire relations of his district but where possible even that of his voters. He should have fused with the municipal life. On this living relationship is based the essence of all democracy. Only when it is present is a structure from the cell to the political top possible. For, the organic idea, carried out to the end, resolves the "opposition" between state and autonomy which is felt as Liberal. According to it, the state is rather developed pyramidally from the individual levels of the autonomy.

The way of men of maintaining contact with one another, the possibility of personally knowing one another, the ability of the leader to remain in constant contact with the persons led depends very much on the situation of technology. In this respect, however, the last hundred years have powerfully changed the face of the earth. For two thousand years, the speed of travel was fixed at the upper limit; the streets of Napoleon I are not basically different from those of Caesar. Then came the startling rise of travelling speeds. Much more significant than the construction of railways, which really do not correctly enclose the country, but only unite the cities, is the victory of the motor vehicles. To them remained reserved the bringing of every district somewhat out of the way to a minimum distance. The most important enlarging of the possibilities of communication, however, we owe to the construction of the telephone system: a district magistrate who had to ride two days in order to speak to the local directorate positioned under him can do this today within two hours. The modern means of communication help thus towards those personal contacts which were recognized above as the presupposition of true democracy. That, in this direction, upto the present moment, no full effect of technological progress has occured is due merely to the following circumstance: the official chancellory proceedings have not kept pace with the modern development. All officials indeed have telephones; what however passes through these does not exist in act. The written act has however become, first and last, the foundation of the bureaucratic work-style. If only the administrative technology is adapted to the communications technology, then not only the greatest simplification but also closer co-operation will be the result.

The bridging of further distances through modern means of communication could mislead one to the conclusion that small administrative unities had passed out of fashion; that a new arrangement must follow which enlarges the administrative unities in the same proportions as the travel speeds are raised. This conclusion would be a fallacy. Certainly, the saving of time makes possible a better employment of human work force. But therewith is not yet affirmed that even the administrative fields could become larger. To such a development natural limits are drawn: through the density of settlement of the area to be taken care of. It would be mechanically thought of to draw only the area into consideration and not the men who inhabit it. They are the main thing. Many country districts which are not more thickly settled than 50 years ago can indeed be united into a new district. Where, however, density of population increased, the work area has not, in spite of technological progress, grown smaller, the burden of work in no way made smaller. In the creation of modern administrative unities, therefore, consideration must be taken of the area, number of inhabitants, sort of settlement, social structure, and development of means of transportation. These are considerations which every administrative reformer should seriously set out and think through to the final conclusions. Decisive in such observations remains the organic point of view: the uninterrupted and personal binding of man to man, from the top to the bottom and vice-versa.

XIII

The new leadership

Two large groups of orders were distinguished in the last two chapters: the purely social, such as the professional order, workers' community, culture (art, science, Church, education); thereafter, the blood-related and land-conditioned orders: family, community. They form the substructure of the political edifice of a nation. From them is developed the "high level" of the state. The ranked structure of a people, which even Leopold Ziegler considers as the essential character of striving for form arising from an organic whole, is the decisive sign of the social doctrine outlined, to be sure only sketchily, here. History knows no repetition in the sense of exactness, but only of similarity. The basic formal principle is timeless, the shape itself time-bound. The state is therefore a time-conditioned form in which a people, legally ordered, strives for freedom.

One however who considers the state as the highest level of a ranked structure must raise the question regarding the bearers of the real politicality. Where are those men who, grown beyond the partial politicality of the subordinate orders, take up the total responsibility for the whole, the complete state? Therewith the problem of the leader treated so often in this work is once again touched on. The spiritual-intellectual condition of the true leader was repeatedly outlined. We have, however, not finished with the demand that leader personalities so disposed should lead the state. It must be explained much more how a correct selection can succeed and what institutions seem appropriate to secure such a selection. In the answering of this question we start from the fact that the world-view represented here presupposes the natural growth of such a stratum of leaders. Mechanical selection processes never lead to the selection of the best. The advantage and the pressure of social institutions is not thereby abandoned. Rather, these can be so disposed that they prevent the natural process of selection, indeed even promote a counter-selection (the rule of the inferiour in the mass democracy). One who recognizes this danger for human society does not banish it in any way when he sets up, in place of the current mechanical selection, a new artificial human filtering machine. Plans are only fruitful when they conceive of institutions which are suited to the organic growth of the society.

The question of the leader, recognized as the burning one of the entire West, is answered differently from different angles. The worshippers of legal democracy, who aspire for the ideal condition of leaderlessness, are omitted in this observation. The materialistic observation of history does not indeed deny leadership as such, but believes that its rise is bound to economic processes. Even this conception of leadership was contradicted. Then there are in Socialism different gradations, beginning with Syndicalism to those which conceive of the class warfare as the way to the coming classless society: they expect all salvation from the educational dictatorship of the "working" class. The elitist doctrine of Pareto comes closer to the genuine idea of the leader. This "elite" however lacks the support from an unconditional value. If a stratum of men is designated as the best, then it must be first established what is socially good. Supposing that the Fascist party were in fact a selection of the best, the character-related good of the individual member in it obtains its standard only in the national mythos. Nationalistically, Fascism has set out very well. But since this work recognized the national - not the truly national cultural - idea as a relative, and not as an unconditional value - at least with regard to its community-forming power - it cannot be the standard for an organic selection of the leaders.

In this gap we encounter now the racial-biologists who wish to measure the social good of a man according to the value of the heridity latent in him.[74] They trace back the capacity for performance, indeed the intellectual disposition of the man to his inherited constitution. The consciousness of responsibility for the general public expresses itself, according to them, in the fact that the superiour consciously breeds his constitution further, and therewith accomplishes an increased performance for the people and the culture. In this activity they glimpse that incorporation into the community which even this book establishes as the characteristic of the superior. A selection should establish the wished for breeding and thus the leading stratum create the biological nobility.

This view ails from the crowding together of sociological and biological thought processes, but, above all things, in the fact that it does not bring the two into the necessary relationship of subordination. Conscious breeding does not yet create a nobility which represents a social stratum, but nobility breeds itself. It is the consciousness of administering special possessions of the society which impels the breeding. The biological inheritance alone does not create this impulse. For, it obtains its value only in social thought, only related to its role as a social leader. The consciousness of being called to leadership must therefore come first in order to benefit the breeding. From this way of thought is illustrated the fact that biologically heridary values alone can found no selection of leaders in the sociological sense.

The plans of Lagarde on the new formation of the nobility, which owe their rise mainly to his observations in England, come closer to the social needs. He considers the gentry, the lower nobility of England correctly as the bearers of the English politics: "The English parliament is worth something only as the

---

[74] One may compare here the arguments of the population political part.

representative of the English gentry: only as this does it represent something; there are indeed no popular representatives in England".[75] From this he draws the conclusion for the German situation, whose chief evil consists in the lack of a lower nobility which replenishes itself in a healthy manner. Nobility is for him therefore not the community of the excellently born,[76] but of all families which consider the family and wish to maintain it as the foundation of the national life. Thereby Lagarde has indeed recognized a basic trait of the noble way of thought which is closely connected to the above-mentioned racial-biological thought processes: the will towards a family and to breeding becomes for him the central point of a new noble character. However, he also sees the sociological side: to the new nobility belong men of certain professional orders who with regard to their lineage fulfil certain preconditions. He thus arrives in the first place at the bureaucratic nobility, which old Russia has already known. That is followed by the immunised nobility, i.e. those families which, in spite of urbanisation, and strong expenditure, and extraordinary performances of individual family members, have suffered loss in the power of their breeding, because an immunising adaptation to the urban-industrial situation has taken place.[77] What Lagarde does in the way of practical plans is extraordinarily useful in a family-political way (economic unity of the race, family wealth, supervision of marriages, etc.). On the membership in the new nobility a political heraldic office should decide.

As valuable as these plans are, especially insofar as the focus of the German people was oriented once again to the moral-aristocratic powers, so lively were the objections which were made against them. One even flung the term "Romantic" against him. Indeed this complaint is hardly apt to harm the moral content of Lagarde's plans; but it may be correct that his plans are not suited to

[75] [Paul de Lagarde, *Deutsche Schriften*, Göttingen, 1886, p.37].
[76] Arthur Hübscher in Heft 5 (1926) of the *Süddeutsche Monatshefte*, [Bd.23,i (1925/26), pp.410-13, "Lagarde über Neugestaltung des Adels"].
[77] Ludwig Flügge in the *Süddeutsche Monatshefte*, loc.cit., [Bd.23,i (1925/26), pp.403-9, "Die rassenbiologische Bedeutung des Adels und das Prinzip der Immunisierung"].

the historical situation of the present and therefore do without the possibility of realisation. Moreover, the newest development has made the building up of a professional order on the already existent foundation and in the direction of the current concept of the nobility almost unimaginable. The difficulty lies less in the fact that, through the falling away of the monarchy, the nobilising situation is evidently lacking; this is in no way a misfortune because princely conferments of nobility were not always fortunate and precisely the nobility as an order needs unconditional autonomy, therefore also the right to the furthering of its ranks. Another circumstance provokes the chief consideration: the historical traditional nobility has conclusively lost its mastery. It would be false to draw the conclusion therefrom that the nobility does not still have its significance for the German people, in the social as well as in the racial biological field. But the fact of lost mastery remains. It is also not to be obtained again. The selection standards according to which a social ruling class is formed are, however, historically conditioned. Once it was more physical characteristics, at another time more spiritual ones, which raised the individual or a family above the commonality. As between the knight and the ennobled businessman there exists an unbridgeable gap, so the future nobility distinguishes itself from the present forms. Always, however, the turning to the community remains characteristic for genuine noble disposition. The true noble is conscious of his responsibility with regard to his ancestors, who lie in the grave, and to his children, who are still minors. (Flügge). Therefrom follows the conclusion that the noble is really nothing else but an exemplary embodiment of man as social being. The order of the nobility is based, accordingly, most deeply on the organic nature of human society. Where the nobility loses mastery, a deviation from its innermost being has, as a rule, taken place: it has become individualistic. Therewith it loses the trust of the people, and ceases to operate in an exemplary manner. A new nobility will therefore arise as soon as a stratum forms itself in the life of the people which develops anew the idea of the social whole and sets it up as an example. The highest form of service therefore founds nobility. The moment when such a stratum forms society and state anew, the nobility also as an order begins to demand its significance. But only the fact of achieved and formed mastery founds the new order of the nobility, of which it may remain an open question what shape it gives itself and whether it fuses in itself parts of the existing and vitally powerful old nobility. For, the born nobility as a whole hardly comes into question for the future nobility, as a consequence of its lost mastery; as little as the class of the educated, so long as mass education and an outmoded educational ideal exist; finally, also not wealth, which lives without obligation. Therefore birth (heriditary disposition), education (even the educated mostly come into their stratum heriditarily), and inherited property remain, nevertheless, the foundations of the ruling class.

With such arguments the contradiction of the people of the "spirit of the age" is naturally provoked who will ascertain with fear that the founding of such a new nobility is based on adaptation. Formal-legally this may be right. But between pure adaptation and inner duty exists the same difference as between formal law and cosmic law. The former arises from power, the latter from inner religiosity. The former is rooted in the material impulses, the latter in the soul.

Accordingly, a last question remains to be answered: are beginnings present which promise the quiet growth of such a new nobility to an inwardly obliged ruling stratum? To answer this question in the affirmative means to express a declaration of faith. The coming age of a uniformity streaming from the total experience will be borne by a leading stratum of men who carry this experience before them as their shield, and strike into the chaos of rampant material impulses and soul-less rule of the understanding the path on which reason and order ride to victory. One who with alert eyes sees investigates the intellectual and social efforts of the present will always encounter that quiet struggle of individual personalities who, distributed in great numbers through the entire country, without knowledge of one another, understand one another immediately as soon even as they come into mutual contact. Never was there in German provinces such an agreement based on the deepest spiritual harmony as it is on the point of forming itself today between intellectually young men who are beyond all party views and world-view remnants. All this is still in a fermenting development. But one begins to recognize one another. And every one who stands in this movement has had the experience bordering on a miracle of getting to know men in a strange city from whom, after a few informative sentences, one gets the feeling that one has known them already for a long time. Here, without organisation, without a symbol, without obligation, a new bonding forms itself which will obtain a striking form when the spirit ensouling it achieves mastery. Obviously, even the beginnings of social formation are present in this direction. In the bonds of the youth, of the generation of the front, exist promising beginnings of this sort. Indeed the community feeling still clings to the common experience of the past. But the time is not far any more when, from it, the prescient vision of a future community comes into being. If this step from the past to the future is made, many bonds naturally disintegrate which do not bear any movement in themselves, but exist only on proud remembrance. Seen thus, the "bond to German renewal" has not yet been founded. It can hardly be organised but can be grown to the degree to which, on the devastated soil of the German soul, a new humus stratum collects.

The thorough professional orderly ranking will accelerate the development of a superiour stratum on which the leadership of the state devolves. It however lies in the essence of every incorporation to press towards the whole, from its own order to the total order, the state. As false as it was to let the city councillor X from the municipality Y immediately rise to a parliamentary representative and minister, so natural will it be that, in a gradational rise, the great autonomous bodies will bring forth men who strive for the final unity, the state. The leader of the professional order is not in himself also a state leader. But the professional order, just as other orders, will crystallise true state leaders who are then classified into the highest order. This development corresponds also to the laws of growth.

Life itself produces the leader. For, as much as the professional politician is to be welcomed, so doubtful is the politician such by profession. Everybody active in the state leadership is supposed to have acknowledged his man, since otherwise the danger exists that the representative type - characterised above - spreads itself as politicians. Against this - so to speak, bourgeois - school the disposition of the genuine politician must enter on national-political thought. It is important to breed this leader-type and not to pursue the illusion of the state citizen by virtue of universal franchise. For, there will always be men who think historically, in nations and continents, and such whose sphere of thought does not go beyond the factories, profession, family, municipality, and indeed the regular circle of party friends.

The state as the highest order of organic community must be an aristocracy: in the last and highest sense: the rule of the best. Even democracy was founded with this claim. Indeed the Jacobins shrink back from the mass in that they differentiate between the *citoyen* and the *bourgeois*. The equalisation of the two however was, as was already demonstrated above, a political philosophical and historical conclusion. The bourgeois has triumphed. If, on account of this remark, the party Socialists should laugh heartily, let it be said to him that even he is nothing else but a bourgeois with a reversal of premises. Certainly, Socialism wants to revive in its best representatives the incorporation into the whole (unfortunately mostly into the class). All these renewers on a purely democratic foundation should however be told that every genuine democracy is in fact an aristocracy. An enmassed people are incapable of "self-government". It always falls into the hands of the Caesars, whether these be adventurers of money or - what stands higher - of blood. One therefore who wants to press forward to the conception of the organic society and the state must demand the turning towards the aristocratic, and indeed to the public aristocracy of responsibility and service, not to the established minority rule of the financially powerful and the demagogues. Nothing characterizes the noble disposition better than the courage for responsible leadership. The true leader begins only where he despises the favour of the masses from love for the people. Genuine love extends itself to the neighbour and to the nation in the idea, not to the consumed human crowds and the philistinism crammed together. The highest law for the state structure is, accordingly, that the state be conducted and led by the selection of the people. Selection, however, conditions living stratification, traditional virtues, firm concepts, social limitation, which are always broken into from below by the most capable. The distinction of the blood is added to that of character, facilitating the breeding of true leaders. Experienced peoples with old cultures, like the Indians, know very well that well-bred families inherit leadership characteristics which cannot be replaced by education alone. The so-called aristocracy of the mind is therefore a phantom of the brain, as soon as it should be transferred from the intellectual to the social realm.

The idea of letting the state be led by an organically grown ruling class is alone suited to overcome the crisis of democracy. It was already argued that this essentially consists in a falsification of the political philosophy of Rousseau, which to be sure takes its beginning from Rousseau himself. The political general will is based, in Rousseau, on the supposition of a common foundation of value of the state citizen; the people should be so uniform that agreement is present in the basic questions. Parties and world-view groupings are therefore as little suited to the political ideal of Rousseau as the division of powers. To this extent is Rousseau a theoretician of the organic state. However, he is at the same time Liberal, and this intellectual attitude becomes a disaster for him: in political practice, he transforms the general political will into the sum of votes of individual state citizens. However, in Liberalism, one becomes a state citizen not by virtue of social performance and political affirmation, but by virtue of birth. Here lies the trap-door of cultural liberalism, and of an ethical world-view, into the field of the political. This Liberal component of democratic ideology had to become a disaster the moment the metropolitan masses were endowed with the franchise and the common world-view value-foundation was lost. Thus arises the crisis of democracy itself, "because with the universal human equality the problem of a substantial equality and homogeneity necessary to a democracy cannot be resolved".[78]

A healing of these serious wounds of democracy, indeed the rescue of democracy itself, which Schmitt paraphrases abstractly as the identity of the ruling and the ruled, is perhaps only possible through the answering of the most difficult of all political questions: how does the general will of the people arise? The mechanical way (vote majority) led to chaos. Only the belief in a social-ethical high standing minority which embodies in itself the highest spiritual-intellectual form of the people remains as an organic one.

---

[78] Carl Schmitt, *Die geistesgeschichtliche Lage des heutigen Parlamentarismus*, München and Leipzig, Verlag von Duncker u. Humblot, [1926].

XIV

The new structure of the Reich

In his finely thought out writing, Carl Schmitt distinguishes from the crisis of democracy the infirmity of parliamentarianism. Now what is parliamentarianism? Ordinarily the instruction contained in Article 54 of the national constitution is understood by it, that the ministers require the trust of the Parliament for the conduct of their office and can be forced at any time to retirement by the withdrawal of the trust. This is, however, only parliamentarianism in the narrower sense and touches above all only the technical side of the governmental structure. Constitutional ordinances of this sort arise from the English situation which has received its special stamp from the two-party system. Seen constitutional legally, determinations like that of Article 54 are not only illogical but also undemocratic; "there is indeed a contradiction in the fact that the Parliament, as the first committee (of the people) whould be independent of the people for the period of the election and is not revokable, whereas the parliamentary government, the second committee remains at every moment dependent on the trust of the first committee and therefore can be revoked at any time" (Schmitt). This contradiction is indeed responsible for the all-powerfulness of the parliament. The division of powers has become as weak as democracy, for the parliament now stands between the people and the government, cutting every connection. The appeal to a democratic dictatorship becomes understandable because it seems suited to establish anew the contact between the leader and the people. Correctly therefore does Schmitt maintain: if, for practical and technical reasons, instead of the people, trusted persons of the people would decide, even a sole trusted man could indeed decide in the name of the same people in place of the parliament without the basic law of democracy being injured.

Parliamentarianism in the further sense is more: social-scientifically its historical transitional position was touched on further above. But even the intellectual essential characteristics, which it is the service of Schmitt to have newly elaborated, found a thorough evaluation in the philosophical part. Schmitt points to the fact that the public nature of the deliberations and the division of the powers are the chief intellectual historical foundations of parliamentarianism. Seen historically, it is a question therefore of a double reaction against the princely absolutism: the secret politics of the cabinet had to be countered as much as the the unrestricted despotism: publicity as the protection against the former, and division of powers, i.e., legal binding, as the defence against the latter. The demand of public representation is only understandable from the world of the Enlightenment: one believed that one could in this way find and legally establish the correct, at least the relative, truth. The parliament thus becomes really the political residue of the Enlightenment belief in the understanding. With the disintegration of the rationalistic age, however, even the sense of parliamentarianism falls away, sealing the downfall of the parliament.

The same is true also, as Schmitt has shown, of the division of powers, which pervades all constitutional law as the basic trait throughout the 19th century. The binding of the state organs to the law, the rise of these laws through "balancing out" of opinions, characterise the modern conception of the system of the constitutional state. Thereby, the opinions waver on the concept of the law. The division of powers differentiates the universally valid law and the decree succeeding in the individual case, the ordinance. The former belongs to the condition of the parliament, the latter devolves on the government. The borders are, however, increasingly erased and Hegel already doubts the legal character of the budgetary law. The later development, which did not differentiate between universal laws and ordinances or decrees which are really governmental decisions, was prefigured especially when the division of powers was practically destroyed by the all-powerfulness of the parliament.

With the disappearance of the monarchy, the division of powers loses its historical justification, which is rooted in constitutional thought. Masterly and comradely forms had to be brought into a balancing equipoise by way of division of powers; through the balancing of these two currents of will, the vitality of the political life had to be preserved. "Here the Liberal idea has joined with a specifically German "organic idea" and overcome the mechanistic idea of a balance" (Schmitt). But this overcoming of a mechanistic system was time-conditioned: it had an inner sense in that historical epoch when to the purely ruling organisation of the state (absolute royalty) had to be opposed from below a comradely formation of the will. In the meantime, the current from below has taken the one from above into itself and consumed it. Certainly, even a democratic constitutionalism (i.e. without a monarchical head) is possible: one may think of the United States of North America; but the division of powers undertaken there is mechanical insofar as the state head derives its power from the same source as the parliament: from the people. Seen thus, constitutionalism on a democratic foundation is only a mechanical substitute of organic vitality. The logically organic political will-formation in a democratic foundation is therefore already prefigured by the actual disappearance of the division of powers in modern parliamentarianism: the 20th century strives for a sole state head, developed from the popular will, who exercises legislation and government equally. The parliament, with its above-outlined, historically conditioned, but outmoded essential characteristics, will thereby fall.

This is the development in the long view. For the immediate future, one must reckon with the weakness of the organic foundation on which a new state unity could grow. As a necessary substitute, constitutional forms transferred to democracy may perhaps be introduced once again. The organisation of the ruling and the comradely elements however results mechanically in constitutionalism - this is the characteristic mark - and not, as in a genuinely organic state, organically. Practical examples further below will consolidate this opinion.

With the basic conception of the system of organic political will-formation obtained thus the reformer of German life may proceed to the real new construction of the state. To be sure, with a necessary self-limitation: it would be false to develop constitutional sketches within the scope of a work like the present. Even here the rule of growth of all organic life is valid. The forms of the state are non-recurring, conditioned by time-relations, the character of the people, territorial political conditions, and political powers. Timeless is the striving for the whole which it created. It can therefore be shown what ways correspond to the political reform of an organic world-view and what lead only deeper into the chasms of mechanistic disintegration. It may also be admitted openly that the life-work of a creative genius would manage to sketch the basic traits and system of on organic law. Perhaps destiny would grant the German people an Ihering of the 20th century. At present, however, practical new political formations can be examined in their content of organic components in some examples of the most recent history.

Thus, Bolshevism has, in Russia, apparently under the influence of the Syndicalistic thought process, but perhaps also from healthy political instincts, replaced the Russian centralism by a federative system of numerous peoples of the Russian territory. This new formation possesses an organic foundation in contrast to Fascism which culminated the French state centralism.[79] The structure of the

---

[79] Whether this development in Italy is a final one may remain open to question.

state power itself is based on the idea of the Soviet in Russia, the crystallisation of the state head occurs by way of indirect election. This is doubtlessly likewise organically thought out. What, however, devaluates the entire system is the perfectly west-European- (Marxist-) seeming rule of a class, is the historical materialistic foundation which plainly denies the natural facts of the social and economic life. Allegedly one wants to reach through class rule true democracy instead of plutocracy. Even the Jacobins could not have grounded their claims very much differently. Fascism is a hybrid of transformed Syndicalism and Nationalism. The Syndicalistic compononents correspond to organic ideas of the state, the Nationalistic - insofar as they are obliged to the popular emotional life - likewise; insofar, however, as they pursue the idol of the political nation, thereby neglecting the people and not developing its powers in an autonomous manner, it is a question of a culmination of western-mechanistic political thought. The real state structure in Italy, apart from its centralising tendency, fulfils the demand of an organic fastening in a characteristic way: the "parliament" arises indeed not only in a mosaic fashion from below to the top, but also through influence from above. Every mosaic requires a means of binding in order not to fall apart. All parliaments which are not borne by a common value-foundation are, so to speak, stuck together by blasting powder. If this value-foundation is present - such as the idea of the nation and belief in the understanding were, uniquely, in the early parliamentarianism - an influence from above is made superfluous in an election. If, however, the politically unifying foundation is lacking - and that will be the case in all ages which know no "this-wordly religions" - the "popular representation" would require the state-maintaining clamp. This translates in political practice to: the parliament cannot form itself independently actively from below to the top without considering whether a unity arises; but the state will has to see to it that the putting together occurs sensibly, and corresponds to the whole of the state. This organic idea was realised by Fascism in the following way: at first a series of unities (syndicates, etc.) nominated the representatives. The list itself is determined by the great Fascist Council, thus, from above. This is followed by the appointment to this list by the elective body. Parts and the whole are thus intertwined with each other, every attempt at breaking loose is in vain.

The *Young German Manifesto* proceeds similarly in its plans: the present leaders of the political unities are selected not only by way of the election, but require the approval of the next higher superiour leader who, in this case, represents the political will. "The election interweaves the will of the state with the will of the people. - In the election, an act of unification is accomplished between the people and the state on the occupation of a leader's position in the national state". The author of the *Young German Manifesto* has thus similarly recognized this law of organic political will formation. All these plans, however, have a prototype which has survived Western history and therefore serves as the model: the Catholic Church. Even here election (right of nominating) and approval (often restricted by political protest) must come together in order to occupy a bishop's position of leadership. Part and the whole are fused most inwardly.

As the building rule of organic state formation, the following principles may be valid:

1. comradely and ruling forms (election and recognition) must be merged into one another in order to secure the life of the parts and of the whole equally.
2. all election processes with the exception of the preliminary election are indirect.
3. the preliminary election itself must be accomplished in such small unities that a social-vital link between the leadership and the led is possible.

In these rules we obtain the standard of examining all state reforming attempts on their content of organic thought. The ways which can be taken in individual cases in order to do justice to the principles expressed here are numerous. Thus the *Young German Manifesto* founds a one-chamber system through the introduction of the election. (The special chambers contemplated by it, corresponding, to a certain degree, to the social autonomy already dealt with, have only the right of counsel with respect to the raising of objections against decisions of the solely legislative body: the chapter-house of the Reich which represents the political chamber. The plan of the Young German Order accordingly takes over a condition already present in parliamentarianism: namely the practical elimination of the division of powers; there is no constitutionalism any longer. The difference between the present-day parliamentarian system and the organic state structure is, however, that the former cannot do without a constitution without the party rule falling, whereas, in the organic state, the opposition between political chamber and government (legislation and executive power) falls away without any further ado, since indeed the opposition of people and government is made superfluous. The political chamber does not "represent" the people any longer with respect to the ruling class, but is the ruling class and the people at the same time. It is the corporate body of the organically grown leaders. Comradely and ruling forms find in it a unified expression.

Nevertheless, even if the organic state manages without a division of legal powers, still in no way does it without a technical one: at least the making and the execution of the decisions of the political chambers results through an independent organ, the government. This can however act only in a freely and in a ruling manner, in the good sense of the word, if it itself is responsible not to a corporate body but to an individual. Therefore the purely organically thought out plan of the Young German Order foresees the appointment of the ministry through the leader of the Reich. Since the latter himself enjoys personal independence - he is "elected" for life - one can, in spite of everything, speak of a certain division of powers. It is, to be sure, essentially different from that of Montesquieu in that it is not of an unconditional nature: the highest leader is not a monarch acting from his own (divine) right.

Naturally, possibilities of substitutes are thinkable to do approximate justice to the basic rules set out above of the organic state structure. One must, however, be clear to oneself on the fact that it is thereby a question of mechanical means (balancing). The fastening of the will of the parts with that of the whole can even result while one perhaps lets a mosaic-like popular representation exist, but sets up a state organ which embodies the pure political will in a hindering manner and distributes the powers correspondingly. To this exigence corresponds the two-chamber system. The popular chamber represents the structure of the people from the bottom to the top, an aristocratic chamber (not in the sense of heriditary nobility) the influencing of the will from above. This system has the advantage that all emergency valves are open to criticism, whereby, to be sure, the rationalistic belief in the "truth-promoting" effect of criticism is presupposed. It therefore works excellently so long as the reciprocal powers are uncontested, so long as the popular representation is restricted to its own tasks, supervision, and so long as the legislation lies, in the main, in the aristocratic chamber. Popular representations which make laws are the end of all true law. The danger of this sort of state structure lies in its swaying balance. The first chamber will tend to self-rule, the popular chamber unfurl the banner of allegedly true democracy in a revolutionary manner. Thus then, even practically the emphasis has always glided into the popular chamber, harmlessly where a gentry rules, but dangerously where the masses and the common people are in the advance. The mechanical two-chamber system is therefore possible only where a mostly predominant organisation of the opposed principles succeeds. It will have no existence in the long run. It remains a substitute form of organic state structure and often only useful for the transition. Precisely for this reason, however, the immediate future of Germany apparently belongs to it. A further question is from where the members of a first chamber who should embody the ruling principle of the state are to be taken. In the feudal state and in the constitutional monarchy, the resolution was obvious. This is today untimely and outmoded. Alongside the appointment through the state head (England, Italy) remains the way of linking a seat in the first chamber to the administration of certain professional orderly autonomous bodies (the Church, universities, etc.). Significantly, the plan of the "Association for the renewal of the Reich" goes in this direction, in that it wishes to see the National Council partially constituted of representatives sent by the National Economic Council. Translated into the language of the organic state programme developed here, this means that the "professional orders" delegate leading men to this first chamber. Therewith the first chamber becomes not a professional orderly parliament but only the rallying position for outstanding heads in the professional life.

The greatest difficulty however is produced by the fact that, in the German state-structure, provincial federalism is taken into consideration (National Council). Here the posing of the question is extraordinarily developed as soon as the different possibilities of organic state formation are held in view. If, for example, the principle of the indirect election is carried out, there exists anyway a practical provincial federalism, since the leaders of the present-day provinces represent the highest political comradely-ruling combination. Provincial federalism and organic state structure thus coincide: there is first of all no place for a two-chamber system, unless the second chamber is formed in a purely aristocratic manner through the inclusion of professional orderly heads or the appointment of representatives by the professional chambers. A second way out is contained in the fact that the elections to the first and the second chambers are based on differing provincial distributions, as this is the case today: on the one hand, by provinces, on the other, by election districts. A possibility of differentiating is further provided insofar as a chamber unites in itself the political will of the provinces, the others the so-called popular will by way of the indirect election. Organic and mechanic will formation therefore would exist next to each other. Now, the direct election must be rejected under all circumstances by the doctrine of the organic state. With the introduction of the indirect election, however, the present-day differentiation between political and popular will falls away. This opposition is finally removed, just as the indirect election logically establishes the ranked structure. Thus there remains only to set up against a political and at the same time provincial federalistic chamber one influenced in a professional orderly manner. Thereby the professional orderly state is not really demanded, but only the classification of the people according to two directions expressed: according to the "provincial" and according to the remaining orders. From the entire investigation, however, the significance of the franchise, which is decisive for the state structure, becomes apparent.

The heads of the state can, according to the organic conception, be crystallised only in a ranked manner. A direct popular election, famed as especially democratic, has its great disadvantage, because precisely the strengthening of the authority of the state leader must sharpen and poison the battle for the highest political position; such an election is especially dependent on the influence of the masses through the press and finance. The danger of unworthy representatives becomes still greater than in the heriditary monarchy. For, in the case of the latter, the responsibility of the monarch nevertheless exists with regard to his lineage: it will mostly work in a restricting manner. Montesquieu considers honour as the principle of the monarchy. It is otherwise in the case of the popularly elected president who can influence history by virtue of his greater freedom of responsibility. One need think only of the case of Wilson. The president emerging for life from a chain of indirect elections is the goal of all organic constitutional politics. With a different symbolism he can also be called an elected king. Even here the model of the Catholic Church operates extraordinarily instructively.

A middle way has thus been found which prevents inorganic rule (alienation between the leaders and the led) equally. From these considerations, it is established how wrongly the present-day struggle for the state-form is set out. Every head of the state must have an original democratic base, no matter whether he is termed President or Majesty. The more reverence and trust there exists in the masses in their leadership, the less they tend to claims to a mechanical participation in the state leadership. Democracy does not consist in the fact that there is, legally, the possibility of a manual labourer becoming a minister. In the realm of the intellectual and therewith of genuine leadership, there are no such envy-filled considerations, oppositions of such a sort between the people and the leader. In all ages, great leaders have come from the lowest strata of the people, without asking whether a formal democratic constitution would permit them.

Thus the entire absurdity comes to light, of seeing in the monarchy the merely undemocratic, and in the republic unconditional fulfilment of democracy. Even convinced legitimists pay their tribute to the democratic basic idea in that they represent a kingship by virtue of the popular will. For a kingship from his own right the time is indeed past, if a collective mass madness does not conjure up a Caesarism. The organisation of the state from the top to the bottom, as absolutism undertook it, stands outside all consideration in the 20th century. In turn, the structure from the bottom to the top has led to the disintegration of every whole. If one considers the matters from this standpoint, the battle proceeds only for the content and not for the form of the state. In the sense that every state form is to be developed from the forces of the people, all Germans are democrats. The true monarchy is the expression of the mythical self-consciousness of a people. Only such a one can justify and strengthen the monarchy. The Emperor, as the highest lord of the Western world installed by God, owes his position to mythical-religious ideas. It is not a concern of the morrow and not of the day after tomorrow, whether such powers awake again and create mythical forms. If direction and order grow out of the chaos, and a spiritual and social situation of peace enters, perhaps for centuries, it could also be possible that the symbol of the crown would radiate with a new brilliance. It is therefore wrong to want to legitimistically affirm the German downfall. But it is equally contrary to break out into a fearful wailing at the word "monarchy". The form of the monarchy which the Middle Ages has handed down belongs to history. Every attempt at a reestablishment would betray an unhistorical way of thought. Therefore only unfruitful minds struggle against one another in that resentment-filled battle position: monarchy or republic. According to the arguments upto now of this work, it may have become clear how outmoded the struggle of those two camps stemming from the Wilhelminian age is. Politically, individualism was as well embodied in the absolute monarchy as in the majority absolutism of modern democracy: two mirror-images which resemble each other to a hair. And, if today these two brothers wish to battle each other and summon all intellectual powers for their agreeement, the coming community-affirming generation calls out resolutely: Away with both, we respect their achievement, but their mission has been fulfilled. A new world wishes to develop, to push new roots into the motherly soil. The form was, in all ages, nothing more than a receptacle of the content. A new generation struggles for the new content of law, society, and state.

It is hard to speak theoretically of powers, for the political practice overrides the paper constitution nowhere so easily as in the field of powers. The political powers easily prevail. For an organic political life, therefore, at most guiding principles of the most general sort can be set up regarding where the present powers should legally lie. Against the financial standard of the state - the most tangible sovereign right - stands always the tax-granting right of the people. These two claims must be balanced against each other, should the state or the people not suffer. The German Kaiser of the mediaeval Reich was forced to go begging among the orders if he wished to protect a borderline of the Reich against attacking enemies. In turn, the present-day state forces its most loyal citizens to such procedures because it dispossesses them through taxes. These two extremes demonstrate how hard it is to maintain the healthy middle line. Today the people permit not only the revenues of the Reich but also the expenses; and this right to permit expenses is exercised by men who themselves bring in small taxes: the unpropertied dispose of the propertied. On the other hand, however, the parliament interferes ridiculously into the expenditure economics of the state. One may think of the pathetic comedy of the battle cruiser which represents only the distortion of all pre-war battles for the sake of the defence bill. To describe how a budget nowadays arises would be worthy of the pen of a Molière: many budget items are only purchase monies which a party pays to the others so that the former may agree to budget items wished for by itself. Stein was a passionate opponent of the expense-granting right of the parliament. Bismarck began his career with a battle, indeed with a constitutional infringement due to this troublesome right. A misled popular representation can take the possibility of self-defence from the state as well as it squanders enormous sums senselessly. Here limits should be set: the tax grants must be restricted by the incorporation of those who feel responsible for the prosperity of the entire economy. On the other hand, the expenditure economy is the matter of the - to be sure, controlled - government.

A great part of the legislation moves to the orders. The real legal formation is accomplished in the organic society not by the parliaments, but by the judges. The paper statutory right is limited to a minimum. What the state then creates still of laws are, to a certain degree, guiding principles of organic life. They should be decided by those in whom the spirit of the people and vitality culminate· and not, as today, by petty bourgeois and philistines. The legislation of good neighbour Müller and Huber, whose politics of interest is then poured by crafty legal technicians into paragraphs, is a contempt of the majesty of the law. - A further principle is: foreign political and military questions do not belong to the broad public. In times of cabinet politics, such Liberal demands were understandable. But a democracy in which the people continually chat in the meantime to the men of their confidence is indeed a denial of itself. Nothing more stupid than the catchword of the removal of secret diplomacy. The public handling of all national life questions has upto now only led to an unheard-of dishonorability of the democratic foreign policy: military secret treaties are concluded and, at the same time, in Geneva, hypocritical speeches of reconciliation are held. One, however, who does not want to give up, even in democracy, a guarding of the ruling persons, because allegedly in the human nature self-ruling tendencies are always latent, may take care to see that the guarding activity is exercised by aristocratic organs and not by democratic ones. The gossipy parliament cannot avoid this necessity, on account of which the popular assembly is systematically incapacitated by committees.

The executive power, however, rests in the hands of the state leader, who transfers their exercice to a ministry freely named by him. As little as the president of the Reich himself may the ministry be only an executive machine of irresponsible powers. One may set up guarantees so that the leadership of the Reich does not come into unstoppable contradictions with the people, although even this must be borne temporarily if it arises from political necessities. Constitutional ways can therefore be planned to force the government to a retreat. But making a favorite game of out of the coming and going of ministers for parliamentary 'children' cannot be tolerated by any nation in the long run. The American model shows how one can govern democratically without parliamentary clauses. It is not acceptable to treat ministers according to the principles of the free wage-contract, to which not even a fortnightly but an hourly termination is attached. The confidence of the people in a government is certainly desirable, that of the parliament however inconsequential, since it has very little to do with the people. But even an organically arisen government may not be exposed to the danger of arbitrary revocations. Therefore, declarations of lack of confidence must result from qualified majorities, if they should force the leader of the Reich to decisive measures.

These plans for the organic state-structure demand self-renunciation, therefore inner discipline, from Germans; they should found, instead of an irresponsible, leaderless financial democracy, responsible rule on a comradely foundation. A final break must be made with the loose talk of the forty million free state citizens who rule themselves. We give to the German people the right to choose their leader in an organic form. Instead of the free way for the party-competent people, we raise the demand of advancement for everybody according to performance and moral preparedness for service. We wish to produce inner freedom and freedom of the orders, both not yet present today. For that, we demand however political discipline, thus uniting ruling with comradely forms: from the top and from the bottom, the forces encounter one another, flow into one another, producing the living current which throbs through the organism. But the ridiculous talking oneself into a leadership must cease. A people has only one right in the political field: to be ruled well.

Where, however, do the parties remain in this entire system? To this question different answers are possible, indeed according to the degree to which the organic democracy is realised. The logical carrying out of the principle of the indirect election would, in general, destroy the parties in their present form. The elective bodies would then indeed be structured not as private associations, but as political organs in the total organism. Locally and within the different corporate bodies there would naturally be parties. They are then, however, of a purely purposeful nature, they are pragmatic (Hellpach); they live not from inner oppositions, but are kindled mostly in their inclination to certain leaders who encounter one another in competition. Parties which pervade an entire nation, without local distinction, are thinkable only where immediate mass elections take place. If a popular chamber remains in existence on the foundation of the mechanistic direct election, there will still be parties as private associations which conduct these elections. But even from them the poison teeth have been drawn, if cultural, economical, and social politics are taken out of the realm of the purely political life. The "world-view character" of the present-day parties disappears the moment the cultural life is divided from the political.

The purely organic state, however, is partyless. One who nags that life must come off badly if every reasonable expression and positive criticism is discontinued lives still in the ideas of the Enlightenment. "The correct" arises not through the balance of thesis and antithesis, but through creative vision which emerges from the experience of the whole. It is therefore wrong to make the complaint against Fascism of the elimination of hostile elements. Every healthy democracy has upto now done that likewise. Indeed, it lies in its essence to undertake this elimination, because indeed the rise of a general will is impossible under opposed efforts. If, nevertheless, political corporate bodies are formed in which the different views find a rhetorical settlement - even Fascism does not give up such a form - then only in order to reflect the powerplay of the whole of the people; to obtain from this mirror the insight into situations on which the leading statesman must be instructed. The purposefulness of these new corporate bodies is therefore organically determined and not by the belief in the creative power of dialectic. Here lies the last difference between sinking parliamentarianism and the party system on the one hand, and the coming organic corporate bodies in the "state of orders" on the other.

The administration of the organic state (Reich) is distinguished conceptually from that which is today understood by it. Today, one calls every acting state authority the adminstration. The borders of the government (leadership) and administration merge into each other, because the modern welfare state has taken over an enormous number of social tasks. Basically, the society should adminster itself, the state however must lead. True autonomy stands and falls with the honorary offices. The larger the administrative unities become, the stronger the need to work with professional bureaucrats. The professional bureaucrat however should be only an expert bureaucrat. A staff of experts is arranged alongside the present political leader of the administrative unity. Never, however, does the bureaucrat himself lead politically. The bureaucrat is an instrument and not the master of politics. He does not need to be unpolitical, he should however - considered internal politically - remain apolitical. His franchises are at rest. It is not fitting that the servants of the state elect themselves to be masters of the state. Much too little is the system of the present-day state recognized as the state of a bureaucracy which, in the most dubious sense of the word, exercises authority. Rudolph von Gneist[80] would, if he had seen the numerous bureaucrats in the present-day parliament, have clothed his thoughts against the bureaucratic rule in much more cutting words than he otherwise did this: "The period of glory of the bureaucratised gentry lasts only so long as it struggles consciously for the raising of the whole against the self-interest of the members. Very soon it comes, as every ruling class, into the situation of considering its privilege as a goal in itself and of struggling for its exclusivity against efforts which are more justified than itself". One who puzzles and struggles over state forms should make it clear to himself how significant the fact of the bureaucracy is and how indifferent the question of who appoints the bureaucracy. At most their number and their quality change, indeed according to whether the monarch or party conduct the appointment of bureaucrats. The bureaucratic rule itself is always the same: equally undemocratic and equally devoid of political instinct.

On the other hand, the new bureaucrat must be a true bureaucrat: namely an expert and a sovereign bureaucrat. Not a professional bureaucrat who fulfils private economic tasks, not a bureaucrat who would like to "regulate culture", but a bureaucrat who exercises the power of the state. The concept of bureaucrat is therefore to be purged of all accessories which were invented only "for the protection of the well-earned right" and derives its existence from political Socialism and the need for income. The bureaucrat may not sink to an all-too modest situation. He should be unpretentious in his life conduct but not petty bourgeois and common. It is an absurdity to frighten away the best heads, the strong-willed personalities from state service with bad pay and social devaluation. Much fewer bureaucrats, but better positioned, that is the way of raising the bureaucracy. To this goal may also serve a new form of selection. The state must be in the position to take up competent men of the free professions and of the

---

[80] *Das heutige englische Verfassungs- und Verwaltungsrecht*, Berlin, 1857.

private sector in its service: men who know the bourgeois life, who do not "develop themselves" at green tables and in chancellory dust. First, the man should give evidence of his ability to endure the battle for life, to nourish and create values for himself; then the state may call him in its state service and pay him correspondingly. Nothing is more pathetic than those figures populating the high schools who, already from the fourth semester, bring into play all influences and relations in order to glide into the army of income-receivers after a strenuously endured examination, thus obtaining security of life and comfort at a moment when a starting cheerful life battle should have been affirmed. The legal scientific training is, of all the expert educations, doubtless the most universal and therefore certainly suited to the bureaucratic career. It however remains a specialist training and indeed one which distances itself increasingly from life. To be legal-scientifically trained is an advantage; to consider certification as the knowledge of the paragraphs and of the juristic phantoms, however, remains an illusion. Perhaps administration is not politics, but it is always the art of perceiving connections and of dealing with men. A bad jurist can be a brilliant organiser; a good jurist a cripple of life. The preparation for public service therefore strides directly towards a new universal educational goal.

Crutches for the weak and a prevention of every personality development, however, is the much famed endowment with "well earned rights". One who has undergone a juristic state examination at 25 receives the licence to fade intellectually-spritually through the rest of his entire life and to be buried alive in the cemetery of the well-ordered salaried classes. 10 years of successful state service and then provision of irrevocability would correspond much more to the demands of life. Already Bismarck pointed to the fact that the irremovability of the bureaucrats, taken over from the self-ruling state, may not be maintained absolutely in the constitutional state. In addition, Oskar Aust[81]remarks correctly

[81] *loc.cit.*

whither the striking power of the army would have reached if even there irrevocability had ruled. Even the administration is subject to the laws of economicality; in its present-day form, however, it is a source of popular economic waste. Soon the number of the tax-consumers is greater than that of tax-payers. Still more disastrous, in the meanwhile, is the endowment of retirement pay. Here a confusion of all healthy concepts truly rules. Thus it is enigmatic why the state - that is said by a man who himself was an officer - pays officers' pensions to relatively young men who have found a sufficient income in richly paid bourgeois positions. Some years of military activity can, however, never justify the receipt of pocket money upto old age. Every employee, every children's maid, everything, strives for retirement pay. Instructresses who bring forward perhaps thirty years of service receive state pension for another thirty years. An old high-level state bureaucrat - throughout his life unmarried and childless - arrives, for reasons of neighbourly love or some other which need not be more closely examined, at the idea of making a twenty-year old shop-girl his wife. This professional official act costs the state, presupposing that the lady has a laudable intention of becoming 80 years old, under certain circumstances some hundred thousand marks. If it is also madness, it does yet have method. Nothing is more uneconomical and wasteful than the personnel policy of the public funds. These funds are really always public. One should pay the bureaucrats, especially the higher ones, in such a way that they can make savings, and perhaps compel them by way of a bureaucratic compulsory savings-bank. The system of pension in the present-day form is however a contempt of competence, selection, and feeling of responsibility: it is simply a shifting of every life responsibility onto the tax-payer.

The most secure weapon against corruption is prosperity. A nation which proceeds against men who have made themselves meritorious conducts filthy profiteering. One should give the unworthy nothing, but to the worthy richly. Instead of unmerited or indeed fraudulent pensions, endowments must come in. The great leaders of a nation deserve great payment. The ministerial pensions of today represent precisely the opposite: they make the minister a receiver of large pensions and help the striver to success, but treat the statesman meanly.

Of the greatest significance for the destiny of a nation is the relation in which it stands to its army. At present, the German nation finds itself in an emergency situation which does not allow it to give corresponding forms to its defence. In addition, there is - perhaps the greatest threat to the German future - the internal agreement of a large section of the German nation to the defence commanded by its opponents. The external lack of freedom, however, will and must be temporary. Therefore the basic question regarding the form of the army and its relation to the state must be raised and dealt with. The structure of the army and forms of strategy have never been accidental, but correspond to the existing structure of society and state. The age of democracy logically brought the universal military service, and the modern mass state the mass army. Seen thus, the world war was the democratic event of world history. On the other hand, it mirrored faithfully the system of financial democracy, in that entire nations were dragged by their financial kings and press leaders to the war (America). At the same time, however, the difference between a people's army and a mass army became apparent: the masses are not the people. The socially dissatisfied who felt themselves forced out of their popular inheritance also began then, logically, to mutiny. So long as the social question is not resolved, the masses not transformed once again into a ranked nation, the people's army remains an inadequate instrument. In addition, there is the consideration whether mass armies have not become outmoded in military technology. The modern war, conducted with enormous technological means, demands excellent nerves, and places apparently higher demands on the spiritual power of the individual than earlier wars. There is no falser conception than that the technological war is unheroic. Only the forms change in which courage and self-overcoming come to light. - People's armies, however, are without quality. They do not at all start from a good average, but are finally forced to press the worst material, indeed the obvious dregs, into soldiers.

Thereby the idea of the military is falsified. If cowards and spiritual cripples are enlisted in the army the war leadership suffers therefrom. It seems therefore as if a culmination of the idea of a people's army has taken place and new forms of army building are in the process of development.

Another consideration leads to the following conclusion: the orderly organisation also presses towards a warrior order. Every nation has men who tend to the business of weapons, are suited to it and see their life fulfilment in it. This group forms the backbone of future armies. Precisely the rise of demands leads to the setting up of voluntary instead of compulsory service. Practically, this situation was established already in the last year of the world war; it was individual volunteers who undertook the advances and maintained the machine-gun emplacements, even the airforce depended on volunteers. The masses of the army still formed only a padding. The war arena of the future will perhaps belong to the technological volunteer army thoroughly trained to perfection. If the age of mass democracy is on the point of falling, then also the age of the mass army. Just as in the state the aristocratic component emerged stronger, so also in the military system. A modern knighthood dawns on the historical horizon.

In this place, fears of the most diverse sorts will come alive. Some suspect in this suggestion mediaeval reaction, others the praetorian rule of the Caesars. There are, however, already voices in the German nation which warn of the present form of the national army and set forth the declaration: in the long run the one in whose hands the army rests will rule. This statement is only conditionally correct. Voluntary armies seize the state leadership for themselves only when the remaining - the larger - part of the nation is asleep and unarmed. Then, only the will to action and the stronger blood triumph. If the West finds itself in a downfall, then the power will certainly fall to great adventurers at the head of audacious troops which still have the courage to counter the rule of money with their own blood. Mercenary armies become dangerous to a nation only when it is socially disintegrated and does not possess any warrior class any more. The

English have founded their world mastery on the mercenary army. In the organic Reich, on the other hand, aristocratic and democratic elements are united in fruitful tension. To the army corresponds the inner readiness for war of the entire people. Thus the army organisation of the future, as von Seeckt[82] has argued, will be a double one: on the one hand, the professional volunteer army of soldierly and technological experts, on the other, the citizens capable of military service, serving in the first place defence. Whereas the professional army is a pure affair of the Reich and instrument of foreign policy, the citizens' army (militia) is regionally organized and obliged to the idea of manliness and the defence of the homeland. Already Frantz characterizes such citizens' armies and provincial armies as the most effective means to establish a living bond in the bourgeoisie through common weapon exercices. One who has observed the federal shooting contest in Switzerland comprehends that such ideas are not "Romantic", but attempt to do justice to manly virtue as a timeless phenomenon. Thus the connection between the people and the army remains preserved, even if not in the sense of the current mass democracy. Böhmer's plan of seeing in the organisation of those who have satisfied their active military service the foundation of a real popular representation seems, on the other hand, attached to an all-too historical reaction. For, the obligation to the defence of the people and the Reich is only a part, the final conclusion from the total service in which the individual stands to the whole. There is an entire series of mostly highly social performances which are accomplished beyond the pure military service. A linking of the political organisation to the military organisation would therefore hardly correspond to the idea of an organic state. It would be superfluous; for, the citizens' armies would coincide in their cells anyway with the smallest unities of state citizens. Decisive for the connection of the people and the military remains the living organisation

---

[82] [Hans von Seeckt (1866-1936), general and politician of the Weimar Republic who maintained a neutral position in the Kapp Putsch of 1920, but participated in the liquidation of the Hitler Putsch of 1923 as well as of left-wing revolts in Saxony].

of the whole.

XV

The organisation of the Reich

If, upto now, the discussion was of the state structure, the concepts, Reich and state, could to a certain extent be equated. For seen from a constitutional legal point of view, even the Reich is naturally a state. That, political philosophically and historically, it represents something other than the state in the western sense this work has already attempted often to make clear. In the last chapter, the Reich was only a higher, richer in content, and more manifold, form of the state. The moment, however, the organisation of the Reich stands under consideration, we turn once again to the real concept of the Reich as it was earlier elaborated.

In the logically organic Reich, structure and organisation coincide. For, the authority of the Reich arises organically from the will of the provinces - of the next smaller parts - to the Reich. The indirect election would not set up a whole developed in another way - as it is today - against the members, but let the Reich arise from the former. But even in this case one does not get over a difficult problem: what are the members of the whole; are the existing provinces to be considered as organic unities, should they be removed, what should enter in their place? To broach these questions means venturing to tread on thin ice, on which today tumultuous battles heave. They have become familiar in the resolutions of the two opposed camps: the federalists and the unitarists. Legal positivistic as the present is, it remained clinging to these catchwords, and held fast to the concept of the provinces as the Weimar Republic established it.

If one translates the two designations, unitarists and federalists, as champions of the uniform state and of the federal state, the wrongness of the opposition already becomes clear; for, even the multiplicity of a state federation wants to be combined into a higher unity and a federalistic voice has never been raised against the uniformity of law, transportation, and currency. In federalism also the idea of a federation is not the solely decisive one. It concerns only one side of the problem, to a certain extent, the foreign political one. It first of all aims at the process of development of a federalistic Reich in which, as a rule, the federation represents the shaping power. Only thus is to be understood that Constantin Frantz made out of federalism a sort of political world-view; his thought was even time-conditioned and stood under the influence of the founding of the small German Reich which he passionately criticized as the representative of the idea of a central European Reich. Not because he combatted the unity of the Germans, but because he considered the small German Reich as an encapsulation and a hindrance on the way to that higher unity. This time-conditioned attitude of resistance against Bismarck made "federalism" seem to him as the highest world-view direction. In fact, he revealed - and that is the timelessly correct in his intellectual realm - the conservative-organic world view. He was one of the few genuine Conservatives of the Bismarckian age; although he had serious misgivings against the Prussian "Conservatives" of his age. A weakness was his deficient insight into the need of the small German detour on which Bismarck as a realist politician had to go.

When Bismarck undertook with a strong hand the shaping of German unity as much as it was possible at that time, the German heriditary dukedom had already been broken for hundreds of years and the young aspiring provincial principalities had emerged in its place. Bismarck[83] characterized the historical situation through the fact that the dynasties as the organisational principle of the Reich had proved themselves stronger than the consciousness of lineage. The lineage organisation of the German people already for a long time did not coincide any longer with the political organisation. Obviously, there are also differences here: while Bavaria politically fused Bavaria, Swabia, and Franconia, the basis of Württemberg was chiefly Swabian. Once again other territorial states simply ignored the basis of lineage. The loyalty relationship between dynasty and subject in combination with the emergence of the modern constitutional state, which was led centralistically by a democratic trained stratum, the bureaucracy, created in many territorial states a not too underestimating political feeling. Most strongly perhaps in Prussia and Bavaria. The Prussians are most of all what one calls a "western" nation. Bavaria, on the other hand, derived its political feeling more from the dynastic roots, because here the monarchy developed early on democratic forms. Nevertheless, the political feeling was too weak in many German territorial states not to suffer a perceptible impact after the fall of the dynasties. The modern state whose rise first made such a feeling possible is indeed a mere hundred years old in central Europe. From this is explained the ease with which many German federal states relinquished their independent life in 1918. In others, the political feeling of the people survived the fall of the dynasties (Bavaria). Nevertheless, it remains questionable whether the development since 1918 is serviceable to the maintenance of this political feeling. This formulation of the question is justified by the following consideration: the Bismarckian Reich was a federation of princes. Legitimism thus formed the bearing component of the Reich founded in 1871. Now, the principle of legitimism however had, since the time of the French Revolution, been often seriously harmed. Numerous German princes had diligently

---

[83] *Gedanken und Errinerungen*, [Stuttgart: J.G. Cotta, 1898, 2 vols.; cf. *The Memoirs, being the Reflections and Reminiscences of Otto, Prince von Bismarck*, N.Y.: Howard Fertig, 1966, 2 vols, Vol.I, Ch.XIII].

mediatized with the help of Napoleon, and even Bismarck had, shortly before the foundation of the Reich, broken thrones into pieces: the greater enlarged their sphere of power at the cost of the smaller. Now, in 1918, the German people became the constitutional bearers of the entire German sovereignty, the idea of the great German unity was also thus necessarily revived. The revolution of 1918 is not only a change of the state form but also a continuation of the Napoleonic politics: the German people mediatized its princes.

Under these circumstances, the revival of the idea of a contract, the idea of a federation, is made extraordinarily difficult. One could perhaps think of an "eternal federation" between Bavarian, Badian, Hessian, Prussian, etc. people. Why should not also more tradition-conscious republics enter into a federation with one another? But this did not happen in 1918. Rather, it was proved at that critical moment of German history that, with the passing of the sovereignty to the people, the multiplicity of princely sovereignty found earlier was replaced by the natural unity of the sovereignty of the entire German people. A state can be conducted always, if it is republican, only by a popular body; and it would be wrong however to speak of a Lippe-Detmoldian[83'] popular body, for example. Only the people who feel themselves as a living unity can operate state- formatively and form a state of historical validity. Such contract parties which could have concluded an eternal federation failed, accordingly, in 1918 and cannot also be artificially created. Only a formal legal way of thought which does not shrink back from the idolisation of the concept of the state could conceive the idea of letting the merely mechanical republics emerge in place of the different principalities. It is, therefore, a straight line movement which leads from the Napoleonic age to the present: from numerous dynasties and dominions to the inner living unity of the German people. A federalism which holds fast only to the state, which would like to perpetuate the accidental political situation of 1918 belongs to the realm of that

[83'] [the dynastic territory belonging to the counts of Lippe-Detmold].

Conservatism which has become tragic to the German people, which clings to external forms, things and conditions.

If one observes the historical development, then the existence of almost a law can be maintained, according to which an unstoppable fusion of the earlier German territorial states proceeds towards a unified state encompassing all Germans. One could ascertain a trend in history according to which the formation of large territorial states is unstoppable and smaller states are absorbed. A historical development could be supposed which leads necessarily from small dominions to the great German national state, from manifold abundance to uniform unity. Therewith, the party of federalism had to be considered as lost and one who fights for it had to suffer the protest of the reactionary.

One, now, who observes the lively relation between the Reich and the provinces which has in the last years produced an entire literature, comes, to be sure, to the conclusion that federalism has, not only in political practice but also in the defence of its intellectual realm, come off badly. Insofar as it attempted to revive historical oppositions, it had to justly suffer the complaint that it threatened German unity. This danger was magnified with great skill by the champions of the unified state, who moreover used the unity often only as a disguise in order to pursue their internal political goals. One constantly conjured up the disruption of the Thirty Years' War and the helplessness of the German federation, which - observed closely - was not so bad at all. It must be said once and for all that the displacement of particularistic tendencies which belongs to the armoury of the political battle of the day in Germany is a hateful means of battle which abandons every serious factual evidence. The German unity is today secured by something which past ages simply did not know of: by the myth of the awakening people. Younger generations, unburdened by personal remembrance, still see the internal German strife of the 19th century only historically and derive from it no artificial excitement. - A further displacement of the question of the organisation of the Reich from the burning point of the essential takes place insofar as the bureaucracies of the individual provinces, with respect to the parties ruling in them, champion their own tangible interests and are in no way seized by the idea of the Reich in its entire depth. A powerful conflict of competence thus rages between privy councillors and ministerial directors, between finance ministers who fight for the tax booty and between small national ministers who are plagued by the anxiety of having to return once again to their petty bourgeois existence. In all ages, the smaller has felt oppressed by the larger and therefore set up the demand for independence. Numerous very small interests of the bureaucracy of the Reich and the provinces come into play and make the battle for the new organisation of the Reich unfruitful.

The question of unitarianism-federalism must be raised from this lower level once again to the heights from which Constantin Frantz judged it. If it is desirable to thereby draw the reality of the political present into consideration, it must also, to be sure, be attempted to treat the entire problem without resentment, from which, unfortunately, such a sharp mind as Frantz suffered. In this goal it is necessary to recognize the principles combatting one another: the western state is the state of centralistic all-powerfulness, the indivisible sovereignty, legally ossified, led by a "fattened" (Boehm) bureaucracy. Against it stands a standardised, atomised, unindependent mass of so-called state citizens; it is the state of authority, no matter whether it is governed absolutely by a prince or by a majority. The centralistic state is a degenerate organism: the head sucks up all the powers of the members, they shrink, the parts atrophy. The result of this process is a temporary artificial rise of power, not to say inflation, of the state. It develops an overstrained power and can also temporarily be subject foreign politically to the states not so tightly combined together (the case of France). In the long run, however, either the power-sources triumph - the province withers - or, insofar as the latter still has its own life, it raises itself to resistance against the sucking up (Elsaß-Lothringen and Brittany). The dismemberment process, called particularism, then begins as a result of the over strain. Against this combats the idea of the organic state, culminating in the idea of the Reich, the balance and the reciprocal action between the whole and the part. If in centralism the emphasis lies in combination, here it does in organisation. Naturally, the danger of particularism threatens similarly in strong organisation; but only when the clamp is too weak. Efforts at separation are, in this case, not, as in the case of federalism, a protest against the strength of the central power, but against its weakness (the disintegration of the German Kaiser Reich). The Reich accordingly is based not on the idea of an immovable, firm situation, but on that of an oscillation. The concept of the Reich can never be thought of statically but only dynamically. Therefore its ideas of law are also not physical, but attached to relations. There is in the Reich no conflict regarding sovereignty, because the idea of degrees of sovereignty is familiar to it. The entire community is to it a unity full of hierarchically ranked multiplicity. Now, insofar as this idea of organic organisation hovers before representatives of federalism, the future belongs to their view. They do not want to threaten the unity of the German Reich but break up the rich soil of the German culture so that it may bear more fruits, i.e. distribute stronger forces. They wish the parts to be independent, so that so much more power can flow to the whole. They strive for the whole from their innermost will, not through authoritarian egalitarianism.

Even convinced champions of the unified state like Erich Koch-Weser[84] seek to adhere to this justified demand in that they have coined the formula of the decentralised unified state. That a Reich has to embody unity, lies already included in the profound term 'Reich'. The concept of decentralisation is however dubious. It perhaps encompasses the idea of organisation represented here; but also a questionable starting point: the one-sided justification of the life of the parts from the whole whereas the right to life of the parts does not attain expression.

---

[84] [Erich Koch-Weser (1875-1944), senior politician of the Weimar Republic who belonged to the left Liberal party. As Minister of Internal Affairs (1919), his main goal was the promotion of constitutional law and the overcoming of the Prussian-Reich dualism for the establishment of German unity].

In fact, the practical plans which that direction made are not very hopeful with regard to the independent life of the provinces. They do indeed live, but only from the mercy of the centre. However, the rule was discovered in this book, as an iron law of organic life, that the parts should exist on their own power. Even in the question of the organisation of the Reich, therefore, a close investigation does not remain spared where starting points to organic life are present, and how an organic solution would be thinkable at present, i.e. in a time-conditioned way.

The Germans are doubly organised: according to lineage and according to provinces, which even the constitution of the Reich gives expression to. Against the present provinces it will be objected not only by champions of a unified state but also by representatives of the organic conception of the state that they owe their shape merely to dynastic arbitration, and are thus present without inner life. Apart from the fact that even "dynastic arbitration" could not often avoid the necessities of history and territory, this opinion is correct only for many provinces whose borders are broken through by the landscape and the closed nature of the administration. Against an organic drawing of borders which to a certain degree will take account of the landscape, and against the removal of small museum states, no reasonable politician makes objections. A political corridor cleaning is necessary. It is somewhat different as regards the transference of this view to the large provinces. Here, the attempt at renewal should have been checked into reasonable paths. The division of France into *départements* which occurred bureaucratically can, as an example, alarm. It is also wrong to observe the provinces historical-politically in the perspective of equality even now on account of their formal legal equalisation in the Weimar constitution.[85] In fact, the historical values of the individual German provinces are fully different: many form a territorial political unity, others have actual accidental borders; some coincide closely with the lineage, others have to a certain extent arisen colonially. Finally,

---

[85] [literally, "through equality glasses"].

there are provinces whose population develops a marked national feeling in contrast to such which, after the fall of their dynasty, abandon the spiritual central point. These facts demand to be taken into consideration. One who, in place of the present-day organisation, wishes to set up the one according to the lineage[86], must first investigate where the consciousness of the lineage still lives and - what is more difficult - how the lineage borders run. Certainly, the organisation according to lineage, because corresponding to the forces of the culture, is original, natural and therefore organic. But these organisms of lineage have been weakened by a century-long development. One could think of a retrograde movement of the restrengthening of the lineage without glimpsing the danger therein of a new division of the German people. But such a process, which is in view of the metaphysical sources of the culture not without probability, requires many generations, indeed centuries. It would also not accomplish itself independently, but would require careful nurture. Seen in the long view, a future organisation of the Reich according to lineage could be drawn into the realm of considerations. For the present, the matters stand essentially more complicated. However, there exist in the form of the present provinces structures which reveal components of organic life: territorial-political bonds and living political character; domestic and economic bonding. The present, therefore, requires a resolution of the question of organisation which takes this transitional situation into consideration, i.e., in relation to the lineage organisation as well as to the one according to provinces. The difficulties of today are not to be mastered by a rigid rule. To every province a particular standard must be set, and its inner system investigated in its organic powers. There is therefore, at the moment, no solution which suits all the provinces at the same time. Only a formal legal way of thought which knows no ideas of mobile law could therefore call the plans of the "Association for the renewal of the Reich" a compromise solution. If its plan,

[86] In this struggle one encounters the Young German Order with many democracts like Koch and Hellpach who attribute a great value to lineage.

whose foundation did not occur ideologically, but betrayed the practical method of a statesman, such as that of the (retd.) Chancellor of the Reich, Hans Luther,[87] tries to rule with a loose hand the situation of North Germany and South Germany differently, then the feeling for the transitional character of our age speaks from such a procedure. It takes into consideration the differences of the historical development, of the political and intellectual structure of the provinces to be ordered anew. This circumstance becomes especially clear in view of the following considerations:

Federalism is - as an organic unsettled situation - impossible if a part surpasses all the others in significance, power and range. If it possesses, as it is clearly the case of the Weimar constitution, the same partial politicality with respect to sovereignty as the other provinces, the latter must not only be suppressed, but the Reich itself cannot develop any independent power beside this excessively large part. The whole must fall into a necessary opposition to its all-too-large chief part. The Bismarckian national constitution already suffered from this Prussian-German opposition. The evil was concealed by the practical union of the state head as well as of the ministry, as it stood between Prussia and the Reich, above all, however, by the outstanding figure of the first Chancellor. The "Prussification" of the Reich had its consequences even in foreign policy: seen historically, that dangerous narrowing of the German field of vision in Europe took place which had to operate in a disastrous manner. Certainly, Prussia had the task of becoming the core of internal German power-building. But its own historical mission, alive upto Frederick the Great: to carry Germany forward into the east and to defend it from the latter, was lost. The more Prussia dedicated itself to its internal German task, the weaker did its external political colonialising power (the pushing of the Polish culture at the German eastern border) become. To a certain degree, therefore, Constantin Frantz is right when he ascertains a

---

[87] [Hans Luther (1879-1962), who served as Reich Chancellor from 1925-26, was a socially and politically conservative leader].

reversal of the Prussian vocation: instead of operating Germanically externally, forfeiting the internal political goal, turning the whole of Germany from a Reich into a state. Frantz thinks that, in this way, the strongest German particularism would have triumphed. In this thought-process there is much that is correct, especially for the one who considers the present-day politics of Prussia carefully. Indeed Frantz overlooks the time-bound internal political task of Prussia. But his presentation contains also a bitter prophecy; for, the predominance of Prussia has in fact necessarily determined the new German development: the Reich has really turned into a small-German "state". And all efforts of the Weimar democracy can be summarised in the one sentence: one wishes, starting from the "Prussian nation" to step forward to the small-German nation. The idea of the Reich and the idea of the European German are thus seriously threatened in their being by the Prussian political idea, influenced by the political idea of the French Revolution. This threat however has become gigantic since Prussia supports in the Reich capital an enormous political apparatus with its own parliament and ministry, whereas, at the same time, the connection with the Reich is torn.

The way to the organic Reich necessarily diverges from the direction struck out in 1918. Prussia has fulfilled its internal political task of small-German unification. There is no more room for a Prussian state, a Prussian nation, within the manifold German nation. The existence of a Prussian government must harm the power of the Reich. To have recognized this circumstance and represented it before the broad public remains a chief service of Hans Luther. If, in the foundation of the Reich, the necessity existed of letting it be ruled by the "strongest particularism", today, after the unity of the Reich preserved itself in the world war, the situation has become different. The Reich should in turn rule over Prussian provinces until an organic organisation has arisen which guarantees independent life. Beginnings in this direction are revealed, on the one hand, by the plan of the "Association for the renewal of the Reich", insofar as the Prussian provinces should by themselves send a member to the Federal Council. On the other hand, by Erich Koch's idea of decentralisation. Therewith, however, the "shattering" of Prussia is not demanded. It reveals a realist political insight when the 'Association for renewal' is thought out on the maintenance of Prussian political power as a whole. The division of Prussia into lifeless provinces would be precipitate and dangerous. New life must first grow and become strong. Finally, the intermediate position of the German Reich between the west and the east is to be thought of. Purely federalistic forms doubtlessly strengthen the position of the Germans in the east. In the west, on the other hand, the rigid national state stands against us. So long as this is the case, the German people cannot in its constitution abandon a so powerful clamp such as the Prussian tradition represents. Even considering its internal formation, the German people find themselves in a middle position. Their political forms must therefore represent likewise a medium. Here no scheme is valid, only living movement.

Thus perhaps the destiny of the German Reich in the following age will be: an intermediate entity between political and national federalism. However, in no way should the view be hauled along that the future belongs to federalism which is built on the people. The age of purely political ways of thought is now past. Treasures still rest submerged in the depths of the German race, in its spiritual peculiarity. The German people must with all their power guard against taking the way of France. The price which a people has to pay for a capital in glittering splendour is too expensive. Therefore the deep aversion of many Germans against Berlin is not directed against the Berliners as men but against the excessive civilisation, the urbanisation, the bloodless and the blood-sucking politics which is peculiar to such a cosmopolis. "For every centralistic politics promotes urbanisation with all its harmful effects for the future development of a country". With this sentence Heinrich Gattineau[88] outlines the consequences of the hegemony which the metropolitan workers' movement has achieved in

---

[88] *Verstädterung und Arbeiterherrschaft*, Berlin, Kurt Vowinckel, 1929.

Australia. Even if the situation of a colonial country is different from the European, a certain possibility of similarity remains which should make the European disconcerted.

If a mechanistic age has been fulfilled, if new life wishes to sprout from the ruins, then organic starting points to such must be seized and used for the construction, no matter where they are to be found. Bismarck's statement of the love for the fatherland, which in the case of the German requires the medium of the love of the homeland, remains the foundation of all political rootedness, so long as states - and that will perhaps always be so - are built on territories. The entirety of the Reich does not need to suffer from this, but receives only a series of bearing supports if, in place of the rootless voting masses, an organized people enters. Federalistic demands which are rooted only in the past are obviously unjustified. That a German dynasty or a German nation supports embassies in foreign nations is a situation that has been overcome. If, however, there is a true Reich, if between pure political right and abstract popular right intermediate levels arise, it is indeed thinkable that members of the Reich may assume a special position with regard to popular rights. One can imagine a Reich whose core is built up political-legally, whereas, in the borders, a transition into popular legal federal forms takes place. The Reich is a deep concept and of a mobility in legal respects which cannot be imagined in a formal legal age. The foreign political part will outline the enormous significance which such a mobile construction of the Reich has for the European situation of the German people.

The new Reich gets its own power, its inner coherence, from the consciousness of a common great European task. From this it is brought about as an obvious consequence that the leadership of the foreign policy and of the army must lie unrestrictedly in the hands of the Reich. Likewise the economic and population policy, insofar as they concern the foreign political position of the chief state, of the Reich. The purely technological necessity of uniformly ordered means of transportation, the healthy distribution of public taxes to the whole of the

Reich, which requires especially a balance of taxes: all these are the incontestable tasks of the Reich.

Thus there remains for the members of the Reich, which can be called at times provinces, at times counties, at times federal states, at times allied states, in the main, the inner administration and the police sovereignty, even on the autonomous economy and culture. Not considering a necessary standardisation of the law, the autonomy of smaller territories cannot go far enough, the constitutional legislators can push the independence of the parts hardly too far. The more free and direct the democracy, the more genuine and healthy. The farther the way from the life of a people to those who rule them in its daily affairs, the more lifeless the leadership. Large states can exist and unchain the last powers of their peoples only when, in the narrower communities of life, life blooms unhindered. Educational leadership becomes so much harder the greater the distance of the leader from those led. One to whom the unity of the Reich is the final goal of all politics must be enraged by the knowledge that parts living on their own rights are only used by the whole. On the other hand, however, prestigious federalistic politicians should give up outmoded demands. Many obsolete customs can fall which should have already a long time ago been sacrificed to the shearing knives of political insight. That every province maintains its own system of certification and examination (as, for example, a Bavarian judge or a lawyer may be professionally active only in Bavaria), that is really an obsolete custom. The legal life of a people cannot be sufficiently uniform; every law demands the greatest possible territorial validity. The Romans have conquered the world with their law. Only a great German orginal law draws culturally weaker peoples under its spell.

XVI

Renewal of the law

All new structuring of the state remains attached to the technological if it does not arise most deeply from a new law. The effort of the whole conditions another conception of the law than individualism had. Law regulates the community life of man. The total experience lends the capacity of "ordering" not only the individual man inwardly, but - to a certain degree as a radiation - also the community. The doctrine of the community as an organism obtains in this way its final justification, is founded in the essence of the intellectual-spiritual structure of man, on account of which Plato derives his concept of order from the whole of human spiritual life. Morality, customs and law thus stream from the same source.

If, however, law is recognized as the emanation of living ordering power, then the connection, the relation (function) emerges into the centre of legal life. Bott-Bodenhausen calls this coming law the functional in contrast to the one valid today, which he characterizes as the combination of individualism and substantialism. By substantialism he understands the holding on to the enduring, to the "quintessence of the body". According to Bott-Bodenhausen, the modern legal development is accomplished between rigid physicality and total relatedness of all things to the central point of the self, seldom advancing into a functionalism which feels the earthly community as the "totality of the self". Thus the law becomes lifeless, overlooks the changing relations and neglects the flowing life. The legal decree makes itself independent, leads an independent conceptual life, provides a model which suits no reality any longer, so that, in turn, the reality must always be translated into the conceptual in order to enable the application of the law in general. Thus law and reality come into an irreconcilable opposition, and especially the law, in any case, is subject to the law of continuity. For, the ordinance must always, in the nature of things, lag behind life. New cultural developments find their outcome last of all in the law.

We have seen above that the doctrine of the division of powers was essentially influenced by the conception of the law of the Englightenment. The latter lived in the belief that it could set up absolutely correct rules obtained in an understanding-oriented way, which then possessed temporal and spatial universal validity. The ordering by virtue of state authority was felt as a command, police order, but not as a law. This rationalism of the Enlightenment, strengthened and borne by the already earlier assumed Roman law, led to the conceptual jurisprudence. An independent realm of legal thought arose which encamped over reality and demanded validity from it and over it. The legal ordinances received to a certain extent an independent physical life, artificial substance. For this reason does Hans Fehr[89] speak of a physical, irrevocable (static) law. Spengler has established that the ancient world, especially Rome, was formed statically in its basic forms. It was otherwise in the case of the ancient German law, which was related to living relationships, and thus revealed a dynamic character. The ousting of the German law by the Roman had therefore to operate in a paralysing way on our law. Only the 19th century has, in a gradual advance, somewhat increased the dynamic components of the German law.

---

[89] *Recht und Wirklichkeit[: Einblick in Werden und Vergehen der Rechtsformen*, Zürich: Orell Füssli], 1928.

Even if on different thought-levels, the functional law of Bott-Bodenhausen and the dynamic one of Fehr are, however, basically the same thing. Both want to remove the formula in order to free life; both want to eliminate the opposition between law and reality. Bott-Bodenhausen is the more relentless in his thought-processes. He wants to destroy the physical aspect of the law to the final remnant, and let only the living relationship have validity. In him, consequently, all law is forged into a final unity: the differentiation of public and private law loses its significance. For functionalism "sovereign right" is "only another direction of the law from that of property right. Both are rights of mastery, expressions of custody". The division of powers also loses its justification for him with regard to the administration of justice, "since the presupposition lying at the base of it, the dependence of thought on heterogeneous rules (ordinances) and the differentiation between thought (judgement) and action (execution) is eliminated. - Legislation, establishment of the law, and execution coincide". These far-reaching conclusions are contested by Fehr[90] in that he objects that a purely dynamic formation of legislation is an illusion; a purely dynamic legal doctrine cannot be carried out in reality. "Where everything physical disappears from the law, the law becomes pure arbitration, the opposite of law". It is, for example, wrong to conceive property merely as a social function.

Certainly, the essence of all life is tension and relation. One, however, who sees only the tension and no longer the poles between which it sways, distances himself once again from the reality which however should be ordered. Making the law independent, its formal separation from the person, means a cult of movement and vitality which does not found - as Bott-Bodenhausen would like - a higher order but bears in itself the danger of the unbounded. The basic world-view character of this legal functionalism resembles the Anarchism of a Proudhon and a Bakunin, the Syndicalism of a Sorel and the life-philosophy of a Bergson.

---

[90] "Krisis der Justiz", *Süddeutsche Monatshefte*, Heft 4, 1929.

Vitality alone is not in itself even a formal principle.

The prophet however has the right to draw the line of his thought into the infinite. At some time, however, it must come into contact with the line of reality. Thus the demand for a purely functional law remains a valuable thrust in order to strengthen the "dynamic charge in the German law" (Fehr). For the future legal development we are indebted to the outline of a functional legal system of most valuable interest. We find explanations for the chief deficiencies which together make up the so-called legal crisis: in the legislation, infringements into private law on the part of public authority are increasing. The increasing limitation of property corresponds not to a positive building up of a new concept of property, but to collectivistic objectives. Individualism thus attains its final highest level of development: collectivism. The multiplicity of equal individuals counted together should replace the personality. Thus the point has been reached at which individualism eliminates itself in the posing of the question - the individual or the masses.

Indeed the ordinances which the administration of justice should apply have increased immeasurably. But they are not applied any more. The logical system of rigid legal concepts is broken apart by the administration of justice; not in the way the free law school, that movement against judicial shackling, wanted it, but in another way. The judge, trained sociologically, decides according to economic and social points of view, according to fairness. He then looks for the ordinance paragraph which suits his judgement and justifies the latter in this way subsequently. Thereby there is no jurisprudence any longer, the belief in the law declines.

Against the phenomenon of disintegration only the deliberate abolition of laws based on effects, on goals, on relation-regulation helps. Today, the powerful economic development, producing new sorts of relations every day floods the law. It cannot regulate and develop any longer the powers which rule there diabolically. The legislation, therefore, will only become fruitful once again when it does not start any longer from multivalent concepts which have become dubious, but expresses the purposeful will of binding - and cultivating - the social life and all effective powers in the sense of a whole. If the spinning of concepts disappears, then the legislation can return by itself to the moderating principle: *multum non multa.*[91]

The administration of justice must, through an application of judicial thought to the fact of reality, become a true legal formation. Law is formed in reality and not in the conceptual.[92] In fact, the judgement should be nothing else but the legal judgement of the reality. The judge's conviction of the law therewith becomes a source of law. To be sure, a legal ordinance will never become superfluous, but "the ordinance can only claim to serve as a guide for the judge, as the methodological doctrine of the accomplishment of the law". Just as the free evaluation of evidence developed from the attachment to evidence regulations, so the free legal judgement from the attachment to legal regulations. The legal sentence thus becomes the highest source, supported on customs and morality, as they exist in a time-conditioned way in the nation from which the judge derives.

This readjustment conditions a change in the structure of the law-court. The appeal madness (Georg Müller)[93] of today serves the mania for contests, the overcoming of the opponent. The jurisdiction of a healthy culture should remind one of the contractuality, and heal the cases of sickness which naturally arise repeatedly and plague the social body. The true law lives quietly operating in the actions and transformations of men. It is only applied by way of judgement in order to heal injuries. But are numerous legal teams, where possible with increasingly more judicial colleagues, necessary? Must the older judge always correct the younger and do five really know more than one? Or is the spinning of

---

[91] [much, not many]

[92] According to Bott-Bodenhausen the fact (the reality) is today first transformed into a conceptual legal fact and then the ordinance is applied.

[93] [Georg Müller (1868-1945), author of *Das neue Rechtsbuch der katholischen Kirche*, Langensalza: H. Beyer, 1928].

concepts not thereby increased immeasurably? The correct way is another: first the elimination of all police penal matters and so-called petty lawsuits from the realm of the jurisdiction, which is endowed with appeals. The "justice of the peace" who has maintained himself in Switzerland, in England, and other countries for centuries suffices for this perfectly. Why should the municipality not elect a justice of the peace who settles by arbitration all the petty lawsuits? Is the law really such a complicated matter that first twenty examination papers hatched by perspiring judicial brains, dealing with border cases, must be solved before a healthy judgement is to be expected? Must every case in which the number-plate of a motor car was deficiently cleaned be examined by two full judicial appeals? As a rule, a factual appeal suffices, a legal application appeal and, in addition, in order to guarantee the uniformity of the sentence with respect to the future creation of law, a law court into which the present-day national court could be turned. It is, in fact, summoned to create law. The famous case: paper mark = gold mark has shown the way to the creation of dynamic law for the future, and has finally made clear the destructive nature of the conceptual jurisprudence.

To be sure, the decreasing of the legal proceedings, the diminution of the judicial colleges, conditions another thing: a new judge. Today, the German judge is burdened with small tasks which the police and the autonomy could attend to. Judicial office and prosecutional officials are merged into each other to a degree which injures the judicial reputation. That a man at the age of 23 decides on a judicial profession honours his efforts. That, however, at the age of 25, he begins his judicial career is a contradiction. To be a judge is the highest office which a community has to offer. The selection can therefore not occur carefully enough. The higher judges should have the right of judicial co-option. The lower judges can perhaps be named by the state, but would be sought from the ranks of jurisprudents and lawyers. Proof of humanity is the most important prerequirement for the judicial office. The social position of the judge, however, demands a corresponding elevation. Today it is, on an average, pathetic. Every proprietor of a large store can clothe himself more respectably than a German judge. It is also wrong to classify the judge in the general bureaucratic system. To him is due a special position which is in every respectable inviolable: it must offer security with regard to national and political infringements, as well as security against every other need. There is no profession which would have to manifest a higher ethos, and hardly a more unskilled hand to preserve this ethos than the present-day party state. Finally, equal pay must be demanded for all judges. Difference of salary by virtue of familial position and service age are justified; but not such which are based on the difference of the law courts in which the judge exercises his office at the moment. Sentencing demands the same responsibility at the lower court as at the higher.

The most important thing has been stated on the institution of a universal legal reform with the demand for the "dynamic charge". Even in earlier chapters, particularly reform-needy positions were pointed out. Decisive, however, remains a basic character of the coming law: the transposition to the final legal goal, the living development of an ordered society. - The present-day civil law exhibits the greatest weaknesses on this point. In the effort to distance itself as far as possible from the "debtor's prison", the modern legal thought has gone beyond its goal. Between the penal fact of deception and the civil legal one of the inability to pay stand today so many possibilities of immoral creditor discriminations that civil process and the system of discharge become a farce. The pauper's oath becomes a licence to freebooting which is not to be arrested by the penal code. Business traffic and the system of credit are in this way injured. The law however has the task of not helping the swindling which slips through the holes of its net, but of protecting the modern economic life.

Therewith the transition to the contested question of penal reform is set forth. Even here the insight is lacking into the essence of the great turning point: it is all a question of the protection of developing legal holdings which arise from a new feeling of connectedness. What arrangement protects the honour of the people, what their fruitfulness? The number of crimes which daily go against the life of the community is enormous; which, as a result of the absence of every moral protection, take place undisturbed, restricted by no interventions from the directorate of public prosecutions. All too large is the field of social life which today lies open and undefended from the attacks of asocial elements. Instead of turning its attention to this, the present-day "dynamism" of new sketches of the penal law exhausts itself in wanting to turn asocial men into social ones. As correct as this effort is in the interest of the society, so ridiculous does this sort of humanitarianism begin to become if the means used here do not correspond any longer to the result. Even here the statement is valid that the protection of the valuable is more important for the community than the care of dubious or only alleged value. The time for basic legal renewal therefore seems not to have come yet. Only when the new value-standard has been adopted will the creation of an organic law succeed.

   Thus even law enters in the service of worth. Its relentless education to high quality, corresponding to the "ever striving self exertion" of the individual, rounds out the picture of a world-view which, as the order of the present, demands the return and the turning to the powerful works of human education. All great political philosophers, all great poets, all great thinkers were educators. What their needy Eros let them unrelentingly strive for their creative Eros wished to form creatively: out of the noblest material on earth - out of living man. The Reich and the law of the future will circulate around this educational work, producing new value and, therewith, genuine culture.

   A new higher connectedness will develop. Socialism, which believed that it could introduce a historical epoch, had to discover "that it it has been only the opposite pole of capitalism, its significance lies in the past" (Bott-Bodenhausen). In view of the present-day division, Anarchism - Communism, both value-destroying forms of individualism, we raise our longing eyes towards a new unity, a coming living whole into which high quality leads. We see before us a movement upwards of history which distances us from the marshes of the swamp of civilisation. We grasp the shining sword of justice in order to encounter the power of matter, the brutality of the understanding, the darkness of chaos. If it must be, we believe in the Holy War, which the enslaved mankind will hail so long as it feels the power in itself of giving evidence of the higher morality of man. Thus does the task of the new German man grow into a world mission and become a combat for God.

We battle for the living community, in order to rescue the soul and the personality. In us lives the spirit of all the great people who, wherever they were, were against the rule of the masses.

We proclaim the new man, who places the society above himself. We teach of the community which recompenses equal service with equal rights. We acknowledge however the natural inequality of men and reject the illusion of equal "human rights".

We acknowledge the right of the community to be led by the best; we demand the duty of the community to take the best from the entire nation and to let them rise to leadership. We acknowledge, however, also the right and the duty of the best to lead and to educate the inferiour. The exercice of power which takes place for this purpose results as a moral duty in the name of God.

In the name of the community, the mistreated individuality demands its right, which was trampled underfoot by individualism to the damage of the community.

With unrelenting sobriety we recognize life and reality in their imperfection. To attempt constantly its overcoming is the tragic destiny of man. One, however, who acknowledges this destiny, triumphing over himself and death, is the true man, the leader to the new freedom.

We preach therefore battle as the purifying form of life. We affirm this battle and raise - as the true disinherited - the battle cry of the new age.

Part Four

Economics

Man, what you love, into that will you
be transformed:
God will you become, if you love God,
and earth if you love the earth.
Angelus Silesius

I

Economics and Community

In order to round out the picture which is produced by a view of the whole in the individual practical fields, a special treatment of the economic life is unavoidable. Perhaps the difficulty of representing the final connections is greatest in this field. For, nowhere has unity been so lost as precisely here. The lack of space, however, prohibits an exhaustive investigation. Precisely in the treatment of economic questions, the author becomes painfully aware of the necessity of self-restriction: he can broach problems of economics only from the point of view of how far mechanistic splitting and organic wholeness, both principles fighting against each other, fight out their oppostion even in the economic life; of how far even here a difficult crisis prevails, and that which has gone rotten demands removal and wishes to become a new formation.

The human impulse to activity operates predominantly in the field of economics. Economics, in the broadest sense of the word, is all activity which is directed to the production of tangible goods. Work is a basic fact of life: "in the sweat of thy brow shallst thou eat bread". Thus, economising is a necessary activity, and work a moral command. Indeed, every work does not need to be belong to the field of economics. But the concept of economics must be limited to material production, in order not to dissolve into indistinctness. Therefore every planned work can, however, be in another sense economic.

Economics should create the material foundation for the self-maintenance of man, who represents a unity of body, soul and mind. Its position with regard to life is a serving one; the less pure economic thought rules men, the more noiseless (Spann)[94] is the economics, the healthier the social order of an age. Economics can never be more than a serving branch of the social and political life. It is the task of economics to take care that man does not have, like an animal, to look constantly for food, but can turn his head to the stars. Culture is hardly thinkable without a minimum of independence from concern for food. On the other side, the fallacy that the cultural stage must grow with the standard of living would be disastrous. There are enormously rich countries (America) which do not bring forth their own culture in the highest sense of the word, and there have been relatively poor nations which left behind powerful cultural works. If, therefore, in Germany one speaks of a downfall of culture, one can with undisturbed conscience maintain that the objection of poverty is supposed to disguise only spiritual emptiness. Hundreds of millions of marks are spent by us - mostly by the public authorities - for the theatre. One cannot say that this expense has brought about a real cultural height. Wealth, therefore, is not a guarantee of cultural development, as little as of political power. Here the materialistic way of thought of the present which falsifies economic power without further ado into life-values reveals itself. Certainly, economics can live within a life-value; but always only in its relation to higher community-values of all sorts. Economics itself, however, is nothing but service to higher life.

The present, in which economics is everything else but noiseless, shows the materialisation of man progressed to the utmost. The materialistic man grants economics too large a place in his thought. The mistreated impulse towards the

---

[94] [Othmar Spann (1878-1950), one of the chief exponents of organic economics, author of *Fundament der Volkswirtschaftslehre*, Jena: E. Diederichs, 1923; see my Introduction in Vol.I of this edition].

whole avenges itself, in that it founds a new "universalism" of an economic sort. First matter is detached from the living life, and then it begins to rule it. The materialistic conception of history is the expression of the perplexity with which man stands before the unchaining of the material instinct. He attempts to rescue the soul, in that he makes it a sort of psychological residue of the economic development. The materialists live on the inversion of the saying: better dead than a slave. They do not feel that an enslaved soul in general does not develop any life. Thus arises, on the one hand, the situation of the worshippers of the age, who consider the mechanising of life under the brazen tread of an "age of economics" as destiny. They do not see that economics does not need to be necessarily mechanistic at all, that it too can be organic and is in the position of preserving the connection to life as well as, for example, science, art or the state can. On the other hand, stand those who perceive with mental anguish the spectre of the impersonalisation of man by economics and summon the power of the blood as a protest against this danger. They are ready to sacrifice economics in itself, only to rescue life. They press towards the desperate act and prefer the catastrophe to spiritual enslavement. A cry of distress therefore resounds through the entire civilised world and clouds darkly form on the horizon from which one day perhaps destroying lightning bolts flash down. It is not the worst men, proletarians, besides, in very small part, who clench their fist against the modern economic colossus. Apparently, it is indeed the most worthy, those in whom the source of life throbs most vitally. But even they persist in the intellectual mistake of the opposite direction: even they forget that economics must not necessarily become a deluge which devours everything alive. Even they lack the final insight into the whole of human life, in which a thriving economics, life-granting and not life-destroying, can be built up.

The nestling of economics in the totality of life is only possible on the foundation which the philosophical part of this work elaborated. The two life-forms are the microcosmic of the individual and the macrocosmic of the community. Obviously, this division is only an intellectual and not a factual one, since life itself indeed is always accomplished in society. It is only important whether the consciousness of being ranked in the macrocosm operates also vitally. If this is the case, then the economic personality will conceive all economic activity as service to the community. Even in the economic life, accordingly, there takes place a fusion of individual human striving with the aiming at the goal of the whole. The foundation of all economics, however, is the living personality with all its driving forces, wishes, conditions and strengths. The creating will of the personality is the source of economics. This natural fact is customarily outlined by the term private economics. The core of the idea of private economics is the demand that man also reap the fruits of his expenditure of force, of his industry, of his endurance and of his moderation by himself. But like his other activities, even the economic activity of the supraindividualistic man is directed to the community. One perhaps produces goods for one's own need. But this itself is related to the total need of the community. Private economics in the highest sense of the word is always also, at the, same time, economics of the community in which the man lives. The higher order which every individual feels above himself extends to the economic life.

Economics is basically not founded on private gain. It remained reserved to the age of individualism to set the interest of the depersonalised individual in the place of that higher economic goal which the feeling of the whole had set up. The economics of the organic age was related to the community in which the man lived, be it the household economics, the city economics, or another form. In any case, it was rooted, exactly as the rest of life, in communities which were founded organically through blood and soil. Individualism undertook to sever the natural bonds and to set in their place artificial connections. This process naturally had to find its residue in the economic life. The individuals were either brought together by the state into a nation or, if this concept seemed too narrow, collected into "mankind". There arose, instead of economics of the people, purely national economics, because the state had proved itself to be stronger than the people. Thus there is, for example, no total German national economics, but only a series of German political economies, of which the greatest is that of the present-day Reich.

The philosophical and national political part of this work attempted to prove that individualism seeks to push forward in two forms to the overcoming of isolation, to an artificial universalism: in imperialism or in cosmopolitanism. In fact, these are also the two economic dispositions which rule the present. Cosmopolitanism is, however, taken seriously by only two peoples: by the Germans and the Jews. By the former, as a result of the weakness of their national feeling; by the latter from national strength. For, since they live in a diaspora, cosmopolitanism is the form of their self-maintenance. In Germany, there exists a juxtaposition of economic imperialism and economic cosmopolitanism. The former more or less unintentionally, because arisen through the German territorial smallness, has brought us much hostility, as the world war showed. It was even wrong to base its battle for existence, with regard to the world as well as to the German people, in an international economic manner, instead of in a territorial political one. One had to coin popular political formulas in order to make clear to all the participants that the nourishment foundation of the German people is too small.

Besides, however - in contrast to the United States of North America, which conduct the strongest economic imperialism - in Germany, there proliferates economic cosmopolitanism, which culminates in the catchword of world economics. The historical school of national economics taught a progressive broadening of the sphere of economics. It therefore did not remain at national economics but spoke of world economics as the next higher stage. This is a fallacy, exactly like the one that the next greater community after the people is mankind. Mankind and world economics are collective concepts but not unities. For, the foundation of popular life and the natural prerequirement of every political system is the soil. But so long as men live on the soil, so long as they owe almost all life necessities to it, so long as they live in states which are stamped with the spirit of a people, so long will the rule of this soil, its structure as a nursery of the people, be the content of all politics. The man who, as a work force, is the most important bearer of economics remains attached to his blood and to his soil. There has never yet been a mankind culture, never a world state. From whence therefore should the world economics have come?

For businessmen and financiers, whose only ware is money, there may be something like a world economics.[95] More correctly, however, their position must be described in this way: their money can plunder the national economies everywhere without any consideration of connections and boundaries. The pirates of money can consider the entire earth as their Reich. For them there is something similar to a world market; the difference of internal- and foreign market disappears for them. With them, private economics had to become freebooting. For there is no community to which it feels bound, to which it can acknowledge itself in service. All relations of purely economic sort aim solely at profit: they serve only the individual and his private gains. Certainly, even the national economies have become world economically entangled. The national economies go with their surpluses to the world market, they carry out the exchange of wares which can be produced only under quite definite conditions which are characteristic for the production or the use of individual peoples. If the international division of labour will have attained a reasonable point of rest - and all signs point to the fact that this may relatively soon be the case - then it will be established that the healthy peoples live from the source of their own economy and the sick, who live off foreign soil, approach an atrophy. Today this development is accomplished behind a veil, which is woven out of deficient insight into the population political connections and blind worship of the idols of world capital.

---

[95] [The reader is advised to read as a supplement to Jung's arguments in this section, Werner Sombart's *Die Juden und das Wirtschaftsleben*, Leipzig, 1911, (tr. M. Epstein, *The Jews and Capitalism*, London and N.Y., 1962)].

From the cosmopolitan, world-economic idea arises that remarkable belief in the reasonableness of world economics which would permit no suppression and impoverisation of the German people. "One needs us", thus runs the consoling speech of that circle. Perhaps it would be more correct to transform it into the formula: "they use us". One lets the German people live only because, behind the numerous beneficiaries of the tributes stand different sorts of interests. If the increased German export may be dangerous to one, as the coal export to the Italian, the second seeks to exert his immediate influence on the German economy for the weakening of quite definite industrial branches, whereas the third leaves out economic political considerations in general and thinks only of the reduction of German power. These efforts cannot obviously be reconciled; they indeed intersect, but in their entirety they are directed unscrupulously at the exploitation of the German people. Walter Funk[96] is right when he thinks: "It is a basically false conception if it is still maintained that the world-politics and the world-economics could not "ignore" a people of 60 million, they will certainly not ignore it but they will subjugate and economically enslave it". The "economic reason" will certainly never bring freedom, but only the displacement of the power relations of German work will.

The cosmopolitan forces in the people strive against the consolidation of internal power. The financial capital has allied itself for this purpose with the party Socialism, which hopes to delude the worker about his deficient purchasing power through rising wages. In fact, however, cosmopolitanism is a luxury which only financial capital can afford. For, money (gold) is valid everywhere. It is bound to no country, no soil, no man. It can be spent where it is compensated for relatively securely, and guarantees its possessor everywhere prosperity and power. Hence also the enthusiasm of the financial capital for parliamentary democracy. Where this exists, influence on the government can be obtained immediately with

---

[96] *Befreiung von Kriegstributen durch wirtschaftliche und soziale Erneuerung*, Berlin, ed. by the Gesellschaft für deutsche Wirtschafts- und Sozial-politik, 1929.

money. States and peoples, culture and politics are, for money, only matters of serviceability and of the acquisition of revenues.

Something different is the advance through the higher technological situation of modern economics to the standardisation of certain economic fields belonging together geopolitically. Here it is a question not of the neglect of natural boundaries on the part of economic cosmopolites greedy of advantage, and even not of their powerful outward thrust through power-hungry imperialism. It is, rather, the attempt to develop thereby the economic power of certain geographic territories so that they become uniform. The present-day means of transportation allow the exchange of goods to greater distances than earlier. The smaller economic fields can supplement themselves through reciprocal raw material supply, whereby expensive wasteful movements can be avoided. Industry obtains the farming hinterland, agriculture markets. The greater the uniform economic field, the better the possibility of producing the necessary material where the cost of production is lowest. Obviously, this statement is not valid in an unrestricted sense but only for the geopolitical, historical and racial group unity of certain territories. Thus the shattering of the economy of the double monarchy was economically unreasonable. Each of the satellite states considers itself obliged to cover its needs with its own production, and therefore breeds artificially an industry which does not do justice to the law of economicality. The impulse towards popular self-maintenance is, in view of this effort, not ignored. But the question is permitted, where the concept of culture and the right to total politicality and autarchy finds its limits. Today, in Europe, national economies have arisen which contend mutually against one another and, to a certain degree, hunger for surplus because unsurpassable borders are drawn to trade. The "closed trading state" does not develop wherever an ambitious little people want it. To this also belongs a series of naturally given presuppositions. The foreign political part will go into this question more closely.

The people, therefore, are not only the foundation and the spiritual

motivating force of the state, but also of the economy. The state is an organic
order of the total community, just as the economy too is. To the state as the
highest order is granted the leadership of the whole; in no way, however, the
observation of those tasks which belong to the economy. Even national economy
is an organic whole, obeying its own laws, which are in turn different from those
of the state. All human activity has its own laws. Family and state are borne by
an inner necessity of a different sort than the economy; in each field, life develops
its own rules which scorn artificial pressure. It is therefore wrong if the state
would like to fulfil the tasks of the economy. If today efforts are present to
nationalise the economy, the latter defends itself justly for its life. It gives
evidence thereby of the greatest service to the state because it prevents it from
perishing in a falsification of its essence, which would mean the nationalisation
of the economy. Obviously, there are here too border areas. For, many economic
branches affect the life of the political and national whole in its very depths. One
may think of transport and public undertakings. But even for these fields it was
recognized that at least private economic forms must be taken up, because only
in this way are bureaucratisation and ineconomicality avoided. There arose the so-
called mixed-economic enterprise. On the other hand, however, it cannot be denied
that the public enterprises tend, through the elimination of competition, to misuse
(one thinks of the demanding price-control of urban electricity works), or do not
work so cost-efficiently as, the private economy. The tax-freedom granted to those
enterprises offers, indeed, a stimulus to bad economic leadership and therefore
burdens the popular economy. Monopolisation and lack of healthy business-sense
must therefore also be avoided in public undertakings. If, however, beyond that,
the state acts national capitalistically in that it wishes to become a big undertaker
in economic departments which can be brought in in a fructifying manner only
according to economic principles, then the sharpest battle must be proclaimed
against such efforts. Experience proves that national economic undertakings are
supported not by themselves but by the tax-payer. "All the economic structures

which have in practice arisen from the basis of a transmission of Socialistic ideas live only as parasites of the private economy" (Funk). But there is another indirect form of nationalisation which amounts to the incapacitation of the economy: by way of so-called tax-Bolshevism, the state mixes itself into the wage-politics and removes from the economy its profits, which are necessary for the forming of enterprise capital. In this way, the capital worked out by the economy is accumulated in public treasuries, instead of becoming useful for the economy. Even this infringement of the state into the economic life goes too far.

In turn, there is also an economisation of the state: just as the state makes its universalism valid by way of its all-powerfulness and total authority, so the economy by the fact that it would like to force pure economic thought onto the political life. Insofar as this effort is directed only to the urging of the state to the undertaking of economic methods in the administration, hardly anything would have to be objected to it. It is otherwise, however, if economic powers determine the political life, if the political will represents nothing more than a compromise of interests of the economic groups. Then the state is exactly as materialised as the individual man of today. There arises in the political realm that soulless, matter-captivated thought which does not see the powers of life any more and inquires only after petty gain. - The characterstic of the present is the erasing of all borders: the state presses into the economy and the economy into the state; both in turn are overlaid and mixed with elements of the cultural and social life. Endless confusion has thus arisen which places the observer before the task of segregation. He can - exactly as in the field of political life and of culture - attain an idea of the whole of the human community only when a pure separation follows at first: the sphere of economic life must be clearly separated, the economy be purified of alien components. Only then can one think of treating the economy once again as a developed unity. Only then can be discovered the laws which it obeys today and those to which it should be subordinated in an organic community. For, all economic activity has its form, which is precisely characteristic for this branch of human activity. One is used to calling the present-day economic form the capitalistic system. In what does this consist, why is its influence so striking, and were do its dangers of disintegration lie? These are the points into which the investigation must enter.

II

Individualistic economics

We live in the age of capitalism. There is no word which is more ambiguous, and the number of definitions of the concept is great. In the scope of this work, it is a matter of finding out the essential component of the present-day economic order which splits up every unity in a disastrous manner. For, somewhere there must be present in the present-day capitalism powers which injure the human soul in such a measure that it falls into an unbridgeable opposition to them.

There has always been capital. The first instrument of the stone age signifies for the man of that time capital. Proprietorship of the means of production quickly sets in and becomes the basis of culture. Proprietorship and accumulation of wealth in a sole hand therefore make up capitalism as little as the presence of men who do not possess any thing apart from their working force. There were such strata in almost all cultures. Even the division of labour, perhaps one of the most marked characteristics of the modern economy, can as such not yet establish the peculiarity of the capitalistic system. Already in ancient cultures it had progressed far. As a further sign there is still the transition to the supply economy. Exactly as the division of labour, however, the supply economy begins to become essential for modern capitalism only when another circumstance first makes this process possible in a broad scope: the modern financial economy. To money itself is attached the necessity of founding a capitalistic economic order, and not from Nature. It is a medium of exchange from the beginning, very often a measure of price. However, its significance becomes decisive when it becomes a means of savings and loan and, in the modern credit economy, it grows into the most powerful production factor that mankind has ever seen.

This development was possible only on the basis of a process which is not of an economic sort but of an intellectual. "Every economic life is the expression of a spiritual life" (Spengler).[97] Man could work with money in the present sense and in the present scope only when he discovered and developed in himself the capacity for abstraction. If previously the property, the ware - to which also gold to a certain degree belongs - stood at the centre of economic thought, in the capitalistic age money does. Money, however, is not a reality, not a factual value, but an intellectual one: a concept. So long as this concept of money remains in relation to reality, so long as money is the function of economics, so long as it represents a value symbol for actual goods - so long does the institution of money signify a victory of mind over matter. Human creativity creates value symbols in order to regulate and to simplify the traffic of goods. It is otherwise, however, if money is no longer the symbol of genuine life goods, of earned real value, but becomes a goal in itself. Money is then no longer a function of life, but a power in itself which exercises by itself further lifeless and artificial functions which violate life. Even here, the process of splitting leads to the victory of the mechanical over the living. Money becomes the centre of influence, thought in terms of money produces money (Spengler). This thought in terms of money instead of in terms of goods is the prerequisite for the formation of modern capital, which does not signify a really resting wealth or a sum of real values but

---

[97] [Spengler, *Der Untergang des Abendlandes*, Bd.II, Kap.V: 'Die Formenwelt des Wirtschaftslebens', Abschnitt A, 'Das Geld'].

the driving force not only of economics but of all of life. Capitalism thus becomes not only an economic form but even a disposition. New streams which arise from the particular power of money set themselves in opposition to the sources of true, natural, life. Thus money becomes the most powerful fiction that man knows, the moving power of mankind.

To be sure, it has been reserved to our unhistorically thinking age to feel this exceptional civilisatory condition as the rule: a proof of the fact that the capacity of thinking in terms of the whole has suffered. Spengler already points to the fact that the political and scientific ideas which our age has of the essence of economics are based on English presuppositions.[98] The fact that the English as the first people developed the modern industry, the recent trade and credit system, that therefore the national economic doctrine of a Smith considered an economic condition of development as a universally valid system, became decisive for the fate of the Liberal economic science as well as for that of its similarly individualistic counterpart, Marxism. Everybody believed in the unlimited increase of capital, everybody worshipped the apparently inexhaustible productive power of money. Thereby it stands firm: that money without the corresponding equivalent in wares, consumer goods, and means of production is a nothing, a phantom. The great currency depreciations have brought forward the proof of this unequivocally. The application of enormous capitals for the construction of places of production and means of production becomes senseless as soon as there is no human working force present to manipulate this means. The accumulation of consumer goods loses its aim if no men are present who wish to use the wares. All supposed goods obtain their value only in the man who must be prepared to use it productively or as a consumer. If the abstraction of money goes too far, if money acquires a life of its own to which no human life corresponds any longer,

---

[98] [*Preußentum und Sozialismus*, Kap.III: 'Engländer und Preußen'].

then the *fata Morgana*[99] of money sinks into nothingness.

The essence of the capitalistic age therefore consists mainly in the fact that man no longer stands at the centre of economics, but money: "The immediate goal of economics is exclusively the increase of a sum of money".[100] The nature of money presses for its constant increase, for capital formation. If the increase would stop, there would be no more capitalism. In turn, however, the perfect separation of money from the present goods will never succeed. The theory of the shortage of all goods which can be countered only by the increase of capital rules the doctrine of political economy upto the moment and seems also - as precisely the creation and establishment of the new currency in Germany demonstrated - to correspond to the economic reality. Only in recent times do ideas raise themselves against it. One concludes rightly that through the shortage of the means of circulation the possible production of many goods is held back, the number of unemployed grows. It is only a logical step to the demand of taking the reverse way and to start with the increase of consumer goods and of the means of production. The purely "capitalistically" thinking person will counter this thought-process with the objection that it is a serpent that bites itself in the tail; for, the capital is indeed lacking for this increased production. To him it is to be replied that this statement is correct in capitalistic parlance; but wrong where the increased production can happen in an uncapitalistic manner: through measures which lie not with capital but with man. An example. All savings - on it is capital formation based - are useless if, at the same time, the existing powers which could be used for production are not employed. But it can be a matter not only of deficient use, but also of bad care of the present working force or indeed of exploitation of the forces of the people, as the population political part argues still more closely. In addition, there is the neglect of the strength of the soil. It is

---

[99] ['Morgan le Fay', a type of mirage].

[100] Werner Sombart, *Die Ordnung des Wirtschaflslebens, Enzyklopädie der Rechts- und Staatswissenschaft*, Berlin, 1925.

imaginable that the financial capital grows, but at the same time the number of unemployed and - what is worse - the devaluation of land and soil do. This is the condition which characterizes the present. In principle, completely uncapitalistic ways are thinkable of increasing the present amount of goods: one thinks of the engagement of the fallow powers of the unemployed which must be carried out even uncapitalistically, i.e., outside the idea that their use is possible only through expenditure of very high enterprise capitals. The moment that the entire economy of a people is not considered capitalistically but from the point of view of setting all the powers of the soil and of the blood in the service of production, the shortage theory loses in universal validity. Whether - as the Englishman Arthur Kitson[101] thinks - it will make place for a doctrine of surplus - he establishes this with the saving of labour through machines - can remain open to question. If it is now established that the capital as on ordering economic power has failed insofar as the fallowness of value-creating powers actually resulted under its rule, the conclusion lies near of granting the state the disposal of the ordering even with regard to the economy (Socialism). This thought-process has, in the meanwhile, missed its mark because the interpolation of the state destroys the most valuable basic power of all economics: the personality; especially because capitalism is not thereby destroyed, but will only assume a collective form which operates in a life-destroying manner to a still higher degree than individualistic capitalism. The relatedness to the whole cannot be established in the economic life even in a collective way, but only with the help of the personality rooted in the community.

If the individual man and the people were placed at the centre of the economic activity, if they constitute the goal of all production, then it depends on their condition whether the production of goods remains equal in its range or a temporary increase takes place. The characteristic of the modern capitalism is now that an uninterrupted rise of production is striven for. One tends to consider this

---

[101] [Arthur Kitson, author of *Unemployment: The Cause and a Remedy*, London: Cecil Palmer, 1921].

sort of "economic progress" as self-evident, without thinking of the causes of this striving. That capital has the tendency to incessantly increase itself lies in the nature of money: money produces money. Generally, however, the process of increase of goods is not customarily traced back to the capitalistic side of the economy, but to consumption. The further question therefore raises itself in order to fully comprehend the essence of modern capitalism, how then that impulse towards increase of real goods, which is at the moment made increasingly dependent on the increase of capital, is to be explained. All increase of production is based on two facts: on population increase and on the increase of needs. The increase of population will be treated thoroughly in the population political part. It may be correct that the progresses of technology, that the modern industrialisation, first made possible the nourishment of the strongly swollen population in the 19th century. It would, however, be wrong to trace it back causally to the upsurge of technology and of industry. More obviously, on the contrary, is the population increase the cause of the technological and industrial upswing; a circumstance to which many social scientists, especially also Schmoller, have pointed. The truth, however, perhaps lies still deeper. It is most probably spiritual, unfathomable causes which, at the same time physically and intellectually increase the fruitfulness of a people in such a way that progresses in the possibilities of nourishment go hand in hand with the increase of the population.

It is generally assumed that, with the regulation of birth and the fall in the birth-rate, the age of capitalism tends towards its end. Not merely because the markets become smaller, although the shrinking of the German internal market is certainly related to the drop in the birth-rate; in the world economic involvement, however, the opening of new markets is nevertheless at least thinkable. Chiefly from the side of the producer does a certain stand-still of capitalistic development threaten: when there begins a deficiency of working forces. Certainly, the technological progress can close perceptible gaps in the ranks of the workers: in the form of the substitution of man by the machine. Capital can actually make man superfluous to a certain degree. But even here the limits to development are set, of which it is hardly to be said according to what law they are drawn. Apparently there exists a precisely reckonable relation between capital and human work which can be displaced without further ado in favour of one of the two factors. It is thinkable that a point is reached where capital simply does not yield any revenue any more. The technologisation of the economy could, since it always depends on man, have a natural limit. One does not need at all to take into consideration the supposition of the race hygienists who believe that the frantic deterioration of the race will one day indeed place the entire technological apparatus in question, because the intellectual capacities necessary for its operation are then dead. The quick collapse of highly developed and also technologically perfect cultures of antiquity can instruct us how immoderately fast enormous establishments fall to total devaluation as soon as human foundations are missing. Instead of investigating the so-called inner laws of economics to the point of conceptual games, it would therefore be far more necessary to discover the connection of the movement of the population and the economy to the ultimate causes.

If the number and wealth of the population manage to rise, capitalism would certainly still have a great future. Nevertheless, in the opposite case, even the capitalistic development is in no way concluded, so long as, on the producer side, an increasing technologisation (materialisation) and, on the consumer side, the increase of needs is possible. Therewith we come to the essential characteristic of modern capitalism, to the relation in which it stands to need. The glorification of wares has always formed an essential component of all economic life, it was already necessary in the age of the pure barter trade. Insofar as the modern advertising is to a certain degree the extended arm of a sales process become elaborate through the division of labour, it is hardly distinguished from those original forms of all trading activity. An economy of division of labour needs finally also its own advertising department. So long as man takes from the offered wares only those which he needs, so long, therefore, as he determines himself the range of his needs, directed by Nature and a healthy culture, so long is he the centre, indeed the ruler of economics. "The modern economy however dictates to the customer not only things which he needs but also things which he does not need. Through advertisement the new need is first aroused in him and then the means of satisfaction for it supplied. The production side rules the shaping of our surroundings. Man becomes a mere customer, i.e., an object."[102] Therewith man has become a will-less object of capital.

Diesel[103] says on this: "It may be a certain principle that men receive nothing, but nothing in vain. Therefore men must pay for all this expenditure which goes beyond the covering of the natural needs, with work, care, capital.

"Now the higher life need does not flow into our modern economy or, not in large part, from natural wealth, from the surplus in life necessities, but from arbitrary accumulation of capital and from the stimulus of desire. Everything is desire, everything is set on the stimulus of desire, indeed, it is indeed considered as especially business-like and moral to titillate desire through the most extravagant devices to the point of madness, without taking any consideration of the natural wealth of a people.

"But that is not the only source of the fact that, with increasing needs, the amount of care and work is not lessened in the broad, joyless, masses of the people. According to a well-known national economic law, a decrease of drudgery and toil is also not achieved by the surprising invention, because with every rung that has been climbed the human need rises. With every rung that has been climbed therefore the external picture becomes more glittering, but the inner expenditure of toil, need, battle for the necessary daily bread remains the same in

---

[102] Theodor Lüddecke in the October Heft, 1929, of the *Deutsche Rundschau*, ["Der Einfluss der Reklame auf das Antlitz der Kultur", p.36].

[103] *loc.cit.* [Eugen Diesel, *Der Weg durch das Wirrsal*, Stuttgart, 1926].

the broad masses. If the parasitical production is increased by that unnatural development of need, the inner care and need of a people finally stands in a grotesque discrepancy to the unleashing of civilisatory hocus-pocus, and men stand all round before a crazed progress and the gnawing need for the daily bread as before a malformed riddle".

Even Lüddecke calls the present-day economics a need-stimulating economics in contrast to the need-serving economics which can be also a reasonable supply economics. He summarizes the effect of this economic form in a simple, but disturbing sentence: "A substantial percent of the so-called poverty is a result of incorrect use of purchasing power". It is, accordingly, certain that the present-day capital, which does without an incorporation into the community and obeys its own laws, enters - with the disappearance of the population increase to which it should naturally owe its striving for increase - new paths in order to satisfy the instinct innate in money for accumulation. The stronger the fall in the birth rate, the more strained the advertisement for the purpose of the increase of needs of the population still remaining. The market is thus produced artificially. Therewith that hopeful edifice of the progress of men through increased capital formation, through the increase of production falls apart. Blessings could grow to men out of the powers of capital, out of the unrestricted production of wares, only if the laws according to which needs arise came from the human soul and not from the capital. A power which is unshakeable must set up the goal of the race between production and need. If production does this itself, then a process arises which can be explained with the following analogy: man resembles a runner in a race who bears before him the goal band with arms stretched forward which he can never bend. He can consequently never touch it with his chest and is sentenced to eternal pursuit. Since however a hounded man is not a man any longer, the tension between soul and capital becomes unbearable. Here, apparently, lies the deepest reason for the anticapitalistic wave which - in contrast to America, where the spiritual powers still slumber - rages through countries of old culture.

But where does the power reside which produces and directs that need-stimulating economics? It lies in the essence of capital insofar as the latter seeks investment and income. For this, however, sufficient opportunity would be offered if the capital applied itself to natural need-serving. The present shows that it does not do this. It rather lets powerful soil-wealth and human work-force lie fallow or uses it for a marked stimulus-economics, acting as if the natural and necessary need had already for a long time been served. A rough example: the peasant daughter leaves the country, which, as a result of deficient tilling, increasingly loses in value, receives in the city unemployment support and puts this aside for rayon stockings which she wears to an amusement arcade. The capital in this case flees the country and turns to the rayon industry and the entertainment business. The costs for the unproductive unemployment insurance however mean a loss in economic power and the wealth of the people. Thus arises an apparently unbridgeable gap between necessities which a reasonable need-serving demands and the paths which capital goes on for the purpose of need-stimulation. A healthy popular economics would have to appease necessary needs, thus liberating spiritual, culture-creating powers. The modern capitalism, on the other hand, lets poverty exist more than necessarily, hounds man in a senseless giddiness of needs, kills his soul and destroys his culture.

However that did not have to be so, even in a capitalistic economy. That it, nevertheless, occurs points to a component of modern capitalism which is hostile to life, denies the needs of life and obeys its own laws. This characteristic of capitalism Sombart finds in individualism. The individual man who, separated inwardly from the true life and the community, manipulates the power of money, made similarly independent, and lives only for himself. "He extends his sphere of influence so far that it corresponds to his will and the perfection of its power, without taking into consideration the welfare and misery of other persons participating in the economic life".[104] Even here we recognize therefore as the intellectual background of modern capitalism two circumstances which actually coincide both in their effect and in their cause: the abstraction of the understanding (money) and the detachment of the individual (individualism) set the seal logically, in economics, on what has similarly occurred in other fields of life: the disintegration of life.

The unrestricted disposal power over money felt only as masterly led to a crisis of the concept of property. Property had experienced in the Roman law its firm conceptual definition; unfortunately, the Germans adhered closely to Roman legal concepts. In the Germanic law, property was less a legal norm than, rather, a social condition. The goal of disposal of goods decided the nature of the property: the individualistic conception of property as an unlimited personal right of rule was not valid. The rigid concept of property of the individualistic Roman law stands in contrast to a view of property according to which it is a "last, merely given form, but one changing according to the situation" (Bott-Bodenhausen). It is understandable that property is contested when it begins to lose its function of creating social values and stands only in the service of personal all-powerfulness. Property in land, in immovables, in means of production, could never deny the relation to life, to the community, to the whole. The unrestricted property of money, however, became as abstract as the concept of money itself and therewith hostile to life. Because it was not recognized that there is still healthy and natural property next to the duty-less rigid concept of property of the present, efforts must set in which deny property or wish to build it up collectively. Communism is therefore only a reaction against individualistic property. It wants to "overcome" it collectively, because it does not see the genuine property in general. For, property is the natural foundation of every living culture, so long as it remains bound, on the one hand, to the personality, as the

---

[104] Hermann Bente, *Organisierte Unwirtschaftlichkeit*, Jena, Verlag Gustav Fischer, 1929.

creative power of all life, and, on the other hand however, man accomplishes all his actions in the idea of service to the whole.

But this collective process which is understandable only as the reaction against the individualistic side of capitalism pervades the capitalistic economics. Even here individualism bruises the personality. This must be constantly repeated, because precisely economic circles understand by individualism a condition in which the economic creative personality is decisive. This is however the case only in an organic economy. If the economy is subject to individualism, it becomes mechanical and collective: the logical execution of the individualistic doctrine of equality. This danger is greatest for the economy at the moment. Not really because the property of the individual is threatened. But for a much more significant reason. If, indeed, the economy is depersonalised, then it loses its innermost power, the creative man, and thereby its strongest essential character: efficiency.[105] The highest law of all economic activity is "the agreement between needs and means of need-satisfaction".[106] This principle must rule economics, if it should not become inefficient. It is true of all sorts of economic activity, to which, for example, even the state administration belongs. That this has, in the broadest sense of the word, become inefficient, indeed carries on a squandering of power and money, is today uncontested, and was even emphasized repeatedly and deploringly by numerous statesmen and scientists. Beginning with Stein and Bismarck to men like Drews,[107] Max Weber,[108] and Eugen Schiffer.[109] But not only in the public administration does inefficiency rule but also in the actual private economy. Otto Heinrich von der Gablenz[110] has described this most

---

[105] In the next arguments the author follows the excellent presentations of Hermann Bente, *op.cit.*

[106] Gustav Cassel, *Theoretische Sozialökonomie*, Leipzig, 1921, [Kap.1].

[107] *Principles of an administrative reform.*

[108] *Parliament und Regierung im neugeordneten Deutschland*, in *Gesammelte Politische Schriften*, München: Drei Masken Verlag, 1921, pp. 126-260].

[109] *Die deutsche Justiz[: Grundzüge einer durchgreifenden Reform]*, [Berlin: O. Liebmann, 1928].

[110] "Industriebürokratie," in *Schmollers Jahrbuch.*

penetratingly.

It is no wonder if public administrations become bureaucratic and inefficient. Here the invasion of considerations and points of view which owe their origin not to economic but to other sorts of ways of thought is made relatively easy. But whereas one could, as a scientist, earlier be considered to be authorized to remind the state of the law of efficiency, the development in the meanwhile has taken almost the reverse path: the state does not become healthy through economic thought, but the economy becomes, on the contrary, sick through bureaucratising. Bente shows the forms in which this happens. The chief cause of the increasing inefficiency he calls the "equalisation of values". Creative and uncreative work are treated equally, creative and uncreative men equated. The inefficiency is only to be explained by the "alienation from life of the elements causing it" (Bente). Thus even economics has its crisis of vitality.

The customary opinion is now that to the development of the modern large enterprise is inevitably bound its bureaucratising. It is correct that the large enterprise fosters bureaucratising, but not that it must necessarily be bureaucratic. Let us recall the example which modern large states offer: they can be as well centralistic-bureaucratic as decentralistic-vital. Ford has therefore given up leading his large company centralistically and has deliberately gone over to decentralisation. Precisely the modern division of work allows this, because the individual work-processes can be distributed to a series of operations which work as simply and independently as possible. Thereby the vitality of production which is threatened by the centralised large enterprise is once again established. However, in it, in place of the creative man, regulations enter. Obviously, regulations are necessary, but only insofar as they arise from the realm of technology. Bente calls this sort of regulations work-instructions. They arise not from bureaucratic centralism, but from the necessity of serving the technological apparatus according to the laws innate in it.

The large enterprise is a child of capital agglomeration which is based partly on the depersonalising of capital. The modern form of business companies, the rise of a special money market, and the stock exchange, have made this development possible. The enterpreneur becomes an employee of capital. The owner of capital and the economic entrepreneur increasingly coincide with each other. This process depersonalises the economy. At least for industry, Marx has made no incorrect predictions; the concerns become larger and more uniform; but the possession of capital is not collected - as he thought - in one's own hands, but is increasingly depersonalised. It can no longer be ascertained whose capital works in an individual case in the modern large-scale economics. With the personality disappears the most important stimulus to efficiency; the competition becomes weaker and the personal risk of the individual capitalist smaller. With the depersonalisation of capital grows the danger of bureaucratising and, therewith, of sterility. The future of economics is, in general, threatened. It loses to a certain degree, its private economic character and therewith its vital impulse. For, the life from which the great economic upsurge arose, taught: "Battle for your life, battle for your possessions, battle for your advancement, battle for your inheritance".[111] The private economic personality is thus removed from capitalism, which assumes collective forms. In no way does it lose thereby that disastraous characteristic, of obeying its own laws detached from the life of the people. On the contrary, there is lacking the living man who alone can form the link to the community. Certainly, the planlessness and anarchy of a private economy, which was set up by undisciplined individuals only for personal financial profit, may disappear. But this does not change anything in the circumstance that collectivism leads to complete despiritualisation of capital and to the final enslavement of the economy. There enter into the economy, instead of the individual, the masses, Socialism sucks up the individuals and thus completes the process of depersonalisation which individualism introduced. The problem of the economy is, however, not

---

[111] Heinrich von Gleichen, *Opposition und Nation*, special issue of *Der Ring*, Berlin, December, 1928.

exhausted in the formulation of the question, individual or collective masses, which are both worth fighting for, but only in that of how one may, in both cases, set up the creative personality once again. Beyond the outmoded contest between Liberalism and Socialism sounds the appeal to the soul of the managing men, to the rights of the working people.

Many derive from the depersonalisation of capital a new concept of property. Others (Sombart) consider the collective development as the end of capitalism. Still others glimpse herein Socialistic efforts, speak of a planned economy and economic democracy. To all these questions, however, an exhaustive answer can be given only by one who examines the most difficult side of capitalism, the workers' question.

III

The workers' question

To preserve the living connection of the economy with the blood and the soil, to maintain it in its serving position, was the task in which Liberalism failed. Not the gold of fruitful ears of corn, but the soulless metal itself finally ruled the Liberal man. Indeed, he forgot even that gold is a gift of the motherly earth, and built on it the international rule of finance which became the disaster of the living soul. The originality and fruitfulness of man were destroyed by it. Certainly, there resulted an incomparable economic upsurge of the unleashing of individual human driving forces. Never would mankind have progressed so powerfully in the mastery of Nature and in making it serviceable for human needs if the human restorative arts had not risen to an unheard-of degree. It is also not ignored that a Faustian trait lies in the economic impetus. But these performances were accomplished at the cost of spirituality, and thus the modern man of civilisation stands with full hands, but with an empty heart, before the splendid edifice of economics. Gradually the knowledge dawns how frightful the price is which was paid for this economic "bloom". The healthy force of the people, once constantly renewing itself from inexhaustible peasant blood, was almost abandoned to destruction. The time had to come when the blood rose against money. The uninterrupted economic forward-movement misled the modern man to the opinion that this tempo of development is natural and the rule. The modern westerner commits the very absurd mistake of relating the history of mankind only to himself and of seeing in the present the peak of a development. In fact, he experiences only a transitional period. Cultures can arise only when the economic security of the peoples has attained a certain position of rest, and the basis of nourishment and economic form are, to a certain degree, stable. It seems as if we are on the way to reaching an end and therewith a repose.

A problematic period of transition is, however, not spared to us until that point. First the wounds must be healed which the economic liberalism has caused to the popular body, to society, to culture. Of which the most frightful is the uprooting of broad masses, of the industrial workers, or - as it calls itself - the proletariat.

The population political part will describe the movement of the population which was the cause of the rise of the proletariat. There the grave "migration of the peoples" which took place from the peasant east to the industrial west will be described. But how is that transplantation of the people to be understood?

If the farming soil is destroyed and no new forms of soil cultivation (intensification) offer the possiblity of nourishing the increasing population, if also no new settlement of the population increase results, then there arises the social division into propertied and unpropertied. Boehmer[112] calls this process "disinheritance" from the correct consideration that the farming soil gains in value with increasing population, but the second and further sons of the farmer forfeit this increase of value, which falls only to the inheritor of the soil. The cause of this disinheritance is, according to him, the circumstance that "the further development of the law ceases the moment the completion of the peasant dwelling makes it necessary". Therewith the possibility is lost for the disinherited person

[112] [see p.96n. above].

of obtaining dwelling and at least a part of the nourishment from one's own soil. He is thereupon instructed to defray his entire maintenance with a salary or wages. The lack of property damns him to the loss of the interest and the entrepreneurial profit which would flow to him from his own property. The difficult position of the disinherited therefore does not consist, as Marxism maintains, in the withholding of the full work-wages, but - according to Boehmer - in the fact that the unpropertied person, as a result of his disinheritance, has no share in the interest and entrepreneurial profit which are, as such, natural.

The increase of men leads to an opposition between space and need of nourishment. It is the lever of the economic, partially also of the cultural, rise of men. Industrialisation owes its origin to this circumstance. When Marx wishes to explain the rise of the proletariat exclusively through pure economic processes, chiefly through the unification of the means of production in a few hands (transition to the large enterprise), he forgets the final cause of industrialisation and of social regrouping: the increase of population. Where such does not take place, no industrialisation and proletarianisation in large measure will be possible. The example of France throws all the calculations of the Marxist doctrine overboard, because it has, as a result of its low increase of population, remained agrarian. Nothing is however more wrong than the belief that the large enterprise will prevail similarly in agriculture. This will not be the case for numerous reasons: first, because mechanising and equalising in it can succeed only to a certain degree; then the weather and soil constitution are different. Next, because the technologisation of agriculture encounters natural limits with respect to the profitableness of machines; because, further, the economisation of the outer district is too expensive in large-scale agriculture as a result of broad paths and the raised transportation costs; finally, because the high salaries which industry pays cannot be borne by agriculture. Farming economy and middling wealth will therefore remain at least equal to the agrarian large enterprise, just as in colonial countries also the farmer enters in place of the large farm, as soon as for some reason the large-scale agriculture does not make a profit any longer. The rise of the salaried working class is thus in no way to be set to the credit of the large enterprise; it arises from a movement of the population which, at the moment, begins to have economic consequences in which the agriculture does not offer shelter any more to the population increase. Industrialisation must then indeed not succeed - one thinks of China -, but there is no industrialisation without the presence of a stratum of landless men who are forced to salaried work.

To be sure, the proletarianising of a people is thinkable not only through the fact that the population surplus of the country people and, later, of the urban population necessarily falls victim to the salaried working class, whereby the number of peasant population remains the same or indeed increases in the intensification of the agriculture. Industrialisation produces, rather, the danger of the devastation of the flat land:[113] and especially the moment that the division of labour makes not only national progresses but also international. For, the further population increase lives on the import of foreign food which is paid for with industrial exports. In order to maintain this, one lets in increasingly cheap foreign food. Thereby the external farming soil gains in value. This increase of value is equal to the decrease of value of the local wealth. It accrues to the one who has disposal of the nourishing soil; work always renders service only to the soil; where the soil does not belong any longer to the working people, this service becomes a drudgery. Import of food, which occurs only for reasons of wage-politics, however enlarges the difference between prime costs and selling prices in industry and in agriculture still more, because the indigenous agricultural products are held down in price. The consequences are a transition of agriculture to extensive cultivation of the soil, soil depreciation, and, therewith, strengthened emigration into the industrial cities, raised bidding of wage workers, increase of unemployed people, weakening of the internal market, sharpened export politics,

---

[113] See also Paul von Sokolowski's *Die Versandung Europas[: eine andere grosse russische Gefahr]*, (Verlag Deutsche Rundschau, [1929]).

and finally once again the rise of the import of food. If the economical politics does not set forward and counter the international division of labour, one's own farming soil will become valueless, and the value being lost accrues entirely to the foreign countries. Losses of wealth of the greatest proportion threaten a nation which conducts such an economics. The German Reich finds itself in the middle of this development. Funk evaluates the loss of wealth of the German agriculture since 1924 at seven milliard marks and thinks that with these means the broad masses would have artificially maintained their standard of living. There is, therefore, no doubt that the proletarianisation increases, if a sharp reduction of population does not lead to the devastation not only of the country but also of the city. As a rule, however, the city sucks up all the forces of the people and ends in a swarm of fellaheen. Thus the proletarianisation of a people is dependent on the movement of population and the economic politics conducted at any time. It is in no way a necessary process due to capital, before which one would have to stand rather helplessly.

When the country proletariat arose, one granted to the unpropertied population surplus freedom of movement and free salary contracts. Homelessness, daily care for one's life and psychological disorder are the true face of that grant. The broad flat lands of the east had offered a paltry life-support, but preserved one from misery; the wages of the industry seemed, in comparison to it, princely. But only so long as they were not devoured by artificial arousing of needs, or, as a result of unemployment, were stopped. That indeed was the frightful aspect of the free salary contract, that the dismissal of the worker could any day push him into the abyss. The one who had become rootless had no resort any longer to the products of his own modest house- or land-economy or to his family. For, in the rent-barracks of the metropolis, even the family life collapsed. Therewith fell the natural insurance against need, sickness, and old age, which the home and family always offer in healthy society. The peasantry, become home-less and property-less, lost in the metropolis its family-forming power. The first generation still bore the home-soil in its heart, the second was already born in the rent-barracks and bore in itself dread. If business fell, if the worker became unemployed, sick or decrepit, he was less than a beggar, who at least possessed experience in his sad "profession". From year to year grew the troop of these uprooted people and, in spite of everything, the healthy peasant blood in them would have prevailed and created from the common need a new social morality, if the rootless and outcasts of the bourgeois society had not appointed themselves as their leaders. In Germany, "education had grown more quickly than the economy" (August Winnig).[114] Consequently, there arose an unoccupied, dissatisfied and poor intelligensia which aroused itself in the radicalism of the French Revolution and, with Jacobin ideas, turned to the new field of advertising which the proletariat masses offered. The ghetto resentment of many Jews, especially of the unpropertied immigrated from the east, concurred with these currents because their social ambition found no satisfaction in Germany. Thus it came to that phenomenon which Winnig calls the intellectual infiltration of foreigners among the working class. The German ruling class, whose duty it was to lead the German worker with his healthy longing for social justice, failed. German Socialism arose in its unusual mixture of doctrinaire credulity, atheism, radical denial, petty bourgeois feelings of envy, and yet reawakened comradeship, moral impetus, and high discipline. The infiltration of foreigners among the German working class became the fate of the German workers' movement, but the latter became in 1918 the fate of the German people. Still no signs are at hand which point to the reduction of the social tension. The triumphal procession of finance uproots increasingly more men who then, as living inflammable matter, threaten every social order. Certainly, a strong disappointment has gone through the Socialist masses; certainly, the enormous army of those ruling and living in the workers' movement have dropped their gestures ever since they benefit from the state. Even

---

[114] [see p.83n. above].

under the hardest attacks on the wealth of the people - foreign debts, consumption of soil capital, depreciation of house property - salaries and social supports have risen to an artificial height. No man dares, however, to think what should happen if the vessel is once emptied. One who believes in the bourgeoisisation of the salaried working class through the path struck out today remains fully captivated in the ideas of capitalism and industrialism. Bourgeoisie and Socialism were indeed only differences of degree, were always the same intellectual basic attitude but with different symptoms. The number of the propertied becomes smaller from day to day. How should the bourgeoisisation then make progress? Is it not rather in this way that the proletarianisation increases? The present-day state Socialism makes everyone discontented; in the end, nobody has anything. Life becomes increasingly more uncertain, not only for the manual labour class, but also for the circles which upto now were proud and contented with themselves. The contagion of revenues - today characterising the entire internal constitution of the German people - must lead just to a bad end, because it delays the creation of real values and impairs the creative powers of the people. Neither bourgeoisie nor Socialism have ever thought to grapple with the basic evil of proletarianisation. Economic liberalism, whether of private or national sort, sits so deep in the thought of the present-day German that he thoughtlessly repels every encouragement to basically remove the "disinheritance" which grows ever larger. This lack of a broad perspective, this psychological narrow-mindedness, which did not foresee what a storm formed itself over the German fate through social causes, bear the blame that a solution of the social questions were not already found at the beginnings of that development which would have preserved Germany from the later collapse. Because the 19th century could not, in general, think in a population political way, and overlooked the great historical connections, society stood helpless before a development whose laws it did not at all recognize. Just as the frugality of the German Parliament led to hundred-fold loss in the German army, so also the small-heartedness of the German economic leaders in the attempt to resolve the social question. Society failed, the state had to attack.

It was the crown which rescued the concept of society. If the Reich had already in 1871 been a capitalistic democracy, like the United States and France, the German worker would have stood today as unprotected as the worker of those states; for, that the working class of North America, as a result of the good business and wealth of their country earns splendidly in terms of natural produce says nothing of their social position and economic security. Just as the situation of a colonial country which reveals almost no population problem is hardly to be compared to that of overpopulated Europe. - It was the German Kaiser who, in Romantic enthusiasm, introduced the powerful work of German social insurance. Socialism conducted itself here in a denying way, without being capable of showing new ways and pointing to more favorable solutions. The Socialistic politics after 1918 is nothing but an unhealthy exaggeration of Wilhelminian social politics. The German working class however helped to remove the crown, which stood in the way of the world-encompassing high finance in its intention to enslave Germany capitalistically. Perhaps the hour will once come when the writing of history seizes the true significance of the world war and draws its conclusions from the simultaneous collapse of the three great and strong monarchies of Europe. Here secret laws rule which do not have their cause - as harmless minds maintain - in a conspiracy, but in the effectiveness of intellectual currents. In the world war, finance set out to destroy the freedom of human work. Therefore the crown, as the protector of the social idea, as the bulwark of mythic ideas, had to fall. Justice therefore forces one to grant to the crown its historical service.

But basic reflection leads to the knowledge that the direction paved in the insurance system of the Reich could not lead to a satisfying solution. For, it is not fitting that society uproot and exploit men in order to leave the security for them to the state. The state in this way undertook a task which had to involve it in an endless conflict with the private economy as well as with the working class. There arose the modern social state which distanced itself increasingly from the system of the true state and thereby lost its own power. In turn, the conquest of the state for the purposes of the "working class" became the goal of all Socialistic politics. If already earlier the knowledge had been alive that the state treasuries are supplied by no other sources but from the economy, then one perhaps one would have summoned to life at the right time the insurance system as a common institution of entrepreneurs and workers under autonomy. But the remarkable superstition ruled that the economy would save something if the state reached into its pocket. Never would the situation have arisen that demagogically influenced voting masses and the representatives attached to them squeeze the funds out of the economy by way of political legislation in order to supply a powerful apparatus which, along with social insurance, discharges an entire series of different aims which have nothing at all to do with its true purpose. The present-day insurance system serves in the first place the maintenance of an enormous bureaucracy which crystallises the party life. With it the worker is in no way helped, the insurance bureaucracy is inwardly precisely as alien to him as that of the state. He considers the functionary economics in the treasuries not as an achievement; that only the beneficiary parties do. The excessive administrative expenditure of the treasuries, both professional and personal, is uncontested. Their performances stand in no proportion any longer to the contributions, which easily consume a tenth of the working salary. In addition, the treasury system proletarianises even the medical profession. One of the most valuable strata of the intelligentsia in this way drives to its downfall. No profession demands individuality and living connection with research and science in the same measure as the medical. All this is omitted by the "treasury lions". An entire literature unequivocally demonstrates how medical treatment suffers under the treasury system. The doctor must work like a machine, without human understanding and without scientific thoroughness. Even the ethics of the medical profession thereby deteriorates.

In view of the medical insurance and the unemployment insurance, the question raises itself, whether cases are present here that are really capable of insurance. The significance of every insurance must be lost if the entry of the insurance case is no longer dependent on "higher authorities" but is placed extensively in the discretion of the person insured. One who pays contributions to the medical funds feels obliged to become sick or at least to benefit from it. The consequence is that, in general, there is no more insurance, but a socialisation of the health system. As everywhere, here, the unscrupulous, incompetent, and weak live at the cost of the superiour. The level of the contribution provokes one to the examination of the question whether - in restriction to the necessary medical need - the immediate compensation of the medical treatment would not be cheaper from one's own pocket. The grant which the really sick and the needy receive today stand in no proportion any longer to the total sum of the contributions coming in. The present-day insurance system is the most inefficient that there is. "The protection for the sick destroyed the will to be healthy, the protection for the unemployed killed the joy of creation, the laws for the protection of the unemployed effected unemployment" (Funk).

Erwin Liek[115] has described the demoralising effect of the treasury system: on the doctor as well as on the entire people. He speaks rightly of the negative selection which the present-day German social insurance conducts. The obtaining of revenue surreptitiously has become one of the chief professional departments of today. The state is on the point of transforming itself into an enormous insurance society: only not on the basis of reciprocality; for, the competent person is gradually sucked up by the malingerers of life who are artificially nurtured. Nowhere has the equalisation avenged itself so frightfully as in this field, nowhere has the state more clearly demonstrated its incompetence in

---

[115] [Erwin Liek (1878-1935), surgeon and author of *Der Arzt und seine Sendung* (München, 1925), and *Das Wunder in der Heilkunde* (München, 1930). Liek distinguished between the true healer and the merely scientifically trained doctor, and sharply criticised the socially deleterious effects of medical insurance].

perceiving social tasks. It wanted to combat sicknesses and it nurtured them; at least those of the soul, often however even of the body. The care by the family, one of the strongest bonds of the family life in general, is made impossible by insurance. For, all free money goes into the general bottomless vessel, instead of into the savings bank of the family. The families with many children thus nurture comfortable and selfish couples. Instead of the living family, enters the bureaucratic treasury which, through its high contributions, hinders the formation of family capital.

The non-Socialistic parties allegedly wish to bourgeoisise the German worker. But significantly they have given themselves in the social politics, from inner dependence and fear of hostile demagogy, to the tow-rope of Socialism. For, the national insurance represents nothing other than an enormous socialisation and proletarianisation. One cannot blame the social democracy for their politics: it needs proletarians and would therefore like to constantly increase their numbers; exactly as the Russian power holders now industrialise Russia for the substantiation of the hypothesis that Communism can exist only in an industrial country. It is however incomprehensible why bourgeois politicians do not also logically conduct the bourgeoisisation of the worker. Along with all psychological pressupositions, it is a question here of the simplest idea that there is: to help the worker to property. But precisely the opposite way was entered on. The present-day national social insurance is however nothing else but the attempt to socialise in good part the wage income of the working class. The insurance contributions have, in comparison to the pre-war period, tripled and quadrupled. For the year 1928, the contribution income of the entire social insurance was evaluated at a meagre five billions (1913: 1,2 billions). The entire levies of the German people for social purposes, including the insurance for the war sacrifice (1,5 billions) amounted in 1928 to a total of 8,8 billion marks, the quadruple of the year 1913. One may imagine what blessing this capital saved all year long by the German people could establish, if it were usefully set up or sparingly spent for real emergencies, instead of being dissipated among the masses with the help of an inefficient apparatus which operates as the incubator of inferiority. Already now crises threaten for individual departments of the social insurance: first of all, for the unemployment insurance, which can claim the sad reputation for itself of having established a new "profession" in Germany: that of the unemployed. One expresses that elegantly when one characterises oneself as a "social pensioner". In a foreseeable time, however, the crisis will seize even the remaining insurance departments, because a rise in contributions is not possible, but the expenses however may surpass the receipts in amount.

Thus the feeling of self-responsibility was powerfully choked in broad sections of the German people. It was made almost impossible for the most competent and economical worker to save capital and to thereby establish private property. What he could save goes into the bottomless vessel. Thereby the contribution sums swell in the course of a working life to a considerable height and could actually secure the welfare of a family. Gustave Hartz[116] has moreover set up a series of calculations on what height the private property of a worker or an employee will reach if he put out the present-day insurance contributions at interest as savings capital. He arrives at amounts which lie between 30,000 and 100,000 marks.

That therefore this sort of deproletarianisation exists for a considerable number of workers and employees is subject to no doubt. If one restricted the insurance to the pure risk department, thus forestalling the miserable search for revenue and the frantic growth of the sickness insurance, the contributions to really necessary insurance could, especially if this were conducted private economically, be reduced by half; the remaining half would serve the capital formation. Natural insurance departments are - if one disregards the insurance of

---

[116] One may compare the arguments of the population political part. [Gustav Hartz, author of *Irrwege der deutschen Sozialpolitik und der Weg zur soziale Freiheit*, Berlin, 1928 and *Neue Wege in der Sozialpolitik*, Langensalza, 1929].

objects, basically only the insurance against accident and death. All persecution which is carried out against the one who has the courage to point to the great inconvenience of the German social insurance cannot prevent the responsibility-conscious German from demanding the abolition of the social insurance before the collapse results. Usually the warner is made out to be the enemy of the people. It may be that small efforts are present to abolish the insurance system in general. But such an attitude contradicts the spirit of this work most sharply. Actually nowadays no reasonable politician turns away from the insight that social insurance is necessary. But not a Socialist one; and what today is called the German insurance system is the worst equalising and value-destroying collectivism. We, however, wish precisely the opposite, since the creation of private property once again for the German man hovers before us as the final social economic goal; the conducting of the enormous means which are today used all year long for the German social budget to their right and proper goal: to the deproletarianisation of the German people.

On the way to this, one can be of different views. The compulsory savings are rejected by the camp of individualistic collectivism. Precisely in this attitude it becomes apparent that, for its representatives, it is not a matter of checking the depersonalisation of the German worker and of creating the foundation of all democracy, men with self-responsibility, but of sacrificing the personality to the idol of equality and the masses. Whether compulsory savings or another way, it stands firm that a considerable part of the present-day social expenses must be used to establish workers' private property. Whether this happens "capitalistically" or by way of a great homestead legislation (construction savings) may remain open to question. A clear division between the self-help of the individual and the tasks of public insurance must follow. Insofar as the protection of the entire popular body (population political tasks) come into question, the state must conduct social politics. Insofar as the individual is too weak, or the vicissitudes of life are stronger than he, there exists the comradely obligation of "all for one".

Here are the great future tasks of the professions, as it was already discussed in the national political part of this work, and it is time that the trades unions become aware of their mission which lies in this field. In addition, however, the self-responsibility of the individual man must be established and strengthened, whereby a great part of the obvious insurance falls once again onto the family. This three-fold division: private, comradely, and purely national, social activity should come to the mind of the reformer who is concerned beyond the demagogy of the day for the future development of the German people.

The tax-levying of today is similarly outmoded and inwardly false. Considered from the standpoint of the worker, it carries out entirely contribution taxes. For, indeed, practically, there is lacking the contribution to one's own salary, which is paid off totally as a contribution to the treasuries. We have also arrived at that limit where every rise of contributions operates in a price-raising manner. From the standpoint of the economy, it is a matter of indifference whether the worker or the entrepreneuer pays the contributions. The employer must always have in view the total cost of production of the ware produced by him, exactly as the employee his actual income. Whether gross- or net-salaries are agreed upon plays no role. Every employee judges his income according to the amount of the pay. In turn, it is a matter of indifference whether the entrepreneur charges the total contributions to be achieved to the credit of the salary or to the credit of the expenses. The present-day division of contributions between the employee and the employer arises from a false ideology. It only makes expensive the apparatus of the payment and of the administration.

The wrong way on which the social legislation has gone has sharpened the class situation of the German worker. Proletarianisation has not been removed, and the "guarantee of an inner peace"[117] has failed. Liberalism has transformed itself logically in social legislation into its enemy brother: into Communistic

[117] Imperial Message of the year 1881.

collectivism. Thus the unity of the German people has remained a dream; for, a great part of it persists in internationalistic ideas which operate disastrously for the battle of liberation in which the German stands. The idea of Socialism operative in the underground, that the war reparations could be shifted to property, impairs the resistance power of the German people against the Versailles Treaty. The craze for wastefulness of the public authorities, on the other hand, makes the reparation sums seem so small that the German foreign policy, in comparison to that of foreign countries which reveals itself to be well instructed of this process, is restricted. Only dreamers believe that the narrowing of the living space of the people would affect only the propertied strata and not the worker. Only men who are used not at all to think economically tend to the supposition that one can settle debts purely capitalistically without performance of work. Thus the position of the worker becomes the pivotal point of the German liberation politics. He would have, in the first place, the inner vocation to be a pioneer here since his life is threatened most of all. Only small circles of the working class have penetrated to this knowledge. It is also not probable that the masses of the Socialistic workers can be moved to a nation- affirming position before it is liberated from the class situation.

The serious mistake of all present-day social politics consists in the fact that it sees only matter and not the soul. The social task lies for it not in the field of the moral-spiritual: it calls the strife for external working conditions and for a share in the work-proceeds social battle. The same absurdity is betrayed also by the so-called social character of today: it corresponds to the attitude of the doctor who provides anaesthetics in order to mitigate at least the pains which an illness produces. The illness itself, however, remains existing. Thereby the self-appeasement of the social conscience - one has done something humane - also plays a great role. It is the weak, compassionate attitude of the well-clad with regard to the ragamuffin, the in and for itself vain enthusiasm to sacrifice something for the latter, perhaps also the wish to redeem oneself. One, however, who tackles the treatment of social injuries should be dispassionate with regard to the individual and only sympathize with a powerful sorrow: that of his nation, which threatens to perish of this sickness.

The class situation of the German worker has a social and an economic, a spiritual and a material side: interlocking with and reciprocally establishing one another. The uprootedness from the homeland ran parallel with the lack of social rights of the worker. These two points were treated further above. It is indeed wrong to set up the unpropertied nature of the worker as the sole cause of the class situation, as the Socialistic and bourgeois materialism do. Certainly, even spiritual conditions depend on it, but property alone can never provide a condition of spiritual rest in a materialistic age. There will always be great masses of people whose only property is their working force. Nevertheless, these consider themselves only in a very small part as positioned in a class situation. Such a feeling arises only when all work effort remains unsuccessful, when no possibility exists of ever attaining property. Especially in countries where the possibilities of advancement for the worker and his descendants are small, a train of hopelessness enters which goes significantly through the entire destiny of the worker. Even the granting of political equality of the worker cannot remove it. The working class will one day recognize that the ballot was a dubious gift, that one gave it stones instead of bread.

The possibility of advancement of the worker depends decisively on the foreign political situation of his nation and on the inner constitution of the society and state. As regards the latter, it should have been demonstrated by earlier arguments that the socialisation of wages, the equalisation of the performances through a false wage- and social politics, the bureaucratising of the entire economic and political life, have reduced the possibilities of advancement to a minimum. It is German Socialism which has conclusively obstructed the free path to the competent person. Some particularly moving demagogues perhaps rise politically and attain success, especially when it is accompanied by a little corruption. But this sort of rise is limited to the political field and affects relatively few. The social and economic rise, much more important, because it comprehends a broader field, has become harder than ever. It is, moreover, dependent on the territory, which the political power may secure for a people as its life-foundation. The smaller the power of a people, and the weaker its foreign political position, the smaller the number of the leadership positions which it has to offer. One, therefore, who promises to everybody the possibility of advancement could as childishly have in view the distribution of the stars. In present- day Germany, a right to advancement and success cannot be assured to the talented, let alone the average, man. One who, nevertheless, does this injures the soul of the people and - as the population political part will show - even the popular body. As matters stand today, if every artificial demand of social rise should cease, the selection conditions, on the contrary, must be sharpened.

But within the limits given temporarily at one time, all measures must be taken to liberate the working clas from the class situation. That social peace is possible is proved by long epochs of history, especially of the Middle Ages. Its exemplary peace of work was based on its economic constitution: not an economics which regulated itself approximately according to individualistic points of view but one which forced everyone into quite definite conditions. Obviously the division of powers which followed in the meanwhile cannot be reversed any more; but even the worker of the machine age can be filled with creative pride if he, on the one hand, grows with his trade, and on the other, receives private property which he can build up according to his will and powers. So long as the worker is not bound to the soil by private property, so long as he moves rootless from one work to another, feels no connection between the prosperity of the entire economy and his personal welfare, so long one cannot speak of a redemption from the class situation.

What are the practical ways to bring the worker to property and an inner share in the enterprise, to the affirmation of his position in life? Two chief directions can be distinguished: one which wishes to make the worker merely a possessor without any consideration of his professional position: and next that which would like to order anew the relation of the worker to the work-giving capital. Both efforts wish to grant the worker the currently lacking security of his existence in some way. Ernst Horneffer[118] has correctly recognized the spiritual side of the workers' question when he says that the result of the life work must be bound immediately to the works and creations arising from this life work. This binding should, according to him, result in the form of work shares. The choice of this means does not seem fortunate. The work share is wrecked by the simple fact that financial value, on which the share is otherwise placed, is a certain quantity, not a work performance. A co-possession by way of work performance contradicts the essence of property, which should be transferable, inheritable, etc. But what happens with the work share, if the worker leaves the trade or must be dismissed? What, if the business collapses? One can also hardly imagine the general assembly of a share-society (a system to be understood only capitalistically) in which 5000 workers appear: but Horneffer demands precisely the immediately active participation of the worker in the administration of the work. This, however, does not lie with the general assembly, which mostly represents merely a well-clad theatrical show. It is somewhat different with the representation rights in the board of trustees. Now, already today the works council is represented in the board of trustees, with what success it is better left unsaid. In this respect, the idea of the otherwise very reasonable works council has gone astray. All attempts with regard to the participation of the working class in the leadership of the business are wrecked by the fact that the reformers, just as in the political field, ignore the double nature of the economic organisation. Even it reveals masterly and comradely elements. One, therefore, who speaks of economic democracy[119] - which moreover is glorified too unjustly as

---

[118] *Die große Wunde*, München, Verlag Oldenbourg, 1922.

[119] Along with the professional democracy, by economic democracy is mostly understood the

"anticapitalistic" - should have first become clear of where the limits of comradeliness lie. The democratisation of the business leadership is a nonsense; it contradicts the actual law of economics, that of thrift. For, every democratisation leads to a centralistic bureaucracy and to a point where the business no longer serves, in general, production, but the person occupied in it. Such a position however makes the one occupied in it occupationless. It is also a delusory hope to be able to reanimate through democratisation of the business that work which has through modern technology become irredeemable. That happens only, as Bente argues, if "the life-related activity" of the worker is once again animated, and not the thing-related one. Bente considers this as possible if the centralistic-bureaucratic organisation is replaced by the organic, in which the creative activity upto now concentrated in the centre is extended to the entire circle of persons involved in it. By this joy of work and consciousness of responsibility should be awakened again, if the business should once again become a nursery for leaders.

The reflections which Bott-Bodenhausen has brought forward should grant a still deeper insight into the nature of business. Starting from the double nature of work (the activity of earning a living - service activity) also ascertains a two-fold essence of business: an economic and a total serving one. As an economic undertaking, it is organised in a masterly manner; as a service centre, in a comradely one. From this knowledge results the erroneousness of all strivings which wish to replace the "monarchy" of the enterpreneur with the democracy of the working class. In a certain sense, a business is even both at the same time. Even the concept of property in the business experiences a doubling in the functional legal idea of Bott-Bodenhausen: in an economic aspect "the enterprise is the private property of the entrepreneur. It is otherwise in the service aspect. In the latter, the business is capable of a binding which excludes the arbitrariness of property with respect to social politics. This binding occurs through the making

collectivisation of capital, a new word for concealed socialisation. Instead of the private entrepreneur enters increasingly the public one, worsening the work revenue and therewith the wages.

independent of the management right with regard to the economic components of the enterprise; for, the social political significance depends not on things, but on the manner of their use. - In respect of the social service right, thus, the business becomes the property (service property) of the business comrades and is subject to the order of service right". There is thus in the new right a bound and a free property. These are different degrees of right. What however is attempted social politically in order to bind the property is not an inner new obligation of property but an attack on the free property. To that belongs the establishment of the wages through political organs, whereas, at the same time, the raising of sums of wages remains left to the free property. This is a natural mortal sin against the law of cfficicncy. The idea of service, which even Bente recognizes as the essential point of an organic economics, demands the exactly opposite position. The service position of the worker also obliges him to the consideration, how he can further the growth of the work and raise the revenues of the business. For, his salary level depends on it. The profit-zealous entrepreneur and worker - that is what they both are today - must turn into service-zealous ones. This binding is accomplished, according to Bente, not really from unselfishness or from some heightened "social feeling", but from the same economic consideration that the advantage of the individual is guaranteed only by that of the whole. The idea of the whole thus operates even in the punctual observation of the law of economics.

The new development of law is concerned with finding a form of gradual division into the field of pure entrepreneurial activity (leadership of business and technological concerns) and the social field. The latter comprehends all relations which arise from the necessary combined effect of capital and work, of matter and man. All institutions which rise to life in this field are of a comradely sort. They are basically to be built up on business and then to be incorporated into a net of associations. Not, as upto now, to be organized horizontally, whereby a local organisation resulted subsequently. Everywhere, however, the worker has to bear the full responsiblity, since nothing must be warned of more urgently than the distribution of rights against which no performance obligation stands. The service rights ordering of the business conditions the fully authorized participation of the worker in all means which the economy allocates for social goals. Indeed, in a logical construction of the so-called leadership of scientific business which, according to the latest researches, can reach a great precision of calculation, it would not at all be unthinkable that the measurement of the salary expense of a business is undertaken in the closest and most peaceful co-operation with the staff. At the moment, this may seem removed from reality, but the actual condtions for it are not very far any longer. For, if the workers' representatives did not know that, at a certain point, the extreme limit is reached, then their demands would have no end. Even today already many entrepreneurs make clear the situation of their business to the employees during salary negotiations. If, thereby, it is taken into consideration that, through the increasing depersonalisation of capital, the entrepreneur negotiating with the workers is in most cases himself an employee, the consideration cannot be rejected that both together maintain a common position with regard to the capital.

In the public today, a battle rages around two catchwords: around the apparent opposition: work community or trade union. It has been mentioned here clearly from the start; but it is still worth a brief investigation how it could arise. Some say the business is the true cell of the economy, the entrepreneur the given leader of his business workers: the worker has to find his social home in the business, the business must therefore be responsible for the safeguarding of the worker. It is also the cell of an economic autonomy that is to be built up. The work conditions are dependent on the way of production, and the latter is different for every business (work period). Only in the business is the differentiation between value- and mass-performance, between competent and incompetent, between industrious and lax working force, to be carried out. Therefore, the standard of a correctly ranked pay can be found only in the individual work. The price monopoly movement which does not employ the performance capacity of a good business and artificially demands the existence of a badly conducted one has found its counterpart in the workers' mass movement which has practically formed protective associations for the inferiour. For, the standard wages did not take into consideration the good performance but nurtured a bad mediocrity. The worker capable of performance is suppressed, the creative power and the powerful impetus of personality get increasingly bogged down. The quality work regresses; already today America surpasses the German nation substantially. If the business does not attain its right, the equalisation destroys every progress. Through the association of the employees outside the business, natural unities are destroyed. The pay contract lies in the hands of the reciprocal interest-representatives and are concluded outside the business. Work community means the "legal organisation" (W. Kupsch) of entrepreneur, employee, and workers of a business. Today, every organic binding between the entrepreneur and his workers is lacking.

To this it is countered from the trades union side, even insofar as it is economically peaceful: Even we would have nothing to find fault with in an economically peaceful constitution if the security existed that such a one would be really observed and the worker not disadvantaged. History has in the meanwhile demonstrated that the worker, isolated, falls prey to exploitation. That he can preserve himself from this fate through the formation of a "work cartel". Against the sole rule of capital the power of work is to be set up; only through association would such a one arise, can the workers aim at sufficient salaries. Only the pressure of the trades unions guarantees a tolerable social legislation and only the uniform regulation of the salaries can prevent wage-reduction by the employer who naturally has a more favorable position. His position is more favorable because, in the concluding of work contracts, a single personality which disposes of the capital stands against a plurality of unemployed persons. Finally, the trades union has a further moral significance: it guarantees the worker spiritual support, incorporates him into a community and in this way prevents anarchy. The work community strives for the smashing of trades unions, and destroys thereby the power of the working class and throws it back irredeemably into serfdom.

These are approximately the arguments which both camps maintain against each other. What now is the kernel of truth at present? The business or work community has for itself a natural growth. It is actually the natural work community, it alone guarantees efficiency and possesses even today life, insofar as pure economic laws rule. Only, it is deprived of soul. It has lost all social, that is, in fact, all spiritual, relations, the human collaboration is limited almost solely to the techonological. The regulation of the social questions was actually shifted outside the business. Thereby the personality worth, the driving force of economic life, was reduced and the production of goods impaired. No doubt that the followers of the work community are right when they see in the mechanical associations of the employers and employees the growth of individualism which reveals once again here its personality-killing effect. But, on the other hand, the association of working masses was necessary. It will remain so until the new economic character has prevailed, until the power battles between capital and work are basically ended and place has been made for a legal regulation of the economic life. It must also be borne in mind that the trades unions represent in part cells of professional associations, that they too can be carried over into an organic life. If, from the present lawlessness, an economic constitution created from the forces of the society and supervised by the state will arise, then the realisation of the work community beckons in the far distance. The author therefore sees no exclusive opposition between the idea of the trades union and that of the work community, even if today a broad gap still exists. Actually it was even attempted to link the two together: in the work council law, which, to be sure, forms a wrong and weak beginning. That, in a perfectly satisfied economy, the in many respects unnatural opposition between employer and employee will be removed hovers as the last goal of every reformer. Perhaps then workers' associations in the present form will become superfluous, especially if closed professional orders have accomplished the incorporation of the "working class" into society. Until that time, however, there must be forces which keep alert the idea of society and combat for its formation. The empoyer-hostility of the present-day trades unions - already strongly moderated, besides - still betrays the utopian idea of Marxism. But the experiences from Owen to the German state Socialism and to the Russian Communism did not pass tracelessly over the German worker. A gradual transposition will take place.

The most excellent goal of our age remains to attain, through legal regulation, economic peace. Borne by the new economic character, the leaders of both parties must find the way to each other, and set up the basic rules of the new order together. It would be the business of the coming national chamber of professional orders to give this idea its legal form. One who is convinced of the necessity of service as the expression of laws of organic life sees the path free to supplement the economic right of the present with the service right of the future. The creative powers of entrepreneur and worker must meet each other in the future autonomous economy in the effort to cure the existing false law with all its harmful consequences through a new law.

A special task remains, of course, reserved to the German entrepreneur. It synchronizes to a certain degree with the process which rules the hour under the catchword of "rationalising". What does one understand by rationalising? Some (Sombart) translate this word by spiritualisation, others by intellectualisation. The goal of rationalisation is the saving of forces, is the greatest possible approximation to the economic law, of obtaining the highest performance with the smallest means.

Practically, this means that every business conducts its own business politics, that, instead of the enormous equalisation through pay regulation, price-standardisation, social legislation, etc., there enters the living power of the individual business which attempts to obtain the highest performance through refinement of the methods in all fields. There begins, in other words, a new epoch of entrepreneurship, which had assumed all-too firm forms in the period from

1890-1920. Perhaps already at that time the entrepreneur built up his business as much as possible, and thoroughly organised it, created voluntary standard social institutions, improved the hygiene and attempted with all means to bind the worker to the business and to establish a spiritual-moral bond. What the entrepreneur undertook then and in the meanwhile brought to consolidation is basically already the perfect work community, only with the deplorable mistake attached that it did not operate as such psychologically. The horizontal organisational movement came in between and produced that business-hostile association which cut all the strings between the entrepreneur and his staff. The entrepreneur can remedy this mistake if he declares his allegiance to that second period of entrepreneurial development which began with the American example. Here unsuspected possibilities lie latent of breaking through equalisation and depersonalisation. Why should a new personnel policy not be introduced which takes over the American methods of the enlistment and examination of working forces, of the distribution of work, of training, of advancement, of professional guidance, etc.? Who prevents the entrepreneur from taking care of the individual worker and doing justice to his individuality? One may think of Ford's method, which selected the worker desirous of advancement and made thereby the surprising experience that most did not want to leave the mechanical work at all. What he therewith attained was the removal of the obligatory idea that no possibilities of advancement are granted to the industrial worker. Today, even in economics, the system of certification begins to effect its evil influence. Nobody prevents the German entrepreneur from throwing this bureaucratic means of selection on the scrap-heap and of introducing economic forms of the examination system, new standards for advancement. A skilled business policy can come upon not only an effective selection, but also measures for binding this selected nucleus of workers to the business. Here a "New Objectivism"[120] is really possible which

---

[120] [Jung is playing on the fashionable term for the latest style in the fine arts; see Part III, in Vol.I of this edition].

brings the law of thrift, of performance and of personality once again into validity. Here the system of the horizontal organisation of our entire economy has a gap through which the entrepreneur can push forward and clear away the equalisation. How easily could such a business community become imperceptibly vital without encountering the resistances to which a clumsy work community propaganda is always exposed. Certainly, the trades unions will prepare many difficulties, they will however in the end, settle with the creative new entrepreneur-type, because the individual staff members affirm him. The experiences which one has had in the introduction of performance wages justify this hope. The indispensable prerequirement is, however, the genuine entrepreneur and not the bureaucratic employee of high finance.

Thus it is brought about that the rationalisation of the economy is not really a progress on mechanistic paths, but the deliberate attempt to initiate life in its rights even in economics. Nothing is more natural than the demand that the working force be not treated as a ware but appointed, developed and evaluated according to their human individuality. There is even a psychology of the work-process which is to be placed in the service of economics. It is mechanistically thought out to treat the work force as a number and to entrust it merely arbitrarily with a partial process of the production; it is lifeless to distribute the work in any other way but according to the natural sequence as it exists in the system of men and of things. What has been accomplished in this field in the last years by individual German entrepreneurs justifies bold hopes.

The technological mechanisation contradicts in no way the demand of organic business leadership. Obviously, the work at the conveyor belt and at special machines cannot be animated. Machine work is by nature mechanical. The worker knows that, in the highest division of labour, he can attend to only a partial process of the production. If he is unclear to himself of this fact, then it must be made comprehensible to him through work instruction what work he labours at. But the division of labour itself can be never spared him. In it, as in a purely technical necessity, also lies, in no way, the danger of soul-deprivation. It is not right that the machine must necessarily deprive man of soul; never will this be the case so long as man remains the master of the machine. If he is aware that he is the master of the machine and that it has the task of facilitating human work, then it can indeed promote ensoulment. In the specialised field of economics, thus, the mechanical rationalisation, mechanisation, can be carried out to the highest level. Decisive is the fact that the human organisatory field of the entrepreneur does not experience through bureaucratisation any depersonalisation. If the ordinance overpowers the living man, then only is the work mechanised. But in and for itself mechanical work does not by far need to make men lifeless.

If all the currents of the age point to the development of a new business community, conducted by the value-creating personality, then the ways must be found to set up the worker outside the business on a new self-responsibility. This is possible only through the workers' acquisition of property, which would facilitate the increased wages consequent on increased efficiency. They will set him in the position to make savings. Upto now, this was impossible because all that the worker could have saved was consumed by social insurance. If the insurance system is led back to the healthy proportion, and performance wages have gained acceptance, then the savings activity of the worker can begin. Does this mean that he should become a capitalist? All attempts with small shares suffered upto now from the lack of capital of the working class. But the question must be raised whether, in the age of depersonalisation of capital, the share in general represents an appropriate form of workers' property. Should the worker appear in the general assembly and debate with lawyers about the balance sheet? If, on the other hand, he lets himself be represented capitalistically by large organisations, for example trades unions, his interest in economics may be hardly less than that of any capitalist who buys shares in the stock-exchange without knowing where the business in question lies.

The financial income does not make one contented, but a property which revives the healthy feeling of mastery and the joy in property which slumbers in every man does. It must, in the final analysis, be suited to make the individual free and independent. It must set him in the situation to pluck and reap the fruits of his work himself. There is only one form of property which fulfils all these conditions: landed property. Böhmer[121] is therefore logical in his conclusions when he wishes to eliminate the disinheritance of the working masses through independent landed property. One may give the worker a little house with some garden and farm land, perhaps even a small car, and he will once again strike roots into the nation and the society. Homes with his own land for spade-culture transpose him into the situation to live freely and to derive a great part of his food from his own soil. The gnawing worry about the livelihood is softened. The masses of unpropertied people will be freed from the "wage enslavement". Without every radicalism, then, the worker stands self-conscious before the entrepreneur. He can still, as the possessor of a home, put aside much more from his pay than before and, in this way, look forward confidently to a worry-free old age. Böhmer has penetratingly described the raising of the means for the great workers' settlement. The author knows that the complaint of being utopian is made against the plans of Böhmer. It may be that the form of his presentation and the harshness of many conclusions arouse this impression. But one never forgets that it is a question, in programmatic work of such sort, always of long-range objectives. One does not see why the construction of houses should not diverge from the barrack-style[122] and pass over to homes, why in the course of the decades a systematic deurbanisation, the transplantation of factories to the flat land, should not result. It is always only a matter of the spirit in which things are practically effected. And this is the reason perhaps of the goals of the work of Böhmer, that a great goal should set in for German social politics.

Even the one who cherishes serious doubts against such plans on account

---

[121] [See p.96n. above].

[122] [i.e. of flats].

of the dearth of capital in Germany may become clear to himself that a great part of the social expenses which are made wastefully today are to be spent productively. That the present-day co-operative house could be incorporated into the great settlement programme, that, finally, the working force of the unemployed which lies fallow could find profitable application. Through the raising of soil revenues and reduced imports, the national wealth and therewith the fiscal strength would be raised. It must also be thought of how the public administration could be forced to savings for the great social work.

All efforts to resolve the social question must culminate in the demand of making as many German men possessors of landed property. Already, the necessity of putting a stop to the increasing ground-depreciation reminds one of this. One can object to this plan - moreover, a very undemocratic objection - that the demands on the thrift of a stratum living on very small means cannot be overstretched. If one places the worker too much on himself, then unsuccessful plans are inevitable and the commonality must indeed shrink. Obviously there is need of education even in this field. A stratum which was for generations unpropertied does not learn overnight to save. But, vice-versa, the idea that an income must come from somewhere to every German should not proliferate further in the present measure.

No people can afford in the long run that considerable parts of it feel excluded from the blessings of life. Whether this feeling has no justification or not means little in view of its serious consequences for the spiritual health of the state and the people. This circumstance was recognized already before the war, after the war it was, to a certain degree, a basic law of German politics. What today is accomplished in the field of social politics does honour, therefore, to the German feeling. But how it is accomplished goes against all reason. One wished to protect the valuable and has destroyed it. To perceive this and to draw the conclusion that precisely opposite paths have to be entered on in order to banish the evil is the order of the hour. Nowhere has the individualistic basic attitude become so disastrous as in the field of economics and of social politics. From this direction threatens proletarianisation and, therewith, the downfall of the German people. The new feeling of worth shows us the saving path. It must be entered with courage in order to make the worker a valuable member of the German nation.

IV

Organic economics

Only where man remains the measure of all things is organic economics possible. One who would like to read into this sentence a confession of an individualistic world-view has not yet comprehended that individualism destroys the personality. That it rather makes objects and forms masters of life. This superiority of objects, especially of money, was recognized as the essential character of the individualistic capitalism, of the materialistic economy. It is that degenerate economic form in which the greed for income disregards all laws of organic economics, indeed that of efficiency. For the business sense and striving for productiveness are two different things.

Money has its inner significance only as a legal amount which operates vitally in a community. It establishes a value relation, is the sign of value and a measure of price. If it makes itself independent and reifies itself establishing the false independent value of capital, then it does not serve the production of goods and the satisfaction of needs, and, in the final analysis, also men, any longer, but it makes everything subject to itself. The quality of the object is replaced by the quantitative concept of money. No longer is the real value the centre of business dealings, but the acquisition of a certain amount of money. The productive powers

in which already Friedrich List[123] recognized the real wealth of a people are
neglected or indeed choked. Everything turns on money, which turns from a
symbol of value to the sole valid expression of value. It fulfils no function any
longer, but becomes a "thing in itself", producing numerous functions which stand
beyond the vital life. The founding of its own value is facilitated by the gold
backing. One of the products present in throughout the world, namely gold, first
makes possible the rise of that which once calls international capital. The
functional character of money would be much better expressed through an
"artificial currency" which is not built on precious metals. The purely artificial
currency would found once again the relations to the real life values and in this
way create the prerequirements under which the production of goods can once
again become the centre of the economy instead of money. The stabilized
mark[124] means therefore for modern economic history infinitely much. It is still
the living proof for the fact that - separated from gold - healthy money can arise
only from the foundation of real economic value. The victory of nominalism is,
accordingly, the final advance into organic thought. It would have to end the
capitalistic enslavement of the nations, because an international artificial currency
is for the time being unimaginable. For there is no currency without sovereignty,
therefore no world currency without a world state. We know only one world ware,
gold. Currency is always the expression of politicality. If in Germany the currency
bank (Reichsbank) is a private undertaking, and the political infringements were
to a large extent withdrawn, then it is in no way said thereby that in the Reich a
sort of private currency is valid. Even the notes of the Reichsbank derive their
validity from the national law, the sovereignty of the currency is to be transferred

---

[123] [Friedrich List (1789-1846), the economist, worked in Germany as well as in America, and
propagated the idea of the Zollverein or customs union in the 1840's. His economic theories are to be
found in his several influential writings including *Das Wesen und der Wert einer nationalen
Gewerbsproducktivkraft*, Berlin: Weltgeist Bücher, 1839; *Das nationale System der politischen
Ökonomie*, Stuttgart: J.G. Cotta, 1844].

[124] i.e. the mark based on land values.

only to a certain degree. If a partial separation of the currency sovereignty from the state has taken place with us, here - along with foreign political causes (London Convention) - even legal reasons were decisive: the state had been responsible for the far-reaching financial depreciation and committed misuse with the currency law. The separation of which from the Reich is, accordingly, a victory of the law over the state which had disregarded the law.

The efforts of many nominalists to abolish interest are perphas utopian in the age of credit economy. Nevertheless, their hostility to interest reveals that deep insight into the real essence of money, which already made Aristotle and Martin Luther take a position against the receipt of interests and business. Certainly, the future development will accelerate the knowledge that money possesses its decisive significance not as an objective power but as a serving instrument. Nominalism will set in so much the faster, the more gold is monopolised; it would have reached its goal the moment the bank vaults of America have swallowed the last bars of the earth's gold supply. Today the United States are forced to pump their gold treasury with all means into the "world economy" in order to devaluate it. The economic imperialism of America is based most deeply on the necessity to maintain with political means of power the international position of gold. The gold-producing and gold-possessing countries are thereby on the offensive, those poor in gold on the defensive. Their only weapon of escaping from the international financial rule is the transition to artificial currency and to autarchy.

The making independent of the money borne by gold has created an unbridgeable opposition between capital and economy. The economy is based on the organic foundations of life: blood and soil, man and nature. Organic economics is the production of goods from these two basic factors. It is self-sufficient and itself produces the capital which presses to and is used by new value-creating institutions. In recent times, as an example of organic economic formation, the enterprise of Ford is often brought forward, because it has existed since its origin almost without foreign money. It developed from the smallest beginnings and by itself produced the gigantic structure of necessary capital. The Ford factories obviously represent an ideal case. Ford worked under favorable conditions: in a country which had disposal of all raw materials, under the protection of high customs, by complete overcoming of the opposition, in a production field which was in the process of a natural rise through the increasing motorising of traffic; but, finally, under circumstances which one can characterise as "war profiteering". One, however, who always points to Ford forgets that the pre-war period in Germany knew the same organic development process. Even the German industry grew from its own power, produced the capital necessary for its structure and created much more bank capital than it, in turn, required. Capital, in the national economic sense, can arise only through work; and an economy which forms capital is therefore healthy. If, on the other hand, it lives continuously on loan capital, it is sick, even if bloodlessness can temporarily produce this condition. The German economy finds itself at present in this situation. The numerous consequences of the war and the financial devaluation have led to its bleeding; the false social and fiscal politics, the state Socialism of the present-day financial democracy, prevent the formation of new blood corpuscles (new formation of capital), the burdening of the German economy by tax payment and foreign credit reduces the profit dividend in a measure which makes reserves almost impossible. One can speak of an alliance of the present-day state with the international finance capital directed against the German economy.

Work is always attached to the soil, to farming and business. The entrepreneur develops this wealth and builds up the production. He does not need profit, or not to the last portion, but sets it up anew in the production. At this level of the development, possessor and entrepreneur are one, capital and means of production coincide with each other. Later begins the separation between capital and entrepreneurship, benefitted by the modern form of business society, especially by the creation of bearer shares. The capitalistic side of the enterprise separates itself increasingly from the economic and gradually forms its own realm.

Just as money makes itself independent, so capital depersonalises itself. If it is collected together, it is not any longer in the hands of the possessor but in those of the person disposing of it. It becomes anonymous, one hardly knows any more to whom it belongs, indeed the owner does not worry at all about what happens to it; he is content if it brings in revenue. All soil- and work-values are, to a certain degree, disintegrated in mobile capital. The national work is, as Spengler terms this, buried under. For "a mobile wealth which can be transferred in a moment through a telegram from Berlin to New York is no longer national. It has detached itself from the soil, it hovers in the air, it is an intangible amount. And if the development in this direction proceeds to the end so that in the large economic fields even the last portions of national wealth are detached from things, then a form of economics is attained which quickly consumes even the currency of the strongest nations. Already today the predominant part of the Germans, English, and Americans, from the entrepreneur to the occasional worker, work for men whom they do not know and who relieve one another unnoticed".[125]

In this way has arisen an artificial, but independent realm filled with enormously effective life: that of international capital. Man and nature are for it only means to the end; they serve the production of financial gain. Therewith the natural order is reversed, life disregarded, the soil made ready for slavery and also - revolution. This realm of capital encompasses the world. It really does not belong to economics; it only uses the individual national economies in order to enslave the life of states, of peoples, and of cultures. Politics becomes a business, war a battle of competition, world-view means of propaganda. Here the emotional opposition against capital comes into action perceptibly in all nations. Upto now capital understood to falsify this tendency into a hostility to economics, in order to remain the laughing third person. The working masses of many nations, especially of Germany, have become unshakeable storming-parties of capital

---

[125] Oswald Spengler, *Politische Pflichten der deutschen Jugend*, München, Verlag Beck [in *Politische Schriften*, München: C.H. Beck, 1932, p.140f].

through Socialism and give a helping hand to it, where it also mobilises and destroys the national values. In this way the international capital becomes a tragically fateful power, a frightful enemy of genuine life.

The opposition between national work and international capital is closely connected with another which was treated at greater length above: between the soil-grown cultures and the Jewry.[126] Certainly, there are numerous Jews who dedicate their powers to the national economy. Certainly, they are in general far from the intention of consciously working for the destruction of the soil-related economy. Nevertheless, it cannot be denied that Jewish and German conceptions even in the economic field strive for different goals. For the Jew there is really a world economy, for, the members of the Jewish people live scattered over the earth; their marked racial consciousness thus provides something like the idea of an economic world state. Economics is therefore for them the platform on which they can give shaped form to their racial longing. Thus the famous saying of Rathenau, "economics is destiny" becomes understandable. Civilisation and world trade, mobile capital and international capital investment, mastery of the states and peoples through capital form the natural life-foundation of a people scattered through the entire world which combines with high abilities a marked will to power. With the illusion of world economy, however, falls also the outstanding position of the Jewry; its destiny is therefore economics.

It can be left out of investigation why the Jews chose business and the system of finance as their most characteristic field of activity. Many explain this fact by the legislation of feudalism, others (Sombart) from the blood-related disposition. For the present, this strife is futile. Decisive remains the circumstance that, in the modern economy, business predominates. This business economics is the presupposition of the Jewish supremacy. In turn, this cardinal point of its disposition has been so clearly recognized by the Jewry that it attempts to pervade

---

[126] [cf. in this connection, Werner Sombart, *Die Juden und das Wirtschaftsleben*, Leipzig, 1911].

the individual national economies with business characteristics. It can therefore be hardly denied that the conflict between the German and Jewish world-view, which will be accomplished fatefully, finds even in the economic life an effect, to a certain degree an arena of a parallel war.

The post-war period stands under the sign of the opposition between economy and bank capital. Obviously, this opposition is only conditionally possible with many reservations and under acknowledgement of very complicated economic processes. Upto now the battle - thanks to the bloodlessness of the economy - ended with the victory of the banks. In order to reveal the difficulty of the problem, it must however be pointed to the fact that even the bank system represents in no way a closed, uniform power. The economy slaves today not only for the private bank capital but also for the state capitalism, which has established an extensive bank system in the form of public banks and savings-banks. Powerful capitals which are withdrawn from the economy flow into these enterprises which, for their part, conduct, with the accumulated monies, in no way economic politics but mostly something else which is not determinable without further discussion. It is a question thereby of a mixture of political, social, communal, and party politics. In any case, the investment of the public capitals occurs not, as it should, according to economic view-points. For, the disposers of these monies are mostly bureaucrats of different stamp: beginning with the trades union officials upto the ministerial councillor. Especially dangerous does this sort of financial economics become through the fact that it sucks up a considerable part of the foreign loans, which are in no way conducted to a really productive use.

The receipt of foreign loans is justified only when it immediately furthers the formation of one's own capital, an idea which Hans Luther[127] rightly brings up repeatedly. The importation of foreign capital should combat the poverty of blood of the German economy, should stimulate production and the formation of

---

[127] *Von Deutschlands eigener Kraft[: Versuch einer gemeinverständlicher Darstellung unserer Lage in der Weltwirtschaft]*, Berlin, 1928.

one's own capital. If the interest burden of the German economy reaches a height at which the formation of one's own capital is no longer possible, or if foreign capitals are not at all invested "as a boost", the foreign debt amounts to the lasting loss of the German national wealth, and therewith actually to the enslavement of the German work. The much contested acceptance of foreign capital can naturally be considered from different points of view. One emphasizes the danger of infiltration of foreign goods, the other sees precisely in the bringing in of foreign monies the guarantee of international co-operation, indeed of the fact that Germany is no longer politically isolated as before the war. Thus it is designated by very clever people as a mistake of pre-war politics that the Reich had not attached the American interests to its own through the acceptance of loans. Obviously, this was impossible, because, before the war, Germany was a capital exporting country, whereas, on the contrary, America had still to pay its debts. The opinion of Hans Luther, that the foreign money-providers are not interested in a Germany reduced to poverty and over-burdened, but in one becoming increasingly healthier through the formation of its own capital, is a correct circumlocution for the fact that investment-seeking money strives for the highest possible interest and the greatest possible security. But it should not be forgotten that not only financial capital but also industrial capital flowed from America into Germany. Whether, herewith, pure investment aims and a blooming of the Germany economy were striven for is, however, doubtful. Rather, this capital seems for a good part to be destined to make the German competition harmless, which always amounts to the weakening of the national work and of the German national wealth. From this point of view are even the foreign participations in the German industry to be judged, because here the danger exists more strongly than in the loan politics, of losing the mastery of the German production apparatus. Indeed one brings up even in such cases the common entrepreneurial interests and therefore considers the immediate participation as more advantageous than the expense of debt bonds. On the other hand, one must always question why the foreigner participates in the German industry; in view of the American economic imperialism one could tend to the opinion that, between the latter and the participation in the German industry there exists an immediate connection. That would mean, however, that the American political economy would like to bring the German entirely or partially under its dominion. Even determined share-minorities can become dangerous to an enterprise. And, in the end, the fact is not to be eliminated from the world that the passing over of great share packages to America signifies practically, however, a loss in German national wealth which can be balanced only if the acceptance of foreign money stimulates one's own economy in such a way that a repurchase of the shares that have left the country is to be thought of. One, however, who would like to make the support a lasting phenomenon conducts a pump economy which has as its result the gradual destruction of the German national wealth, unless one stands in the revolutionary standpoint and says: Enterprises which lie on German soil remain always German, no matter to whom they belong. It may be that national revolutionary currents one day will oppose the blood to the international capital. For the time being, Germany cannot think of conducting such a desperate politics.

The foreign money can institute blessings in our economy if it serves the improvement of the production apparatus. But is the great creative reform which represents rationalisation basically thwarted by the increasing mastery of the economy on the part of the bank capital, the horizontal associations which mechanise everything and, finally, by the bureaucratising? It was however maintained quite often that the German cartellization (paragraph cartels and trades unions on the one side, consumer organisations on the other) is not, in the first place, an economic, but a purely capitalistic process. It serves more the safeguarding of the capital revenue (to be differentiated from the business profitableness) than the removal of all-too unlimited competition. The cartel economics reckons only with mass forces and excludes the entrepreneurial personality and the free economic will. The effort to bring the wares as much as possible without competition to the customers also choked the impulse to produce quality. The creative entrepreneurial power was impaired especially since the German cartel politics directed the prices according to the inefficiently working businesses, so that for the better working there existed no necessity of rationalisation. - The horizontal associations are children of need. Foreign political distress made a closed appearance of the entire German economic department as necessary as the horizontal mechanical associations of all working forces forced the employer associations through trades unions. Even business, as the chief customer of the creative economics, conducted the association system to the point of over-organisation. All buying and selling is regulated by association rates. It must therefore be established that the real impulse to the horizontal formation of economics has begun from the trades unions and from capital. Once again, the narrow relation of Marxism to finance capitalism is revealed. Both press together towards international cartellization, working against the new tendency towards autarchy. The creative economics stands between these two powers and defends its bare existence, wherefore it was forced similary to make use of the means of power of the mechanistic associations.

In this situation, the question regarding the future of economics becomes apparent. Some see in the thorough mass-oriented organisation of the entire economic life the way to economic democracy. It is practically a question here of Marxist thought processes. Accordingly, finance capital and trades unions dispose of the depersonalised economics together, bureaucratising and artificially regulating the economy. On the workers' side one hopes thereby for the hour when the collected capital, detached from the entrepreneur, could be socialised. For the economy itself, so non-Socialist economic scientists maintain, the circumstance of in whose hands the capital ruling the economy lies means little. "We will have to finally accustom ourselves to the idea that the difference between a stabilised and a regulated capitalism and a technologized and rationalized Socialism is not a great one, and that it is considerably indifferent therewith for the fate of men and their culture whether the economy is formed capitalistically or Socialistically. What is important is: the way of work is in both cases the same; in both cases the entire economy is based on the ground of intellectualisation. One may ask oneself, however, in what way a great comradely- and a capitalistic warehouse, a Communist- and a capitalist blast furnace factory, an urban- and a capitalistic tramway, are differnt from each other. -- Here the fate of mankind will decide: whether the most important component of the human activity, the economic activity, should belong to the realm of the soul or the realm of the intellect".[128]

Sombart's conception has something to say for it insofar as organic economics is always a co-operative one. Thereby it remains, as Ford also thinks, considerably unimportant who the owner of the creative capital is. Whether the administration of the means of production happens for the common good is more decisive than the property situation. Here, even the future development of the concept of property will be decisive. If property is once again felt as a duty and a fief, the individualistic and materialistic attitude of capital will disappear. It remains maintained however if the capital assumes collective forms, be it in a large capitalistic or a socialistic sense. For, at this point, the most important of all questions of the future becomes possible: whether the future will bring a reversal from the collectivistic and individualistic to the organic conception of economics. If the separation of the capital from the economy and therewith its rule over it makes progress, that necessary relation of service between the economy and the people will never again be establishable. The economy then may receive its final laws from inorganic forces which stand outside life. It would inwardly ossify, become entirely bureaucratic and therewith inefficient. It is however organic only when it is private economy. For, only through the economising personality, who is at the same time aware of his self and of the connectedness of his self to the

---

[128] Werner Sombart, in the October Heft, 1926, of the *Deutsche Rundschau*.

community does the necessary incorporation of the economy into the totality of life take place; only man can establish as the point of transition the connectedness between the economy and the people. For he alone can experience at the same time his self and the whole. The core question of the future is, accordingly, how the pure private economy can be maintained, but, on the other hand, how its individualistic attitude, conditioned by the mastery of money over the soul, can be overcome. It cannot be repeated often enough that private economy does not for a long time yet need to be an individualistic economy, as little as a capitalistic economy must lead to the rule of capital.

In a similar direction move the thought-processes of Bente[129] when he emphasizes, in opposition to Sombart, that the future of economics is perhaps capitalistic, but no longer individualistic, but total economic. Decisive for the future remains the circumstance that, instead of the individualistic economic character, the service character emerge. To be sure, the depersonalisation of capital cannot lead to making it an unconditional ruler over the economy. If, therefore, Bente maintains that it is the character of the future development that the depersonalised capital does not remain piled up once and for all in individual enterprises, but flows through the entire economy so that even the interest of the capitalists of certain businesses turns to and from the entire economy, that, further, the tendency of the stock-exchange as the expression of the total economic prosperity will become more important to it than the situation of individual entrepreneurs, then here an alternation is present: namely, between the laws according to which the capital moves and the national economic laws. The stock-exchange capital does not know anything about an organic economy, it has no relation to the community of the people and to the national economy. It works with assumed values which can daily fall or rise in billions. Through impulses which often have nothing to do with the economy any longer. What sort of service

[129] [see p.213n. above].

should dwell within the capital separated from the enterprise? Whom should it serve? Mankind? That would be an empty concept and a falsehood. It however always serves the striving for profit of the individual. The capitalistic service character, however, is only possible in the entrepreneur. If he makes the capital serviceable for the business, production and therewith the national economy. "Perhaps the direction of the class struggle will be thrown out from this. The struggle against the capitalists as the owners of capital becomes without question senseless to the extent that the capital becomes part of a depersonalised total apparatus and its profit is for the most part reinvested" (Bente).

If, therefore, everywhere associations result and are evaluated as signs of a new age, then it is important to distinguish whether they are in truth the final lengthening of the individualistic-collectivistic epoch, or they give expression actually to a new service character. The renewer of German life, however, must be able to explain what is mechanistic and what organic. In this way it may be established that all collective forms, all centralistic bureaucracies, all value-destroying associations, are to be combatted even in the economy. That, where the need of the age has nevertheless allowed such bonds to arise, the effort must exist to replace them with organic ones. This is only possible through the new business policy which creates the prerequirements of a future work community. Through gradual transformation of the pure pay trades-unions into professional orders. Through the limitation of the cartels to that measure which is definitely necessary for the maintenance of a powerful economy. Through the formation of those work communities identified above which unite the entrepreneur, employee, and worker, finally all the economic departments of a certain field which no longer serve collective mass interests but are adapted to the organic process of production. Through the reestablishment of the principle of the greatest efficiency. Finally, however, through the liberation of the creative economy from the purely financial capital.

But this independence can occur to the economy only when it is placed in the situation of forming its own capital. Today it is in such a way that finance capital and the worker have united to prevent the efficient capital formation. It is important to break up this union and indeed from the side of the business while the creative entrepreneur obtains his workers for the thriving of the business at any cost. The worker belongs to the economy and not on the side of money. The entrepreneur can combat capital only with his own capital, and this arises only through economic work in the business. However, the reformer must, in addition, seriously examine the question whether the present-day condition, that economic profits are obviously left to the international bank capital for further use, should be maintained. In the comradely movement one has comprehended that only a bank system of one's own guarantees the fruits of work. If the capitals employed in an economic department do not flow back into the latter, but are invested according to the particular laws of finance economics, the idea of self-help loses in this way its penetrating power. It becomes virtually a chief concern of the German economy that the capitals employed in it also remain in it. Certainly it brings the weakness of capital with it, that the greater part of the work profit is paid out in bank interests, be it to national or foreign banks. Here for the meantime there will be little to change. But in no way is it necessary that the enormous sums squeezed from the economy with the help of the tax screws and the social legislation, insofar as they look for investment once again, are lost to the economy. The denationalisation of the social insurance will make a change possible here. Basically, all monies of the economy should remain in it and only a balance of national and international monies result insofar as it is necessary. Accordingly, the following strucure of the bank system would be brought about: the greater part of the capital remains in the individual economic department and is invested anew therein. Surplus monies are supplied through a national economic bank to needy groups of the national economy. Finally, a bank system remains for international balance of payments. For the realisation of these plans the diverse beginnings are present. The comradely movement has recognized the basically correct, but so has industry. To be sure, too late, and today restricted by the emergency. That, however, the knowledge in this direction makes progress indicates the sharp battle position which an industrialist of intellectual wealth and the creative power of a Ford has assumed in opposition to the bank capital. He has recognized the powerful opposition between economy and finance capital as the pivot of modern economic development.

Capital can fructify like a beneficient rain; it can destroy like the roaring flood. It depends on man to make matter serviceable to himself, and to organise unleashed instincts. In the final analysis, therefore, the question of the future economic formation is whether a new type of economic man prepared for service is on the point of arising. This question can be answered in the affirmative. There are still creative entrepreneurs, there are still economists ready for responsibility, perhaps more than at the beginning of this century. Their powers, however, lie in chains today. The collectivism extending itself in many forms hinders their development. On the purely capitalistic side, however, the personality attached to the people does not triumph but the individual obliged to nobody and ready for no service. Thus the battle for an organic economic formation can be rendered in the formula: here the money-grabbing individual - there value-creating personality. If the idea of the whole, of service and of the people triumphs, then there will be once again a national economy. The phantom of individualistic capitalism will be avoided and the blessings of life enter in place of the all-ruling Mammon.

A false concept of freedom, a lack of inner connection, even in the economic field, have been responsible for an anarchy which is matched by life-killing collectivism. Here therefore the same process as in the realm of social, cultural, and political life. Even here, almost more than anywhere else, helps only: the freeing of the personality. Nowhere does the call for true freedom sound so penetratingly and so warningly as in economics.

V

Supraindividualistic economics

State and economics serve the people in an equal measure. The highest regulation of the popular life is incumbent on the state. The state as the highest order sees to it that the economy fulfils its office with regard to the people. If an economic system becomes a goal in itself, if the non-economic life of a people begins to overgrow or indeed denies service with regard to the people and subordinates itself to other masters, the state must then take action. The inner formation of the economy can thus become so erroneous that it no longer does justice to its task of support of the people, it can undergo such a weakening that the health of the people begins to suffer: at that time indeed has the hour of political bargaining struck. On the state, however, devolves the careful treatment of the economy and its being set in a relation to the non-economic life of the people. Economic policy can therefore not be conducted successfully without social- and population policy. On the other hand, it is wrong to make political decisions of any sort without a consideration of the economy, which however always guarantees the foundation of life. Thus social policy can, following its own goals without a relation or, indeed, in opposition to economic policy, operate fatally for the economy and therewith for the life of the national body.

The modern economic development strives for systematic arrangement. No term is more wrongly conceived than the concept systematic arrangement. Already in the formation of the term there is a source of error which constantly reveals itself in misunderstood interpretations. The expression 'system' is ambiguous: one can think of an arbitrary plan by virture of which artificial effects should be aimed at; of mechanical attacks on organic life, which always bring about disturbances. One can, however, also start from the fact that under all human activity there lies an organic systematic arrangement, that order is the spritual-intellectual basic law of all life. There is to this extent also a plan according to which the economy must operate, from which every deviation is harmful and life-destroying. An example. Every attack on the economy, whether it come from the side of thc finance capital or of Socialism, which eliminates the creative personality contradicts the higher systematic arrangement of the economy, its inner laws. Thus even the economy requires an order without which it must become stunted or degenerate. Systematic arrangement in this sense is, for example, present when wild excesses of underselling are cut off, when unprofitable businesses are suspended, or when a rationalisation of the work-method results. Here belongs especially the modern tendency of creating large enterprises which produce everything from raw products to refined ready-made wares, in order not to be dependent on trade and on the market. Thus business unities are created which enter the market only with their final product, and achieve in themselves the greatest measure of self-sufficiency. This so-called vertical association does not occur according to business points of view but for the purpose of systematic production.

A planned economic politics must however correspond to the inner systematisation of the economy. Both phenomena point to an internal but not an external connection. Indeed it is wrong to want to reach a "planned economy" for the sake of the state, through attacks on the economic life. But no state can give up influencing the production of goods according to a total plan which aims at the guaranteeing of the sustenance of the people. Even this plan is nothing artificial but included in the essence of national economy. The state must see to it that the health of the nation does not suffer, that the national body is powerful in its population policy, the spiritual capacities of the people are not blocked and the social peace remains maintained. Translated into the language of economic policy this means: every nation must strive for the highest measure of economic autarchy (self-support) if the foundation of its existence should not be threatened, especially in tumultuous or war times. At no time of recent history was the tendency towards self-support of the peoples more alive than today. It is understandable to everybody who has perceived the powerful danger which dependence on international finance capital means for a people. The German people must have experienced to its horror in the world war what dependence on foreign markets means. Post-war Germany has unfortunately drawn no lesson from it. Every economic politics which does not establish the necessary balance between industry and agriculture, between industrial export and internal market, but indulges in world-economic dreams sins against the German people not only politically but, as it will be shown later, even economically. It is no accident that one of the strongest exporters in the world, namely Ford[130], combats the overgrown foreign trade with the following words: "We must wish for each nation that it learn to support itself so far as possible. Instead of striving to see that the other nations are dependent on our industrial products, we must rather wish that every nation create its own industry and a culture based on a firm foundation". The world war, which for many years excluded Europe almost fully as an export land, benefitted the rise of overseas industries. This circumstance could however have taught our economic politicians that the earlier situation in which a few peoples provided all the others with industrial products is not reestablishable. Especially the machine industry must say to itself that it exports production machines only in order to finally sacrifice the export of ready-made wares. The considerations which Böhmer has

---

[130] Henry Ford, *My Life and Work*, [Garden City, N.Y.: Doubleday, Page and Co., 1922, Ch.XVII].

set forth lead to the same result. He argues that the so-called market politics, which England developed out of its special position as the then leading industrial power in the world, found its final expression in the world war. One of our best economic experts, the erstwhile Chancellor of the Reich, Hans Luther, has clothed this idea in the clear sentence that the world war was a powerful anti-dumping measure. According to Böhmer, however, the politics of the forcing of ware markets is an artificial one. The development which is conditioned by population policy proceeds to endow all developed countries with self-supporting industries. All attempts to restrict this impulse to self-support are nothing more but attacks on the life arena of the peoples. The market politics is therefore a marked capitalistic politics, a politics of the perpetuation of the lack of freedom. This sort of world economics is not a politics of reconciliation of nations but of force. The disinheritance of the proletariat is followed by the disinheritance of entire industrial nations in favour of farming nations. The reversal sets in when in the industrial countries unemployment assumes a permanent form. This consideration of Böhmer's is to be agreed with and similarly his conclusion that economic development strives once again for the self-support of the peoples. For supraindividualistic nations it is naturally much harder to attain this condition to secure for oneself in time an internal market which is so capable of assimilation that the unemployment is dispelled. Logically, therefore, even Böhmer develops the settlement plans already treated above.

If in this way the connection between economic, foreign, and population policy is made clear, the erroneousness of our present-day economic politics will become apparent. It does not place at the centre self-support on the foundation of a thriving economy, but dreams of the saving help through a capitalistic world economy. It weakens the internal market and prevents the formation of industrial capital of one's own: the decisive prerequirements of a healthy national economy.

In no way is a position thereby taken against the industrial export or the food import. No reasonable man denies the necessity of bringing in the necessary foreign exchange through export for the payment of imports. The German economic leaders even suddenly act under the pressure of maintaining the working masses in their existing situation. On the other hand, the exports cannot be choked at will, since it is based on reciprocality between two nations. But one must distinguish between the politics of the day - which there is also in the economic field - and the long-term political goal. Seen in this way, there can be no doubt that the control of the internal market must enter in place of the striving to raise the export at any cost; that, then, the self-production is to be raised in order to reduce the import; that, finally, an educational influencing of needs should take place which prevents the superfluous import. A real rise of exports - on account of the raising of reparations really a foreign political demand - is wrecked by the circumstance that two persons always belong to export: one who undertakes them and one who tolerates them in his market. This natural limit cannot be crossed, even if we reduced the price of our export wares to the point of economic self-destruction; then indeed anti-dumping measures would come in. Even Hans Luther brings in a series of weighty reasons for the fact that, on the export side, the German balance can hardly be bettered, that, on the contrary, the dangers which are manifested thereby within the German political economics becomes increasingly greater. If he sets a certain hope on the export of German quality goods, the provident economic politician must bring in the doubt whether the industries of other nations are not on the point of reaching a lead even in the field of quality goods which may make us ponder. The suppression of the creative personality in the German economy, from the entrepreneur to the skilled worker, the equalisation which our social politics is responsible for, the destruction of the working quality through standard wages, have placed such limits to the production of quality wares that the freely working foreign country (America) is already superiour in many departments.

The stability of our balance of payments will in the main be possible on the side of imports. That requires that the German nation control with all its powers its present-day lack of food. One seeks to realize the idea of the organic whole logically - as was explained above - within the economy through the fact that the private large enterprises secure their own raw material bases. It is enigmatic why the insight into this necessity is apparently lacking in the field of national economics. However, one knows that a powerful internal market is the prerequirement for exports. "The internal market is our economic dynastic power" (Luther). Nevertheless, post-war Germany, like England at one time, is on the point of abandoning its agriculture. The first goal of all German economic politics however must be the maintenance, where possible the strengthening, of the German agriculture. The social philosophical expositions of this work have now demonstrated that the present day social- and political form as such operates in a way destructive of farming. The author would therefore like in no way to conceal the opinion that through the continued existence of the present-day finance capitalistic, urban, parliamentary mass state, the downfall of farming is sealed. The question of farming is not to be dealt with in a pure economic political manner. Agriculture is not a profession, but an original form of human production which as such can never be evaluated capitalistically. Capitalistic income and agricultural profitability are two concepts which lie on different planes.

No other economic department projects so much into the field of the general national policy and population policy as agriculture does. Already for that reason it is wrong to leave it to its fate or to self-help. This is moreover made more serious by the fact that the combination of the financial system and of industry cannot correspond to a rectified process of an agricultural sort. For, in agriculture, it is a question of millions of individual businesses with different needs and diverse soil- and work-conditions which can never be standardised. A conduct of agriculture through a few leading heads is therefore excluded. Certainly, the encouraging way of the comradely system must be entered on more deliberately than before. Especially the market associations obtain, in view of the rising demand for agricultural proprietary articles, increased future significance.

Essentially, however, the state-help remains related to the structure of the agricultural credit system. The burdening of the agriculture is today too great, the exchange credit unsuited for agricultural relations. Agriculture is indeed not a business and the fact that "national economic productivity and private economic profitability do not coincide at present to a really considerable degree" cannot be denied. Indeed, one can go beyond this statement of Luther's and ask whether, in the age of finance capitalism, such an agreement is in general possible, whether we must not accustom ourselves to the idea of abandoning the use of the customary concept of capitalistic profit in general in agriculture. Obviously not profitability, the basis of all economics. Never should agriculture become the boarder of the state. - The experiences in colonial countries, especially in America, demonstrate that really only the large farm concern corresponds to capitalistic requirements. It is, however, often connected to an extensive economy which a thickly populated country cannot afford. With us rationalisation of agriculture means intensification. The small holding will perhaps be able to exist alongside the large holding. There should not be a "transfer of the soil to the best landlord" amongst us for popular political reasons. Latifundium[131] business has upto now not been received well by any nation for long. The technologisation of agriculture has still a great future, even if perhaps more in the chemical than in the mechanical field, even if more through basic training of the farmer than through mechanisation, which has its limits. The most important assistance, however, which can occur to agriculture exists in a favorable influencing of the market for agricultural products. What does the raising of the production help if the market leaves something to be desired! In this field we live in anarchy. Today, the international big business rules the German corn market. There are businesses which by themselves - established only for competition and profit - force an import of food on the German people. The same agricultural products are imported

[131] [related to large estates].

which are remarkably brought from the German internal market for export. The corn price is already established by the corn trade for the future harvest. All these are conditions which ruin every hope of the farmer and weaken the internal market to the utmost. The basic needs of a people become in this way the object of the most blatant speculation. On the other hand, combatting the corn monopoly is a two-edged weapon. Switzerland has had no good experiences with that. The pooling of the Canadian corn producer which has been brilliantly accepted by Canadian farming could serve as a model. To be sure, it is doubtful whether the German agriculture can build up from its own power such a corn trade organisation.

Luther evaluates the part of the food import which could be produced without a simultaneous decrease of other agricultural products in the German Reich at 1 1/2 billions. Mussolini's corn battle has shown what the deliberate will of a powerful economic politician can do. The corn production of Italy has been, in the last four years, even on a conservative calculation, increased by half; but apparently more. How do things stand with us? Whereas our rye production recedes, we introduce enormous amounts of wheat and do without any instructive measure with regard to the people in respect of its consumption. Therewith an important side of the future economic politics is touched on. Import prohibitions, since the German political economy is not conducted in a closed island (Luther), may represent a little useful means for the regulation of needs. It is also topsy-turvy to stare as if transfixed at the consumption of foreign luxury wares, which signifies relatively little for the passive side of the balance of payments, even if it works so painfully from an ethical point of view. Decisive remains the mistake of every economic educational politics with regard to the consumption of mass goods. Here food and textiles play the chief role; among food items, however, especially the luxury items. With increasing motorising, even the petrol- and oil-question becomes increasingly more urgent. The progresses in the coal utilization have in no way been able to reduce these import items. And yet the economically thinking man must question where the advantage lies which allegedly the German economy should experience through the hundreds of thousands of motor vehicles. Sober judges see, in the main, foreign cars which burn up foreign products for unnecessary trips - apart from the fact that they incidentally kill numerous men. One may stand helpless before this phenomenon; to the matter-of-fact observer, however, such determinations cannot be spared. In all these fields, a deliberate economic policy would have to be set up with a great training programme. The future economic politician will never see why a community should give up having an influence on the psychological regulation of needs instead of leaving it simply to the artificial stimuli of profit-seeking capital. There is also an education to national economic thought. Liberalism, however has, as everywhere, neglected the idea of education and in practice transplanted it only to the field of scientific education, where it worked in a community-destroying manner.

Forceful attacks on the economic life, especially monopolies, are not fruitful here. For these attack precisely economic departments which are ripe for this on the basis of firmly established needs. All attempts to regulate the economic life itself through influences on its inner organism have led to damages and failures. Where the need exists and even technology has reached a point of repose, a transition from the supply to the need economy will be possible in a modest measure. It is, to be sure, hard to say when a conclusion of technological development is present, when the need reveals firm outlines. But, nevertheless, there are such economic departments: not only in the field of the transportation system, of the water-, gas- and electricity supply, which are therefore indeed partly conducted in a community economical way, but also in the free economy. The need for coal or of food is not to be reckoned too severely; the increasing cartellization for the purpose of the markets proves this. It may be that a great part of the present-day cartel has no stability. The future will show whether a series of private monopolies arisen for the reason that in the concerned economic departments the highest degree of performance capacity has been reached, are not already organically ordered for production and the market.

In any case, it is time not to leave the regulation of need solely to the "business sense". A goal-clear economic politics can, without infringements into the internal economy, basically influence the entire national economic development. Industries which serve the necessary needs can be looked after, industries which work for artificially aroused needs suspended. In the case of the former, the need is approximately predeterminable, in the case of the latter, it depends on business skill. If such industries which owe their existence only to the competitive instinct have arisen at one time, then the opposition to them is usually crippled by the frightful apparition of threatening unemployment which could arise through suspension. Only the enterprises serving pleasure and luxury, the production of things that are national economically entirely superfluous, are strengthened in this way. Behind such objections lurks self-interest. Indeed, regularly, even the entrepreneur of such industries experiences the support of the workers, since the advantage is a common one. Thus the development of the exhibition system was not combatted by workers' parties because remunerating earnings arose thereby for the farmworker. This attitude of the workers is understandable, but does not change anything in the fact that instead of splendid exhibition halls dwellings would be built much more correctly, whereby workers and manual labour would have similarly benefitted from them. Every economic activity is to be examined on whether national economic need or pure capital politics represent their motivation. Obviously, both could run parallel. But that wrong economic policy, thought out to its grotesque end, leads to the fight for the treatment of mental patients because otherwise the wardens of the mental asylums would become breadless; leads to the burden of opium intoxication and cocaine-sniffing, because otherwise those occupied in this trade would lose their income. In this way, the interest of the whole which is national economically easily attainable through national economics is forgotten in favour of the personal advantage. When the railways conquered Europe, it was asked what should happen to horses and drivers; the predicted frightful consequences naturally did not appear. And if, for example, the film industry had not arisen, the national economy would have certainly found ways of supporting the men occupied today in it in another way. Everywhere that a superfluous need is artificially aroused, the justification of planned attacks on the part of the economic police cannot be contested. Next to the new order of the competitive franchise system, an increased carefulness of the legislator with regard to advertising provides the means for the removal of that outgrowth. Perhaps a transition to a pure need economy will be hardly possible. But it means still giving up the blessing which the healthy capitalism could spread, if the capital decides on the needs and not the consumer. Advertising reveals economic individualism at its high point. All attempts of its beneficiaries to point constantly to the need of propaganda cannot eradicate the national economic truth which runs: first bread, then cars; first homes and then radio sets; first necessary clothing and then silk stockings. The present-day consumption feeds on the purchasing power of the people and perpetuates poverty. Never must it be forgotten that the perfect solution of the social question is frugality. There is no greater lie of history than that frugality coincides with lower cultural levels. Precisely the original cultured peoples of the far East have crowned their culture with the education of the individual to limitation of needs.

In this way alone will even the capital formation be possible once again. Thrift is the foundation of all economics, not only of private individual economy, but also of the national economy. Certainly, the capital formation, without which neither industry can thrive nor agriculture be intensified, can be furthered even through rationalisation of the production: when one enlarges the margin of profits between production costs and sale prices. The profits arisen in this way can immediately benefit the production apparatus. But even the raising of wages, the enlarging of incomes, can lead to capital formation, if thereby the consumption, especially of foreign imports and luxury goods, is not stimulated. If every income increase is totally consumed, the prices must in the long run rise, because indeed no raised productivity stands against the over-consumption. Perhaps people are saving once again today, but too little. In the individual household the consumption has, in comparison with the pre-war period, risen to a degree which cannot be explained by the usual experiences of financial depreciation alone. The search for luxury, a consequence of one-sided this-worldly affirmation, has grown. In this way does the individualistic intellectual attitude operate even disadvantageously for the economy. In addition, however, there is another form of squandering outside the individual human situation: the enormous expenditure of the public authorities. Nothing is more fatal for the savings undertaking than the economics with foreign monies. Practically, however, the expense economy of the authorities of all sorts represents nothing but a disposal of means purchased from others. Luther has summarised the basic idea of all healthy economy in the witty sentence that everyone has the right to make a fool of himself at his own cost, but only at his own cost. (The organic world-view must, besides, contest even this sentence from a popular political point of view). The rise of the savings undertaking is perhaps one of the foremost demands of an educational economic politics. That requires however that even the self-responsibilty for tasks of all sorts is established once again.

Along with the fiscal politics, of which more is to be said, the customs legislation remains as the chief weapon of the state for the influencing of the economic life. How seldom one thinks in terms of national economic ideas, how little the gaze of the individual camp goes towards the whole, is illustrated by the stubborn resistance which the party Socialism offers on almost all occasions against the tariff protection. One should, however, believe that the simple consideration of how harmful the import of food is for a national economy which can produce by itself may open one's eyes to the business interests which often conceal themselves behind the demand for free trade. Certainly, the question, free trade or tariff protection is not to be answered in favour of the one or the other in a way that is valid for all times and for all situations. It is established only that, not the adaptation of the market price to the world market price, but the stabilising of the national economy must be the goal of all tariff politics. Certainly, it is a high goal to manage without protective tariffs; perhaps to be realized when the individual national economies in themselves are stabilised. Unconditional protective tariff can weaken the economy, especially in departments which thereby obtain a monopoly situation. It can harm every forward effort. But, vice-versa, the protective tariff can even operate educatively. It raises the production and cheapens thereby the cost of living. "It is a supserstition that the protective tariff worsens the standard of life of the broad masses" (Funk). Upto now, no country has fallen through protective tariffs, but perhaps the English agriculture through free trade. Today, the tariff walls grow everywhere and no exhortations to free trade, no Geneva settlements, restrict this development. Every nation stands under the law of the movement of its population and must reach the highest possible self-support. For that reason, earlier agrarian nations which now build up their own industries protected their growth through protective tariffs. They could lay the foundations of this industry under conditions which operated more strongly than every tariff wall: in the world war. The powerful tendency towards self-support and, therewith, towards an organic economy of one's own which today - opposed to the world economical dreamers - pervades the entire world shows the direction of the future development and can teach us what the order of the day is: to protect the national work before holes are torn within its ranks which cannot be closed any more. The opposition between national economic productivity and private economic profitability in agriculture is even to be bridged only through protective tariffs.

Earlier there existed a public tariff-political conflict between industry and agriculture. In the age of market politics, it is understandable, even if the victory of free trade over the agriculture betrays a short-sightedness of the general English politics which avenges itself bitterly today. England had to conduct numerous wars as a result of its free trade politics. Already Goethe maintained, "War, trade, and piracy are three-in-one, and not to be separated". Germany has avoided that mistake, but is however apparently well in the process of repeating it. And, indeed, for the reason that the finance capitalistic and business powers have in the meanwhile undergone a considerable strengthening. On the other hand, the knowledge of the significance of the internal market has grown in industrial circles, especially among the key industries. Today no one sets up the equation: market equals market, no matter where it lies. One knows now that internal market always means strengthening, foreign market, however, an advantage for the national economy only under quite definite circumstances. This sign is encouraging. But the insight into the national economic connections should have gone further. One should have recognized that genuine economic politics is basically social- and population policy. If it is today placed in an artificial opposing position to this apparently political special department, this only proves that the economy was forced out of the totality of the idea of the people through purely financial powers (all-too world-economic thought) and began to obey its own laws which contradict those of the national economy. The moment that there is once again a national economic consciousness, however, economic-, social- and population policy coincide. The economic politics of the future will therefore, in all its measures, set up the preliminary question of how they operate on movements of population, population formations, ways of settlement, migration, rooting in the soil, and finally on the spiritual constitution of the people.

In order to make clear the significance of this thought process, it is necessary to represent the soil-rootedness of the economy. Almost all the raw materials which are needed for food, clothing, and dwelling arise from the soil. The war has revealed how it stands with a people without sufficient raw material basis. One should have thought that, under the pressure of this knowledge, a wave would have set in to give agriculture its economic key position once again. The opposite, however, is the case. Through consumer politics directed to popularity and delusory individual welfare, agriculture was conducted in an extensive-economic manner in the post-war period and after the introduction of the stable currency, the credit question treated in such a way as if the farmer were a speculator or a stock-brocker. The mobilisation of all soil-related values began; the furious battle between agriculture and industry on the one side, banks on the other persists upto the present.

The state should have protected the soil-related economy through its economic policy. That occurs only when it does not measure the individual economic departments and professions with the sham standard of an alleged justice which should be valid for all, but evaluates its present significance economic politically for the nourishment of the people. For, this is not the same in all economic departments, exactly as little as the performances of individuals in the economy are equal in value. Indeed, among the raw materials, in the fire-trial of the war, those were discovered which are indispensably necessary and those which are superfluous or at least dispensable. From the standpoint of the maintenance of the national culture and of the securing of the food basis, the following ladder can be set up at whose top the economic activity grown most inwardly with the national culture and the state, and at whose bottom the competitive department which tends by nature most strongly to cosmopolitanism are to be set.

Uppermost stands the farmer, and indeed the self-economising one before the one who lets his landed property be ruled. Agriculture is more than competition, its practice the highest of all professions; it gives the personality the widest space for development and can therefore come to satisfaction, indeed to the goal of its existence, earlier than every other activity. It gives the strongest support spiritually because the binding to the soil and narrow division of labour make possible sowing and harvesting and, therewith, the joy of creation. Human creative power and natural growth meet each in a creative union. The thriving of the fruit is dependent not only on the power of the hands and the cleverness of the senses, but also on the mercy of the heavens. The work of the farmer thus becomes, at

the same time, the gift of Nature and of God. Landed property is therefore more
than every other property. It is not destructible, it is a piece of the motherly earth
and must be tilled, should it bring fruit. It signifies, to a certain degree, the power
of disposal over a part of the state sovereignty, to which also the sovereignty over
the soil belongs. If the state sovereignty right should ail, then also the power with
which the farmer is rooted in the soil. And, vice-versa, no state can in the long
run live without the peasant adherence to the soil. The farmer is, in spite of his
lack of "bourgeois patriotism", the maintaining basic matrix of all states and
peoples. He nourishes man and propagates him. Farming was always the apparent
inexhaustible emergency reserve of competent and healthy men which the modern
metropolis does not bring forth in sufficient number.[132] From this knowledge
grow the guiding principles of all economic politics: stabilisation of the
agricultural property, checking of the emigration from the country, intensification
of farming, a concern to form it profitably through healthy fiscal- and credit
politics, securing of its markets, and the organisation of the market.

Next in the series of economic departments may perhaps come industry,
with the provision that the obtaining of raw materials is ranked before the
production of ready-made wares. The transition to the vertical associations indeed
leads to the erasing of this difference, but nevertheless there are still enough
industries which are differentiated by the fact that some fetch their raw materials
from German soil and others derive it from world trade. Common to both is the
landed property. Also, both economise with the soil-related means of production
which exists: the German man. Against the soil-relatedness of industry, especially
of the key industries, it is objected that it had entered in the last years into inter-
state connections. From this circumstance one seeks to derive cosmopolitan
thought-processes, as this happened last in the treatment of the pan-Europe plan
of Briand. This way of observation is, however, all-too mechanical. Apart from

[132] Compare the population political part.

the fact that the associations in the coal- and steel industry have, to a certain degree, a geopolitical basis, and thus correspond similarly to a certain soil-boundedness, they point in no way to the beginning of a new economic epoch. The approximation of the west European coal and iron economy rather resulted for the reason that the national heavy industries sought to obtain from this advantages for their national economic position. Belgium and France wanted to secure the advantage obtained through modern reconstrution and war gains; the German heavy industry drew from the German situation of helplessness the conclusion that it at least steered into conditions remaining unchanged and protected from powerful attacks. The moment the actual power relations do not correspond any longer to the bonds entered on, these economic contracts would be dissolved. They are differentiated from even political bonds by the fact that they are built on calculable goals, whereas the latter are based on man, who, in his utlimate core, is moved in an incalculable manner. This will result as soon as national economic necessities force the heavy industry to a regrouping.

Within the industry exist, accordingly, two camps which emerge especially in tariff political battles: the production of raw materials tending to the idea of agriculture and the approachable ready-made ware industry accesible to business points of view. All too easily does the latter forget that even it has to administer an expensive national wealth: the German workers. If it wishes seriously to protect the worker from exploitation, then it must also think national economically and help to secure the German food basis. It must therefore participate in the protection of raw material production and may not wish to conduct free trade at any cost through short-term greed. The common duty of industry, today recognized and followed by it everywhere, is the most careful administration of the human wealth. In the choice of industrial location, in the establishment of factories, settlements and homes, national economic points of view must enter into the foreground. The factory support of the German entrepreneur has upto now produced exemplary things. But even it is limited to the protection of the individual; it did not think national economically in the higher sense; otherwise, many industrial cities would have been set out differently, would have had another style of building, indeed would not at all have arisen perhaps in their present stony relentlessness. The national economic politics has to take care that the population political relations between industrial workers and farmers does not become unhealthy, that the urbanisation does not increase, that superfluous industries do not entice country masses who in the end fall victim to unemployment benefits.

In 1882 the members of the professions in agriculture and forestry made up 40.0 out of hundred of the entire population, in the census of 1907 it was 27.1, in 1925 only 23.0, out of hundred. To it corresponds also a decline of the agricultural tillage flats since 1913. In other words: the farming core of the German people is, relatively, becoming increasingly smaller, and its soil-related component increasingly smaller; for, the decrease of those occupied in agriculture and forestry did not really benefit industry and manual labour, which have hardly changed their share from 1907 to 1925. It is around 41 out of hundred. The casting away of the soil-relatedness strengthened rather a professional department which is relatively less soil-related: business.

Business has sociologically no uniform structure. For the most part, it belongs to the professional middle class and is often amalgamated with manual labour. Insofar as it is the middle class, it has, especially in the small city and on the flat land, a certain soil-relatedness. It often disposes of its own landed property and is closely bound to the stratum of its buyers. It was weakened through war and financial depreciation, through the advance of the large business (warehouse). But the limit of this regressive movement seems to have been reached. It is self-evident that, on account of its personality worth, the middle class must be maintained with all powers. To be sure, it is constituted of diverse components: as significant as a healthy craftsmen's order is for the national economy, so doubtful is the inflation of the small business distribution apparatus, which could be replaced partly by the consumer associations which of course may not serve specific goals (the party). The shrinkage of handicraft, on the other hand, is always a serious national economic and national political loss. Even if the result of the census of 1925 is hard to evaluate fully, because no clear difference resulted between handicraft and industry apparently, yet, through comparison of the numbers of the people occupied and of the businesses, a clear shift to the large business can be ascertained. The number of businesses has increased from 1907 to 1925 only around 2.5 out of hundred, whereas the number of the persons occupied in them has increased around 29.1 out of hundred. There must have resulted in handicraft, therefore, a relative regression, whereby the independent middle class has undergone a weakening. Handicraft must, however, in no way compulsorily dissolve. The level of industrialisation at which industry does not dislodge handicraft, because certain production processes are bound to the handicraft way of production, has long been reached in Germany. If handicraft nevertheless has receded, this proves that the German economic politics has failed in the care of the craftsmen's class.

The king of civilisation is the businessman. Only the abrupt infiltration of individualistic thought-processes explains the awakening of the business class in Germany. There were always businessmen and always must be. But, along with the necessary business, arise members who insert themselves at any place in the chain from the producer to the consumer in order to make profits. This parasitical business characterises the most recent German economic development. The numbers of the professional business census of 1925 have thereby a directly cultural-historical significance. Whereas since 1907 the number of businesses in industry and manual labour has increased only around 2.5 out of hundred, it has grown in business around 64.1 out of hundred. Even in respect of the number of persons occupied, the increase in business was greater than in industry and handicraft; it amounted here to 29.1 per cent, there 62.4. Not less than 1.2 million men more are occupied in business in 1925 than in 1907. Apparently not only without an increase, but even with a reduction of returns. (That of this increase

475,000 are of the female sex may give instructive information to the observer of German family life. Even here, we may refer to the population political part.) If one now compares large and individual business together, then a perhaps greater increase of individual business concerns must be ascertained. In the small business, the number of middle class positions seems to have increased; whether, of course, to the benefit of efficiency remains doubtful. On the other hand, the throng of the persons newly occupied in business is distributed in the same relation (1 to 2) as existed in 1907 in respect of both sorts of business. Even the large business underwent a significant inflation.

These figures speak not only an economic, but also a sociological and a moral historical, language. The productive power of the German people is healthy. To the need of income and the impulse towards insurance corresponds the desire to make effortless gain. If, however, one draws the shortened work-hours into consideration, then one attains the result that all progresses which are made through rationalisation do not benefit capital formation, not an increased production of goods, but greater comfort and a widespread tendency to live as well as possible with the least work possible. The unemployment insurance and the swelling of the public administration can be considered as a further circumstance which burdens the total productivity of the German people. It is therefore clear that the value-producing powers of the German people are receding. We are on the way to becoming a business nation, without England's geographical situation, without English power, and without the deliberateness of English politics. We neglect agriculture and let our farmers perish; a people without farmers is, however, a reed in the wind, even if it extend ever so proudly to the heavens. We speak of colonies and forget that urbanised peoples also lose their colonising power. England possesses the soil of half the earth; but its masses do not emigrate to the colonies any more. The blood has become weary, and the English unemployed prefer to be nourished pathetically in the homeland. The German people, however, show the same weakness in their eastern border, where they become increasingly pushed back by the Slavs.

The commodity large business, especially in the produce- exchange, which already deals with representatable wares which it partly does not see, has lost the last connection to the land and the soil. Its empire crosses all borders. From it it is only one step to the business with gold and money. Just as gold became an abstract ware, which stands over all other wares, so also the bank system stands over the economy, often indeed over the states and the peoples. It would not have been able to become a world danger if the nations had remained conscious that money is a symbol of the values created by them and not a value in itself; if everywhere pure economics had been conducted and the delusion of world economy resisted; above all, however, if the financial capital had not come to power over the press and the state, through the parliamentary democracy and with the support of Socialism, and destroyed all organic community. The world war was its war: the national economies collapsed and become dependent on it. Since then, it leads an unconditional independent life, not alongside, but over the economy; it seeks to bring the production into increasing dependence on itself and to "control" it, according to the point of view of profit-aiming. Not national economic productivity, but only financial economic income is the goal of this development, which is called high capitalistic. The significance of all national economics is, however, the securing of the nation's food and not the individualistic capital income. Thus there rages today the hard battle between the creative economy and the rigid power of the financial capital; its decision will depend on whether it finally succeeds in leading the present-day raiding party of capital, the Socialisitic working class, once again into the camp of the economy. This is a life and death battle, of tragic greatness and decisive for the culture of the white race.

Half of the totality may yet be mentioned, that the system of economic credit is different from that of guarantee credit. The guarantee bank belongs to the realm of the political. It has to regulate the blood circulation of the national economy. But woe if it is supervised and influenced by foreigners, especially if the latter pursue capitalistic goals. It must be an essential goal of German politics to free the guarantee bank from international capital influences.

In the setting up of the economic ladder according to the degree of rootedness in the soil, the professions which cannot be considered as markedly economic were temporarily   left out of view: the bureaucracy and the free professions. The bureaucrat is by nature state-supporting, since his existence is interwoven with that of the state. If, of course, he is no longer obliged to the pure idea of the state, but to the present state leadership, the state can, if the latter deals in a party political way of thought, be disintegrated. Even if this bad case does not emerge, there nevertheless exists the danger that the bureaucrat satisfies himself with the mere support of the state. He has then the attitude of the employee who would like to basically use his employer but not basically destroy him. This conception, which does without the deeper moral bond, unfortunately obtains increasingly more room. The trades union association of employees has reached over from the economy into the political life. Bureaucratic trades unions are, however, destroyers of the true concept of the bureaucrat. As understandable as the idea of the trades union was for the economy, so disastrous does it become in the political realm: the recognition, also only theoretical, of a bureaucratic right to strike signifies the collapse of the idea of the state. To conceive the state as an employer, just as one considers the private employer as a being with professional sense, is the application of private economic thought to a situation alien to economics. For, the state has no professional will and should have none: it embodies the community. To strike against it is anarchy; for that superiour community-will should in fact be represented by the bureaucrats who strike.

. In the free professions there exists similarly a connection to the culture, which, to be sure, occurs mostly purely intellectually by way of the cultural consciousness. Precisely in the free professions which dispose of a great developmental wealth do most of the personalities arise. There are indeed, in them, men who are glowing nationalists, and such who are born cosmopolitans. But, nevertheless, precisely the personality development which is possible in these strata will bring about an intellectual attitude which tends more to subordination under the community than the mentality of dependent men does. Therefore the free professions have always had an extraordinary significance for the national culture, have contributed essentially towards the intellectual intensification of the national culture. Precisely in the present age, the clearly historical task of working against collectivisation devolves on the few independent men who still exist.

So much more deplorable is the decline of the free professions, numerically as well as in respect of their economic situation and inner power. Many doctors have become alienated from the scientific work through the treasury system and are accustomed to bungled work. The overfilling has led to sordid competition which similarly damages the total worth of the medical profession. Here is a stratum of intellectual workers, valuable for the whole, on the point of falling victim to the practical Socialism. Similarly lie matters in the lawyer's profession. Apart from the disastrous intellectual transformation which consists in the fact that the lawyer feels himself to be increasingly less a lawyer of the justice, and, rather, a representative of the party which only too often demands of him that he should find out the gaps in the law in their interest, even the professional ethics is threatened by external causes. One has not yet been able to decide to remove, through the introduction of the *numerus clausus*,[133] the unworthy situation that the badly graded part of the jurists turn to the lawyer's profession. As a result of the sharp competition, the founding of serious lawyers' chancellories has become increasingly more difficult. In this way there arises an employee proletariat of lawyers out of second and third class lawyers with dubious side incomes. These hungry existences take up at random dubious tasks and seek to make justice out of injustice. The public therefore increasingly more sees in the lawyer a mere

---

[133] [a restricted number of entrants admissable to an academic institution].

instrument which can be appointed to any even immoral task. This dubious situation of the lawyer's profession is indeed commonly recognized, but, as everywhere, the wrong conclusion is drawn from it. By a sort of comradely socialising it was attempted to free even this profession, like the doctors, from the worst need; a plan which had to take away from it its great scientific and cultural significance. For, there entered in place of the personality placed on its own responsibility a devoted syndicate type; the law-creating power of the lawyer's profession was blocked up; one of the few possibilities to bring it to economic well-being with intellectual work was finally lost. Even here the worst mediocrity would suppress performance.

There is for a nation no better sign of inner health than the presence of a stratum of free professions stablised in itself. The more independent livelihoods, the stronger the foundation of the state. Through the absurd promotion of the university study now, a dangerous transformation of the academic career has doubtless emerged. Nevertheless, the relative share of the free professions has declined. There were active in free professions, administration, Church and army:

In 1882 .... 4.9 per cent professionals
In 1895 .... 5.7 "   "   "
In 1907 .... 5.3 "   "   "
In 1925 .... 4.7 "   "   "

Thus the post-war period has already brought, according to these figures, a remarkable decline. If, however, one thinks of the fact that the entire administration is included in them and that this is enormously swollen, then without further ado there is produced an overview of the loss which the free professions have undergone. In the figure of 1925 the professional army is also contained. There remains therefore very little for the free professions.

An organic economic politics will constantly hold in view the ranking of the people according to professions, sorts of vocation, business forms, and so on, will always set up considerations regarding which economic department is especially necessary for the national economy, which social stratum must be maintained at any cost, and which checked. It will thereby struggle through to taking care of this department, and cutting off the other. Nothing is more wrong than to start here from universal human considerations. The productivity of the national economy and the health of the national body are the highest law of all economic policy, which should also pitilessly ignore the individual. Today, it takes care of the individual only as a mass being, because all individuals have joined together in a horizontal organisation according to power, and thus exert a collective pressure. It lies in the essence of the personality that it cannot do that. Thus it comes about that the roller of equalisation sweeps over it.

If, however, the highest order of all economic policy is the care of production, then the circumstance must be suspiciously right that - in spite of the general impoverisation and in spite of the emergency situation of the German people - the relative number of those who are without a profession and professional evidence has doubled from 1882 to 1925. It may soon have amounted to a tenth of the German population if the development did not change. In this figure it becomes evident that the idea of service has been pushed back in the German people by the system of beneficiaries.

A creative economic policy will therefore try to banish with all means the weakening of the German productivity as it has become clear from the figures brought forward. It has two weapons in its hand: the economic police and the general economic policy which culminate in the fiscal legislation and in the customs system. Often, the limits of both these realms of duties are erased just as those between economic-, population-, and social policy. Indeed it is to be expected that even general state politics and foreign policy must go hand in hand with economic policy. In the organic community, there is no unconditionally valid division between the individual departments of the leadership, because all strive for the same goal: for the organic whole of the people.

The idea of common service leads in a straight line to the question of compulsory labour service. Already the "Utopists" espoused it. Is the compulsory service suited to this? As a pure compulsory labour service, it has, upto now, been introduced only in Bulgaria, somewhat diluted under the pressure of the Entente. The emergency service for the army, on the other hand, has, since the world war, become a frequent phenomenon and has found diverse forms in a series of laws: thus in France, Italy, Holland, Switzerland, Russia, Roumania, Poland, and the United States. For the German compulsory labour service plans from the Socialistic and military sides are present. As a way to the Socialistic future state it is to be rejected. The maintenance of the wealth of a nation devolves on free economy. The idea of compulsory labour service moves indeed between the economy and the state, between uncapitalistic economic aims and moral educational goals.

Against the compulsory labour service many things are objected. Thus one fears, on the one hand, the formation of a "reserve army" operating against the economy, especially against the worker. Every pay demand of the workers can be replied to by the entrepreneurs with a resort to the cheaper compulsory labour service, and the strike can indeed be made ineffective. Further, it is said that, with the introduction of the compulsory labour service, the workers' market would form itself even more unfavorably than today since many work opportunities would disappear. There would be very little for the work suited to labour service in the economy. It would demand chiefly trained specialist workers. The development of the wasteland has its limits, the profitability of canal building would be contested. In addition, there would be the difficult accomodation of those under compulsory service, which however should be in proximity to the work places. The barracks would conceal a social danger in themselves. The compulsory service army would produce a new bureaucracy, under circumstances indeed a further squandering of means which one could lead in to the economy. It would not counter unemployment thoroughly since the unemployed are predominantly constituted from higher age groups. The most weighty consideration, however, is raised by Gottfried Flügge.[134] He contests the educational possibilities of the compulsory labour service for a series of notable reasons. Among them is decisive that the compulsory labour service can in no way be compared to the army service whose concept of sacrifice is a quite different and a much higher one.

All these counter reasons have something for themselves and are in part hardly contradictable. On the other hand, there is a political number of economic tasks which are not derivable from lack of capital, yet must be attacked for the advantage of the community. Where one can economise only "capitalistically" there is no place for compulsory service. There is, however, an economic activity whose use lies beyond the capitalistic income, namely in the field of the national economic advantage. The high capitalistic economy has shown itself to be incapable of it. Even the great technological performances of the East, of antiquity, and of the mediaeval West, give evidence of such community work. Tasks of this sort are set even before the present-day Germany. Let one remember only the dearth of homes, the condition of the streets, and the broad plains of the wastelands. Work force lying fallow (unemployment) is an irreplaceable loss and a sign of sickness for the national economy. Certainly, even capital is required to set this work force in action. But not so distanced as within the capitalistic scope. It must, therefore, occur even outside it. During the war, the government did not perceive this and nurtured a grave dissatisfaction, in that one granted the soldier only a miserable honorary salary, in the homeland however an hourly payment of marks. It is not fitting to nourish a million men in a public manner and, at the same time, to leave a considerable number of national tasks unresolved. The national constitution guarantees to every German a right to work. Why does one not establish the duty to work? The lasting unemployment and the contradictory unemployment insurance basically owe their existence to the capitalistic thought-processes. Here a change must be brought about.

---

[134] Gottfried Flügge, *Arbeitsdienstpflicht?*, ed. by Werner Best, Berlin, Kranich Verlag, 1929.

Whether the introduction of universal compulsory labour service, especially in the form of a work army, is the way leading to the goal should not be decided here. The basic idea of the Bulgarian compusory labour service, which in short-hand is called a tax, is however correct. It then argues further that it is really thought out national politically that the idea of tax may not remain with money but must attach every state citizen through his work immediately to the totality of the people. Against this nothing serious can be brought forward. It is simply not appropriate that a people increasingly decompose into two halves: into one which toils in a coolie fashion, and another which grasps at revenues. Behind the idea of universal labour service the pressure of a law must be set up; how, remains left to the particular hour and to the creative impulse of the legislator.

The following however becomes apparent: the downfall of the universal army service is a hard blow for the moral, civil, and practical education of the German. With the increase of age, every German must, in an organic state, be subject to a training process of comradeship, of performance of duty, and of ranking. No doubt that the ideas of protection of home and fatherland, of the manly mission and of the war sacrifice signify a moral high aim which is not to be reached on other bases than the army service. Therefore the German foreign policy must work with all its power for the downfall of the army limitations. Switzerland, which has a strong army, proves that military competence and peaceful politics go well with each other. Until then, however, interim solutions must be striven for; perhaps a binding of sports training and public work engagements. We need a far-reaching, practical, political life school which makes a man of the youth, a conscious community-servant of the individual.

VI

Exploitation or financial economics?

If the community, especially the state, should fulfil its tasks, so must the people provide the means for this. The service of the individual extends not only to personal service, but also to the disposal of wealth and money. The "bringing together, administering and paying" of the monies serving public goals is called financial economics.

A healthy financial economics seeks to fulfil the political tasks as perfectly as possible with the smallest expenditure. Standing between the economy and the state, it forms a middle entity, obliged to both in equal measure. It must collect the necessary means which the public administration needs. It is, however, also forced to consider the performance capacity of the economy, and to take its norm from it. The state is in the position to break through this private economic law through pressure. Related to the individuals, it too has a right to it. For, it takes care of, not the individual limited by time, but the indefinitely lasting community. It must think of future generations and may not spare the living in certain circumstances. But seen from the standpoint of the organic community, even in financial economics the rule of performance and counter performance is valid. The state may not become the exploiter of the people, the people not become the boarder of the state. The present-day financial politics is an instrument for the satisfaction of the collective mass state. The fiscal capacities are determined by the expense side of the Mammon state. What driving forces operate here decisively the national political part of this book has presented. The equipoise of the powers between the people and the state, the basic law of all organic life, has been lost. Nowhere therefore is the crisis more threatening than in financial economic fields; here the catastrophe stands at the door.

The financial need of the public administration in the German Reich (the Reich, provinces, and municipalities) rose from 7252.6 millions in the census year 1913/14 to 14,477.9 for the year 1925/26. That is almost exactly double. Thereby the forward movement is in no way concluded. The quarterly incomes from the national, provincial, and municipality taxes rose from 2774.3 millions in the first quarter of 1927 to 3111.7 for the same period of the year in 1928. One can therefore, taking consideration of the public administration at the moment, reckon the financial need at 17 billions. If one reckons, in addition, even the contributions to the national insurance, then there emerges a total public burden of around 22 billions. That the pre-war national revenue had not at all grown to this annual expenditure, let alone the present-day one (50-60 billion marks), is illuminating without any further explanation. For, the German national wealth increases more slowly than the populations and its needs. The German balance of payments produces in the years from 1924 to 1927 a debit balance of over 11 billion marks. Upto the end of the year 1929, the German foreign debt should have risen to the level of 16 billions. To be sure, these amounts stand against 5-6 billions of German foreign possessions. Even the growth of savings monies to about 7 billions must be taken into consideration,[135] as well as the newly formed capital which was invested once again in the economy, but is hard to evaluate. In any case, one's own capital formation is insufficient because indeed, otherwise, no

---

[135] Loan and transfer of German wealth to foreign hands.

foreign help would be necessary. Luther evaluates the present-day annual debit balance at 3 1/2 to 4 billion marks including the war reparations. From this it becomes clear that we find ourselves on the downward path. The smaller part of the foreign monies is really invested competitively. The greater was consumed along with the above-mentioned 7 billions which are to be registered as the wealth loss of agriculture. The German Reich and the German people therewith conduct the credit economy of a bankrupt. The first result is a sell-out of German economy, much more threatening than that during the financial depreciation. But even the self-importance-seeking financial economy corresponds to the "borrowed standard of living" of the German people; indeed they rise reciprocally. A leaderless people, whose government is overcome by the enticements of demagogy, is capable of continuing this financial conduct for a still longer time. Values are present, thanks to earlier industriousness. Along with the production of matches, there are many economic departments which can be mortgaged or auctioned for the highest bidding following the Balkan and the South American example. Unfortunately, however, the German Reich lacks the possibility of an enlightened revolution which could reestablish the national possessions situation. That under such circumstances a flow of capital has set in of unsuspected proportions is no wonder. Here there is no use of an outcry over the state-hostile and immoral conduct of capital. One should, on the contrary, ask oneself whether immorality does not already begin in the present-day expense economy and in the fiscal politics.

"Every tax, it may have whatever name it wishes, must be borne totally by the national economic production and is shifted by the latter onto the consumers. At the same time, however, a tax can restrict the taxed production department at least temporarily in its development. In the final analysis, there is in the national economy only income taxes, which are shifted onto the consumers".[136] This

---

[136] Friedrich Aereboe, *Agrarpolitik*, Berlin, Verlag Paul Parey, 1928.

opinion on the system of taxes corresponds to the idea of the community represented by this book. Only one who is concerned to rely on the economic body, which represents a unity based on the community, as such, for tax discharge acquires the standpoint from which alone a just taxation is possible. Just, not in the sense that it hurts nobody but in the sense that the interest of the economy, the national welfare, and the political necessities remain equally preserved. There exists an inner connection between the individualistic world-view and the fact that the tax-obligation today is related only to the person, be it the natural or the legal one. The entire fiscal legislation of recent times aims at the individual, his manner of thought and his advantage. Already further above, the contradiction of the direct taxation of the burcaucrats, employees and wage workers was criticized. Aereboe rightly calls the income tax from the salary and wages a childish mischief. It is enigmatic why even today that outmoded idea of the educational effect of the income tax can continue to exist in the ridiculous attitude that the state grants salaries from which it pays over to itself a certain percentage as so-called tax through an involuted procedure of calculation. Who then reckons with incomes which he never really has? - The conception of tax in terms of the individual then harms the economy most seriously. Apart from the fact that it benefits the financial capitalists, because it can undertake tax evasions by way of self-appraisal which are never possible to immobile property, such an individualistic conception of tax basically considers first of all the effect of the tax on the individual, seldom that on the entire economy. In this way also, then, do entire tax theories of the last fifty years start from the question of how a tax affects the individual and how the taxation of the one operates psychologically on the other. Besides, the taxation is not directed to the point at which it harms the production power the least and disturbs the economic development the least, but to the individual whose entire economic attitude is however different. Consequently, the principle often pointed to in this book is confirmed: that the individual always comes off worst when his interests and his sensibility should be preserved; that he, on the other hand, can be treated justly only when the measures affecting him start from the idea of the community. The number of the fiscal laws and forms of taxation present today stands in an inner connection to that of the numberless individual interests and special wishes which are made valid in the existing discussions of the fiscal laws. The uniform basic idea, which can be only of an economic and not a personal nature, is missing. On the other hand, numberless envy-taxes raise their poison-swollen head, which are raised gladly especially by the municipalities, whose city parliament has a property-hostile constitution. Then there come about also mis-taxes, as the present-day taxation of house property reveals. Originally one wanted to subject the house owner once again to the laws to which he owes his existence: namely to the pure economic ones. This praiseworthy tendency was reversed by the state hungry for income, along with the assistance of the property-hostile powers, into its opposite. A tax of precisely unheard-of economic absurdity arose. The emergency situation in which the state was immediately after the introduction of the stable mark is totally acknowledged. That, however, such a tax could maintain itself for years in its entire range is the best proof of the planlessness of the German fiscal politics. Similarly hostile to the economy works the trade-tax, that scourge of the middle class which is absolutely hostile to the people. Industry and agriculture were burdened by the Dawes obligations, in respect of the debt to the revenue bank in a way which made every capital formation impossible and the desirable profitability unattainable.

In fact, there are only two sources which can be tapped fiscally: for current tasks the national economic revenue, for others the national wealth. A recourse to the latter can result without raising of taxes through the imposition of loans; in a fiscal way through the proclamation of wealth taxes. Every attack on the wealth should have been possible only for very special reasons, for very special aims and finally under very special circumstances. An essential reason consists in the fact that the sums which are necessary are to be raised from the current revenues.

Special aims are to be given in general only when foreign political tasks of basic significance for the nation await their solution. The special circumstances are dependent on how high the savings monies of a national economy are. These three points of view must be weighed against one another. In general, it is true that a consumption of the basic stock of the national economy for current political goals reminds one of the procedure of one who saws off the bough on which he sits. The destruction of property, from hostility to property, may however never be the goal of wealth taxation, because thereby the national economy is destroyed irredeemably. If a national economy has consumed that which has been saved up by a series of generations, as this was the case with the stabilisation of the German currency, the capital formation must be furthered under all circumstances and, as far as possible, every attack on the wealth therefore avoided. What however remains fully unbearable in these principles is a current wealth tax such as exists at the moment in Germany.

But even if Germany would know no non-recurring wealth tax nor a current wealth tax, still the veiled wealth taxes remain to be objected to. This veiling occurs by way of the income tax. The great economic conference in Vienna as well as Valentinus[137] have brought the view to light that the direct taxation in general has no justification and that the doctrine of the social injustice of the indirect taxes is a fairy tale. The so-called indirect tax is one on consumption and already therefore more just than the direct which, to a certain degree, punishes industrious and economical work. It is now objected against the indirect tax that it hits the poorer strata relatively more harshly than the well-to-do. For, the increase in price of the wares effected by the consumer taxes reduces the pay-receiver in similar measure in his standard of living. That is not right. In healthy economic conditions, the pay follows the price. If this were not the case, the high salaries in North America would be totally inexplicable. The level of the

---

[137] *Steuererleichterung*, Verlag der Berliner Börsenzeitung.

salary takes into consideration, on the other hand, the circumstance whether the worker pays indirect taxes or not. In addition, there is the psychological side. Why do the workers' parties defend themselves against the indirect tax? One must point at first here to the often-mentioned circumstance that the worker is really led by the financial capital, which wishes with his help to plunder and smash the immobile property by way of the tax treasury. Then, however, the obedience which the salary receiver shows in tax questions as opposed to the businessmen becomes explicable only through the circumstance that he is conscious to himself of the meaninglessness of the income tax raised from him. That means, he feels himself not as a tax payer, because, in wage discussions, he shifts the tax rebate to the entrepreneur. The excise taxation, on the other hand, he feels as an actual tax payment, even if it comes to his consciousness not so much in individual points but rather as a whole. In this way is surprisingly emphasized how topsy-turvy the current conception of the educational effect of the income tax is. Quite on the contrary, today the situation has formed itself that a relatively small number of taxable people contest the state expenditure on behalf of the masses, whereas the latter have to a certain degree incapicated themselves fiscally.

A more precise observation of the manner and method by which nowadays the taxes are raised leads to the same result. Every tax is overturned or, as the case may be, returned, wherefore the direct tax operates at least similarly to the indirect in the setting of the price. Thus it cannot be seriously denied that every businessman registers his entire taxes and payments to the credit of "overhead expenses", which he includes in the price of the ware. This procedure was especially promoted by the system of tax pre-payment. If it is so, then the maintenance of direct taxes cannot any longer be advocated. Now, one says that the battle for the final burdening with an overturned or a returned tax decides the economic situation. In times of favorable business, the consumer will have to bear the tax finally, in case of unfavorable business the producer. Here the losing businesses of the entrepreneur would then step in, i.e., his wealth stock would have to suffer. In this way does this sort of taxation arise from a wealth tax. That is a veiled sort of wealth tax which nevertheless still has the advantage of being at least bound to an economic process. It has, as a rule, the shutting down of weaker businesses as its result, whereas the stronger remain maintained. A certain economic justice cannot be denied to this process. Today, however, it is in such a way that, through the progressive income tax, the large and performance-capable business is subject to a much higher tax than the weak and small. The level of the price is oriented to the numerous and, as a result of progressive taxes, dearer, wares of the industries running well. The weak and inefficient business are thus fiscally indulged and the price level is not thereby reduced in the least. If, now, one would remove the special tax of the large business, which is conditioned by the progressive income- and corporate tax, along with all direct taxes, the price would apparently become lower. For, the smaller businesses would either have to work efficiently and calculate more conscientiously or perish.

It would lead too far to elucidate that, even in the free professions, especially among the "intellectual workers", the direct taxation works in a value-destroying manner insofar as the person earning well (because clamorous) is likewise in a position to shift the tax whereas the one earning poorly must bear it. Thereby a culture-bearing stratum falls into need. Just as in the pure economic field the economically inferiour are maintained artificially according to the current tax system, but the economically superiour are forcefully suppressed, the present-day taxation of the free professions operates in general in a culture-destroying manner and leads to the injury of a superiour order. The direct taxation of creative intellectual work is a crime against the mind and becomes directly a sin if the progressive income tax indefatigably punishes the creative person for his diligence. If he may shift it, the immorality of this tax experiences thereby no justification.

From all these considerations which space prevents us from substantiating individually, the new financial science attains a doubtful position with regard to the direct tax in general.[138] Many plans therefore have been made, all of which boil down to taxing the national economic income at the most appropriate and harmless point in an indirect way, and thereby to making an entire series of taxes and forms of tax-raises superfluous. Let one remember the "production tax" projected by Rabbethge[139] and the great value-added tax similar to the production-tax which, according to Valentinus, would make the entire direct taxes as well as a considerable number of simultaneously existing value-added taxes superfluous. The abandoning of the income tax would, to be sure, require a rethinking all along the line. Its retention is harmless only when it is so low that it does not undermine the capital formation and - without being shifted - is felt as "a self-explanatory reduction of the income" (Valentinus). If the tax-free income is essentially raised, it loses in general its universal character. According to Stolper's plan, 11 twelfths of all salary receivers would be freed of the income tax. Why then not go over directly to the excise tax? - However one may stand with regard to these plans in individual points, the general line is to be agreed with. For the author, it is important only to emphasize, within the scope of his economic observations, even the significance of the way of thought starting from the community for the tax system.

If in this way the idea of the community attains a breakthrough in the tax legislation, and thus every infringement on the national economy resulting from individualistic reasons were rejected, the result would be a fundamental new attitude to agriculture. It is obvious that as little as the current credit policy also is the present tax policy justified by the new conception of the special position of agriculture in the culture and state. Its promotion is a chief question. The rise of the agricultural income therefore conditions, from the larger perspective, a fiscal preservation of the greatest proportions. The removal of the income tax, which

[138] So also the former national finance minister, Peter Reinhold and Gustav Stolper in *Der deutsche Volkswirt*, Berlin.

[139] *Verfall oder Rettung*, Magdeburg, 1923.

Aeroboe calls the worst enemy of the farmers, would effect no wonder here, especially if it lost its excise-tax appearance. A production-tax on the basis of turn-over would be bearable for agriculture without harm, and the pressure of the land taxation would disappear. For, the present-day revenue taxation is too immobile, the evaluation procedure too crude. - The internal market, the indispensable prerequirement of every healthy export, would be strengthened and thereby also the payment of a higher real wage to the workers of the industry made possible. - Even if, in the second part of this book, a quite special sort of inheritance tax (wealth tax) was projected as a national political measure, let it be expressly emphasized here that, as a rule (in the presence of a certain number of children), no inheritance tax should be raised. Basically, however, it is to be evaluated as family-destroying and as a damaging of capital formation. But it is not unjust to the plan to raise, in the case of lesser number of children, and of a certain level of estate, the wealth tax, from which the basic stock could be formed to settle anew the sons of farmers with many children. An application of this means, obtained through the inheritance tax, for the current payments of the state is to be rejected. In the settlement and improvement of families with many children, the author sees a task for which the wealth of those who refuse fresh blood to the culture could be seized as an exception. Agriculture, however, must in all cases assume an inherited special position. Instead of smashing entails, the German people should much more correctly have worried about how the destruction of the farm wealth is avoided on the basis of an individualistic inheritance right such as that of the civil statue book.

An entire series of reform plans, reasonable and usable, are at hand: so especially the idea of improving the crude house-rent tax or of replacing it with a rent tax (Reinhold), or a home tax (Aereboe). Aeroboe thinks that the tax progression, in the case of income tax immoral, could be therefore transferred to the excise. Whether a home tax is population politically clever, whether it does not hit the national health, would have to be seriously examined. The window-tax in France is discouraging. Monopolies however play an especially great role in the reform plans. Alcohol and tobacco stand there in the centre of the deliberations. It may, especially for the tobacco trade, be correct that here chaotic conditions exist, that small businesses are spreading which feed on the national economy. On the other hand, however, the idea that the economy of the public authorities could be enlarged with a new department fills one with horror; a new army of "tobacco bureaucrats" would - apparently founding a new trades union - enter on the stage. The counter-movement against the collectivism of our age would be perceptibly thwarted by new monopolies. For irresponsible finance ministers there exists, moreover, the temptation to sell off monopolies to foreign countries or to make them indebted thereby. Nowadays it is difficult to decide where the borders between monopolisation, socialisation, and international financial rule lie. Therefore one must be warned of new monopolies. However, measures are thinkable which rationalise the tobacco economy as well as raise its fiscal revenues. Through indirect taxation, significantly more can be elicited from alcohol and tobacco, exactly as in England, than today.

The standardisation of the tax system and the discovery of the point in the economy where a payment from the national economic revenue can be best made would result most speedily if this concern were left to the economy itself. The financial need will maintain itself for a foreseeable period at a calculable and equal level. Even then, if numerous state tasks are transferred to autonomous bodies, the total tax-yield for the public tasks would not become smaller for the time being; later that can become different, if the advantages of a healthy autonomy, which is always more thrifty than the bureaucratic one, obtain an effect. Stolper[140] projects the determination of public expenses for ten years in order to combat the tendency to rise in expenditure. To be sure, it is also thinkable that emerging circumstances force one to a reduction of the financial need. But

---

[140] [cf. Gustav Stolper, *Ein Finanzplan: Vorschlag zur deutschen Finanzreform*, Berlin: Der deutsche Volkswirt, 1929; *Das deutsche Wirtschaftsproblem*, Berlin: Der deutsche Volkswirt, 1928].

this must be striven for, to already check the present-day collectivism. Total change alone produces the reversal from the Mammon state.

The carrying out of taxes through uniform offices can be maintained, but a closed economic body would be able to accomplish the proclamation and allocation more expertly than the present determing political departments. Already further above the principle was combatted that, in general, the person permitting taxes also would have to take care of the raising of the taxes, that therefore the person paying must also speak for the security. If now one imagines that the economic bodies reveal a local organisation which can coincide with the present-day municipalities, provinces, and counties, then ways can be found to carry out that healthy principle. Thereby the greatest attention must be granted to an idea of Valentinus: that urban corporate bodies do not burden the industry of their sphere of autonomy with taxes, which as a result of the increase in price of the wares must be paid by the country. It is clear that such measures must lead to the inequality of the general price level, to the migration of entire industries and to the exploitation of the country. The progressive trading licence existing today belongs to those taxes which exert this disastrous influence.

The establishment of tax districts indeed arose often already in discussion. And the more the economy is collected into large structures, the more the finance officials are directed to good agreement with their management. If one pursues this direction further, it is then only a small step to that condition where the chiefs of the tax officials negotiate with the chiefs of the economy on the financial need of the public authorities and moreover leave the raising of this means to the economic autonomous bodies.

All financial reformers are agreed on one thing: that the financial balance between the Reich, provinces, and the municipalities should be basically organised anew. The present-day transfer economy is much more unbearable than the pre-war situation. If then the Reich was partly the boarder of the provinces, it is today vice-versa. Only, with the difference that the expending positions do not themselves raise the financial means but must force it in a distasteful battle from the headquarters of the Reich. In this way the worst businesses get involved with a perceptible lack of responsibility. This may not in any way become a permanent situation. Already before the war, the plan was made to allocate to the Reich the indirect taxes, to the federal states the personal taxes, to the districts and the municipalities the revenue taxes. Perhaps that was too mechanically thought out; but ever more correct than the empty intermingling of today where, in general, no separation exists and every public corporate body economises wildly as a result of it. Some want now to assign direct taxes along with the municipal surcharge right to the provinces once again, and to leave to the Reich the indirect taxes. Others (Stolper) plan the reverse. On the other hand, it is objected that excise taxes must be universal and equal, so that the price level does not suffer. The allocation of the excise taxes to the provinces and municipalities would signify a return to the 19th century. The same is maintained, however, even by those who wish to see the income tax maintained by the Reich. They therefore think of a surcharge right of the provinces and municipalities to the national income tax.

In general, the mistrust of a far-reaching tax-granting right of the provinces and the municipalities is great. The petty parliamentarianism ruling in them provokes the justified doubt whether one should totally consign important taxes to it.

Therewith, however, it becomes apparent that a financial reform is not to be resolved through tax-methods, but must go hand in hand with the new distribution of the powers. But even this is in turn a part of the national reform: the new order of the relations between the Reich, provinces, and the municipalities, the working out of genuine autonomy, as the second part of this work treats it.

The carrying out of the financial reform, however, arising from the basic curtailment of the financial need and from the real tax reform, will never succeed under the present-day interest- and demagogic system. That even Stolper perceives when he maintains that the financial reform which is required today can be only "the fruit of a great popular movement". But his hope that the financial policy would at one time be borne by the passion of an entire people is illusory. This remark expresses a disastrous ignorance of the total situation of the German people and of the basic forces of history. Certainly, the German need is especially apparent in the financial political realm. But the "simple man on the street" does not feel basically affected by it. One does not move masses, and one does not make history with financial programmes. A nation is not a business, but animated life. Nevertheless, even the author believes that the curing of the German financial economy can be the fruit only of a popular movement; to be sure not of a financial political one, but of such a one as restoringly encompasses the entire cultural, social, economic, and political life because it has leaders who experience and strive for the whole. One of the many fruits which a renewal movement so constituted will bear is even the German financial reform. For, life is a whole, and one who does not feel that will perform even in economic and financial policy only a partial work.

Part Five

Population policy

I. Of the concept of population policy
Historical glance. - Maintenance of the people as a task. - The present-day social politics.

II. Population movements in Germany
The fall of the birthrate. - Falling mortality. - Birth surpluses. - The unhealthy age division. - "The mortgage of death".

III. Causes of the shrinkage of population.
The dying out of the peoples an inevitable natural law? - Not a physical depletion. - Not a decreased number of marriages. - Decrease of conjugal fruitfulness. - The true cause of the shrinkage of population. - Wealth situation and number of children. - The bureaucrats' lack of sufficient number of children. - Metropolises.

IV. The uprooted
Decrease of emigration. - Immigration from foreign countries. - Industrial-district-Poles. - Foreign migrant workers. - The advance towards the west. - The rise of the city proletariat from the country proletariat.

V. The effects of the shrinkage of population.
The law of least resistance. - The biologically young Europe in comparison to the biologically old. - The example of France: population reduction. - Infiltration, racial mixture. - Political consequences. - Immigration of foreign races.

VI. Economic consequences.
Economic dangers of underpopulation. - Workers' security. - Regression of agriculture. - Devaluation of the soil: the example of France. - Wars and sicknesses.

VII. The treatment of the ailing national body.
The darkening of the situation. - Complaints against the state. - France's battle against racial suicide. - Plans for improvement. - Family insurance. - Family or honour. - Means: morals and laws. - The present-day "morals". - Furthering through the state and school. - Political colonisation. - Advantages and errors of the settlements. - New settlements. - Migration.

VIII. Science as a signpost for the healing of the ailing national body (the doctrine

of racial purity).
Significance of racial hygiene. - The concept of race. - The doctrine of heredity. - Selection in antiquity. - Counter selection in culture. - Practical conclusions. - Science and state.

Part Six

Foreign Policy

I. The concept of foreign policy.
The flawless classification of the concept of foreign policy. - The inner strife of German politics. - The state forms the people. - The people form the state.

II. Western rise - Europe's downfall.
French rise. - Loss in the west. - Loss in the east. - Triple Alliance. - The disintegration of Europe. - The painful picture of the present. - The reaction of 1871. - German culture without power-political support. - The unnatural predominance of France. - The German complaint.

III. Individualism in foreign policy.
The saturated German Reich. - Deficient defence. - The acquisition of colonies. - Naval politics. - Berlin-Bagdad, English-Russian alliance. - Imperialism and cosmopolitanism. - The English-German opposition as a result of that politics. - The pacifistic cosmopolitanism.

IV. The intellectual foundations of the German post-war politics.
The attitude to the colonial question. - The false new economic imperialism. - Increased cosmopolitanism. - The present-day bearers of the foreign political course. - The materialistic pacifism of action. - New catchwords. - The association of nations. - Internal political pacifism and foreign political tactics.

V

National cultural foreign policy

The constant preservation of the same direction is guaranteed only when the sense for the higher purposefulness of the existence of the people has come alive once again. Then the political instinct awakens to new life. Leaders arise who balance their own will to the popular will. The significance of the national community in the scope of the world-view resting in the suprasensual has already been made clear. The nation is, to it, the earthly individuation of the Divine being, in which the individual himself may continue to live. If God reveals Himself to the individual man, it is only in the spiritual form which is conditioned by the special spiritual condition of his own people. Thence the significance which the person obliged to the communal worth attaches to national culture: he wishes to acquire the vessel in which he may continue to live the Divine being which has become manifest to him.

Besides, however, he recognizes also the necessity of an order towering above his own people. The total experience obliges him indeed not to work for a mere concept of mankind of the individualistic sort but for the creation of a higher order in the life of the nations, in which the totality is glimpsed, at first of the peoples of the same territory and interconnected history. In the chapter, "People, race, Reich" the philosophical foundation for this demand has been given.

Since the intellectual concept of culture is bound to the physical aspect of the people, there follows therefrom the affirmation of the self-maintenance and security of the national existence as the first law of life. But also attention to foreign peoples. Besides, however, the German recognizes the special position of his people in every advanced spirituality, which calls the German people to make the next step to human perfection: to the establishment of a right legal order among the peoples, at first of the European territory, in his immediate neighbourhood. Charity begins at home. Human perfection however means the approximation of man to the divine and the distancing from the barbaric. Thereby the striving for perfection remains a goal in itself, the goal eternal and unattainable. From the recognition of the German duty towards humanity grows the feeling of a mission. The insight that national culture as such must be developed freely and unrestrictedly in order to be able to serve really as a vessel leads, in connection with the consciousness of a special task, to the pressure to create for this culture a spiritual leadership role among the other nations. That is not overconfidence, which leads to presumption, but a necessary impulse to the furtherance of spiritual development. If lower self-seeking utilitarian instincts work against this effort, the German is obliged to counter them. He must fight for the validity of his culture, if necessary even under sacrifice of his own life. Therefrom are effortlessly produced two foreign political directional points for our age:

The entire German people is to be made the foundation even of its political thought and existence; it must strive for the position which is suited to its spiritual powers and necessary for the exercice of its missionary vocation. Only then do unequivocal foreign political goals arise from intellectual facts, from the basic spiritual attitude, consciously in the case of the leaders, emotionally in the case of the entire mass of the people.

The way to these goals is conditioned by circumstances which prescribe a quite definite direction. For, a people does not stand, as a spiritual vessel, to a certain degree in a void. But it is bound and linked to the destiny of the earth which it shares with other peoples, whose fate is more strongly connected to it than the individualistic way of observation recognizes.

The German people holds the centre of Europe. In the north, west, and southwest of the settlement area of the Germans live - round the centre of Europe - "old" peoples, almost entirely with national states of the western stamp: mostly with clear national and linguistic borders. (The political borders have, to be sure, advanced since 1919 over the German national territory). In the northwest, east and southeast of the German settlement area on the other hand - still within the inner European territory - the peoples are interlinked to one another in terms of settlement. Here there are no border lines of peoples, but broad, simply drawn borders of contact. The political ideas of this territory must therefore be different, more mobile, corresponding to the situation. If the pre-war solution of the problem of peoples and states was already unsatisfactory in this mainland territory, still more so the present-day one. Here in the heart of Europe a powerful task of resolution persists: to find new forms for the living together of the mainland peoples who lack clear territorial borders.

That is the prime task of the Reich German foreign policy which has for the time being only to act in the west and remove the mistakes of the Versailles Treaty as much as possible. For the moment the German people has nothing to offer the west, unless indirectly through the east. There lies the key.

These - in no way new - national and territorial political foundations of the German foreign policy were ignored and therefore forgotten by an instinctless age inclined to illusory ideas which considered only the individual peoples. Thence the collapse of German foreign policy and the lowering of its perspective, therefore its lack of tasks and direction. The foreign political thought of the pre-war period however was conducted only in states and not in peoples. It was not based on the enclosedly settled Germans in Central Europe, but only on "the inhabitants of the Reich", who however were only a part of the entire German people - at the borders besides mixed with foreign peoples - and also not on the territory which the entire people inhabits and on the radiations of this territory and of the entire people.

Here lies a goal of the highest significance which perhaps the materialistically thinking person grasps partially when he arrives through different ways at the understanding of the Great-German Central European. Foreign policy must be interlocked in the people and the soil, the idea of the political union of all German culture and of the mastery of the German cultural soil must therefore be basic. German foreign policy must therefore strive in two ways, in terms of the people and in terms of Europe:

for the Germans, who live in Central Europe on the closed national soil: a political entity of "Germany", which there is not yet today; for the Germans outside Great Germany: living space, that is, secure self-rule of its national cultural affairs within its host state,

for Europe: new order beginning with the central, near eastern and near south eastern territory and progressing from there to the borders, in the form of a European states union.

Both goals are more closely linked to each other than a fleeting examination allows one to suppose. They embody the idea of the historical Reich in its present form suited to the present circumstances. For the same right to a national state and to security of the foreign positions not encompassed by this must be granted even to the remaining peoples of the same territory through an international legal order.

The complaint that the setting up of such far-reaching goals in this time of German powerlessness is without a prospect of realisation is false. If powerful performances are demanded of the German people, even a great thing must be held in view. Victor Hugo, imprisoned in the forms of French political thought, swore, on the occasion of the transactions of the National Assembly at Bordeaux on the Frankfurt Peace of 1871, the reconquest of Alsace-Lorraine, Mainz and

Cologne! Only one who wishes for the whole makes great efforts. Giving up from the start and lack of a goal lead to the background. Moreover, anything else is impossible. For, colonial and overseas policy is unattainable while these goals are to be justified ideologically, historically and economically. The inner lack of peace and the economic situation of Europe cry directly for a new order.

Public declaration of far-reaching goals of foreign policy does not only frighten. It also conceals advantages. Even enemy policy can prepare itself on clear political lines. That is proved by the success of Japan, when in the nineties it proclaimed much more wide-ranging and thereby really self-aggrandizing goals. Uncertainty on goals dissatisfies more strongly in the long run: it spreads mistrust, because no foreign statesman can calculate what will happen if unexpected new events enter. That was precisely the most terrible mistake of the German pre-war policy.

VI. The national cultural goal.
The significance of the German-Austrian merger. - Border German liberation.

VII. From the national cultural political idea to the idea of national rights.
Reich and foreign Germans. - The atrocities of the western national state. - The impracticality of total separation. - The new conception of the state. - German popular rights.

VIII

The European goals

The future federal politics is basically different from that of the pre-war period. The latter knew only two form-groups: the free federation or the firm states union. Two forms of federation were further in use: the genuine federation between two approximately equally strong states which joined together with equal rights for the common attainment of this or that goal under preservation of their full sovereignty (in the sense of the western conception of the state); then, the treaty between a power and powerless states which had more or less lost their independence. For example: the treaties of the French Revolution government and that of the first Kaiser Reich, England's "federations" in overseas territories with Indian princes, or those of the American Union with Central American states. If one wished to move closer together one required to enter into indissoluble bonds. Monarchic personal union does not need to be taken into consideration in this connection. Commonality between certain state institutions characterizes the state unions, lasting unifications of two or more states for the purpose of uniform or similar exercice of sovereign rights, without needing to consider "the union" and its organs in order to undertake government transactions within the individual states. A still closer bond was the federal state on the nature of which the science set up many mutually divergent doctrines regarding the question of where the sovereignty lies, whether it is divisible, etc. Unconcerned about this conflict, throve such federal states foreign politically uniformly directed and defended, to be sure not always without inner frictions. Actually it is a matter of whether these structures have arisen from the relaxation of older historical unions (Austria-Hungary) and whether the tendency towards the separation still continued to predominate, or whether related or otherwise - mostly through language-community or blood mixture - closely linked states were in the process of binding themselves to one another still more firmly (the United States of America and Brazil).

All these models do not suit Europe, for it requires a full new formation. Such a one was, however, upto now observed among nations of equal origin and language. Multi-national Switzerland looked back, before the Confederation assumed its present form, already to a centuries-old common history. Much less does the model of the Geneva national federation, of a loose state union, suit, in spite of some determinations making dissolution harder, and above all not the new British one of 1926. The British state union has become uniquely historical: bound externally only by the crown, internally however by community of language, by total clogging of British interests, and by the sea-ruling navy. Where the community of language is not perfect lie the weak points (South Africa). The union of nations, however, brings so many congenital mistakes openly to view that only a superficial observer can plan to "order" Europe according to the model of the union of nations or indeed as that of its subdivision. Rather the internal new structure of Soviet Russia can offer suggestions. For, in many respects, there were there similar tasks to be resolved which arose from the multiplicity of peoples. The difference lies, however, in the fact that the Bolshevist total state, ruling over the · entire territory, was at first already present and then split itself up subsequently, for the facilitation of the administration, into partial republics - according to language and race, in order to preempt dangers which would have to arise from the dissatisfaction with the standardising tendency of the administration.

Nobody forced the power-holders in Moscow to it. They did it out of free pieces, partly from considerations of utility, partly in order to realize old Socialist-Syndicalist doctrines of the earlier age.

Still more differently stand matters in non-Communistic Europe. It decomposes not only into languages and races - in extreme cases awakening races like the Ukrainian -, but into many large and old political peoples: full of marked racial personalities with much famed history and hard outlines, with a peculiar intellectual and economic culture, with a more or less established state system. Next to these we find small- and medium- nations, younger and poorer in tradition, still with so much more reckless nationalism, mostly stuck still deep in their adolescence. Preferred in the conclusion of the Versailles treaty, they unjustly received their own states with all-too broadly drawn borders in which they could rule freely, thanks to the victory of the atomistic French national state doctrine, without consideration of the foreign national parts wrongly apportioned to them, of their neighbouring nations, or of the European community. The self-interest of states therefore stands today in full bloom. It produces evil fruits.

The untenability of the European map arisen from 1918 to 1920 is admitted by the public opinion of all nations. To repeat the causes and reasons of this condition would be a waste of space. They are not only of an economic, but also, in high measure, of a political sort. The deficient resolution of the question of nationalities shelters visible dangers. The powerless and chained German people poses to the European politics more of an enigma than earlier the powerful did: an idea which Stegemann has brilliantly developed in his *Illusion of Versailles*.[141] The doctrine of the self-determination right of the peoples directed against the Germans and the Hungarians once announced in the "Declaration of Lausanne" adopted by Wilson during the world war, is today turned against the artificially inflated would-be victor states. It begins to work in favour of the

---

[141] [Hermann Stegemann (1870-1945), *Das Trugbild von Versailles: weltgeschichtliche Zusammenhänge und strategische Perspektiven*, Stuttgart: Deutsche Verlags Anstalt, 1926].

Germans and Hungarians and destroys the European state picture of the Versailles treaty.

Thus there sounds everywhere the cry for a new order of Europe, to be sure, differently tuned according to the standpoint of the appealer and according to his way of thought: in western Europe, in the better established national states, more cautiously, even if the economics there, stifled by military burdens and out of fear of America's competition, wishes for real establishment of peace. In the satellite states, most loudly. There the economic self-sufficiency (autarchy) striven for at present was quickly recognized as a chimera, even if upto now the state leadership holds fast to it. The scope of these state economies is indeed too small. Larger economic structures seem necessary. All attempts however to reestablish the earlier Hapsburg Empire at least as an economic Danube confederation were wrecked on political oppositions. Austria wants it as little as Hungary.

Need then indeed promotes plans to organise Europe, but not the solving formula: what as such was offered as allegedly new, was indeed partly extolled like a trade ware, is old wine in new bottles. Anxiously concerned to maintain the present distribution of power, without really undermining the present-day western state - Socialist varnishing does not change its system for the better - all the following mentioned reforms wish however finally only a sham-democratic state federation. The catchword of equality and freedom are transferred from the internal political to the foreign political field. One wishes to transform the whole of Europe into a gigantic mass democracy, and raise the lies of the equal and free rule of people into a proportion of immensity.

IX

Ineffective or wrong plans

At first, economic plans were submitted to the public by Socialists, but also by the "capitalistic" side. They recommended almost throughout a European customs union, partly according to the previous private economic union.[142] Esteemed economic unions emphasized in announcements, and at the various conferences, the necessity of the economic "co operation" of the European states. Traffic conferences wanted to remove Europe's turn-pikes. A manifesto coloured in the free-trade style wanted international financial people to tear up Europe's economy-restricting customs walls. In Geneva, the economics conference, in Paris, the international chamber of commerce, was concerned in the same way.

Others recognized in advance that the European question is however not, in the first place, determined by considerations of utility. "To conceive it from this point of view is a way of observation which reminds one of the politics of the pre-war period, in which we expected everything from economic and power political organisation, a standpoint which has led finally to our present-day chaos.

---

[142] [Paul] Göhre, *Deutschlands weltpolitische Zukunft*, Berlin, Kurt Vorwinkel, [1925]; August Schmidt, *Das neue Europa*, Berlin, Reimar Hobbing, [1925]; [Wladimir] Woytinsky, *Die Vereinigten Staaten von Europa*, Berlin, J.H.W. Dietz Nachfolger Verlag, [1926].

Even this attitude betrays a not all-too deep insight into the forces determining the development" (Kleefisch). The historical-Catholic "West" movement seeks therefore to revive once again the universalistic idea of the Holy Roman Empire of German nations. Accordingly, the Austrian prince, Karl Anton von Rohan undertook to bind the conservative ruling class of the European nations with his *Europäische Revue* and through conferences. "For the supplementing of the communication work of the governments" arose further a union for European communication, into which famous politicians entered: Luther, Stresemann, Wirth, Vandevelde, Briand, Painlevé, Albert Thomas, Ramsay MacDonald, Fritjof Nansen, etc. But this union must fail because good words and dispositions are useless; for action, however, this circle is organised in a too motley manner; its forces eliminate one another.

The reach of all these efforts was, and is, small, their powers are modest; they consist at the present of a book and a journal or of one or two conferences in the year which give an opportunity for expression. Their objectives are either economic or cultural-intellectual. They do without the comprehensive, pick out only details, without giving firm outlines to that which is demanded. Thus their effectiveness too remained small. Even for the future nothing is to be expected from them but relaxation through criticism.

It is different with the so-called Pan-European movement. It sets in with easily comprehensible recipes which are immediately coined into catchwords, promoted by a charlatanly advertising campaign. Their founder and their driving force is Count Nikolaus von Coudenhove-Kalergi ·in Vienna.[143] Of his way of thought one gets the following idea in his book on the aristocracy:[144] "The man of the distant future will be a mongrel", so prophesies the son of an already mixed "Austrian" aristocrat and a Japanese woman. "The eurasiatic-negroid future race,

---

[143] [Count Richard Coudenhove-Kalergi (1894-1972) continued his belief in the Paneuropean movement upto the sixties].

[144] [*Adel*, Leipzig: Verlag Der neue Geist, 1922].

externally perhaps similar to the ancient Egyptian, will replace the multiplicity of the peoples with a many-sidedness of personality". On the leaders of this future development he says: "Instead of destroying Judaism, it has ennobled Europe against its will through that artificial selection process (steeling through heroically borne martyrdom and purging of weak-willed, intellectually poor elements, of which he has spoken in the earlier sentence) and trained it into a leader nation of the future. No wonder therefore that this people, arisen from the ghetto, develop themselves into an intellectual aristocracy of Europe. Thus a kind providence has, through the grace of the spirit, gifted Europe a new noble race the moment that the feudal nobility fell, through the emancipation of the Jews". To this half-coloured mongrel the concept of race and national culture means nothing for understandable reasons.

In 1923 he published a programme piece, *Paneuropa,* and won with it European fame, especially in circles which were in advance favorably disposed to him on account of his book on the aristocracy. His introductory statement, "This book is determined to awake a great political movement", he has made true. Externally, Pan-Europe was a success: not alone thanks to propagandistic performances, through its easily comprehensible symbols - the sun-cross as the sign of humanity and reason - and through the timely capitalisation of a need of the time, but also, above all, through its penetrating criticism of the conditions of the present-day Europe.

Its foundation is, of course, wrong; for he says, "The entire European question culiminates in the Russian problem. The main goal of the European politics must be the prevention of a Russian invasion ---." "If Russia succeeds, through some harvests, to revive itself economically, before Europe is united - then Europe's fate is sealed. The future state form of Russia is thereby irrelevant. As soon as the opportunity offers itself to Russia to bring Europe into its dependence, it will make use of this possibility - whether it is now red or white". That sets the facts on their head. Soviet Russia is weak in economy and army,

apparently for a long time. Certainly, the fact of the disappearance of the
predominantly Nordic ruling class in Russia is highly significant for the future.
Only the knowledge of this circumstance preserves one from the politics,
dangerous for Europe, of democratising and capitalising Russia. A Pan-Slavism
of the nihilistic sort of a Dostojewski would thus grow up with a dangerous rise.
The western historical conception therefore saw correctly in the Russian field
European colonial soil, in the Russian peasant masses men who must be ruled in
a European manner. There are, therefore, with regard to Russia, only two political
ways, of which one is hard to enter: to bring Russia once again under the rule of
a European ruling class; the other is outlined in 1914 by the history of the Middle
Ages and the battle of Tannenberg, one of the few which has true world historical
significance: to push the European culture towards the East. Later generations will
praise the destruction of Russia as the great performance of the German people;
as much more tactically correct it may perhaps have been to preserve it at first.
It means, however, to ignore the present-day situation of Europe if one does not
perceive in the forcing back of the Russian Empire one of the great possibilities
for the German foreign policy. From a broad perspective therefore partial consent
could be granted to the thought processes of the Pan-European Count if he
advocates a truly European policy against Russia. Never, however, can such be
conducted if the emphasis of Europe lies in the west. A French anti-Russia politics
must always treat Germany and central Europe as an intermediate territory. In fact,
however, the emphasis of European self-maintenance lies in the European centre,
in Prussia. Without this even the Rhine and, therewith, France are lost.

Coudenhove acknowledges the Paris peace treaties, which signify to him,
in spite of his criticism, "politically a progress in comparison to the pre-war
situation". He glosses over its consequences: "As unjust and damnable also as
these supressions of parts (Germans, Magyars, and Ukrainians) are: to these
suppressed peoples of today at least there remains their own state as a national
resort and as a free cultural centre - whereas, before the war, European cultured

nations were in their entirety robbed of their national freedom. In spite of this remnant of national suppression, for the removal of which every good European must work, a progress is accordingly to be recognized in the political structure of Europe of the pre-war period". For this reason, the much-mixed Count also teaches the irrevocability of the borders drawn in Paris; for this reason, too, his hostility to annexation: one who works for a change of the German borders must conduct war politics. Thereby did Vilna come without a war to Poland, Oedenburg to Hungary! The Belgian cabinet decided in 1926 to sell Eupen-Malmedy to the Reich. If this decision too was repealed once again on Poincaré's insistence, it still shows the erroneousness of Coudenhove's thesis that one must make the best of the Versailles drawing of borders: "One who attacks these borders - attacks the peace of Europe".

Coudenhove's plans have perceptibly experienced extensive rejection in serious political circles. Even from national German parties, whose thought arose from the same individualistic root, the following was smaller than the criticism. Even leftist circles in the Reich rejected Coudenhove because his doctrine takes as its point of departure the work of the Paris treaty and makes the hegemony of France the chief column of his system. Nevertheless, Coudenhove found for years his chief support among the Berlin bank circles, while one overlooked in France what useful assisting peoples the pan-Europeans could become for the guarantee of the things acquired in the work of the Paris treaty. Finally, however, the French foreign minister, Briand,[145] explained in the summer of 1929 in a commision of the French chamber that he would submit plans for the "United States of Europe" to the powers in the autumn; Coudenhove approved Briand's plan in a public announcement.[146] Now the connection is clearly established.

---

[145] [Aristide Briand (1862-1932) served eleven times as Premier of France, in addition to holding the post of Foreign Minister for many years. In December 1930, Briand put forward his plans for a federal union of European states].

[146] [See Richard Coudenhove-Kalergi, *Paneuropa, 1922 bis 1966*, Wien: Verlag Herold, pp.64-66; *History of the Paneuropean Movement*, Basle and Vienna: Paneuropa Union, 1962, p.10f].

The foundation of Coudenhove is the individualistic national state with its formal democracy. He instructed in 1923: "Europe as a political concept encompasses all democratic and semi-democratic states of continental Europe with the inclusion of Iceland --- The remaining territory of European Turkey belongs politically to Asia". The Europe to be founded by Coudenhove "reaches so far to the east as the democratic system; the question whether Russia belongs to Europe the Count sees as "made essentially simple" since it has placed itself outside Europe through its break with the democratic system. "The addition of England and Ireland to Pan-Europe would be possible after the disintegration of the British world empire".

Pan-Europe should thus consist of 26 larger and 7 smaller territories with 300,000,000 inhabitants. In addition, even the overseas colonial empire of the Pan-European powers enter with 53,000 inhabitants in Africa and 78,300,000 inhabitants in other continents. - What is such a union of states with 431 million inhabitants? Super-imperialistic formal democracy with all the mistakes of the past, a product of megalomaniac intoxication of numbers!

Coundenhove's strict advance limitation of the future union of European states, which he later sought to moderate somewhat, ignores territory. Already for this reason it is superficial and false. If forms, however, the essential factor of his individualistic thought "in states". In addition, it is, because cumbersome, awkward. Western way of thought in a pacifist variety conducted to the highest degree, already almost to a caricature, robs the European construction plans in advance of every freedom of movement, what Coudenhove moreover does not overlook entirely. Dull and uncreative, but for that reason easily understandable to like-minded people, Coudenhove knows only states and state nations but not peoples, not driving cultural movements. To want to prescribe firm borders means to ignore that Europe is, historically, intellectually- and religiously, communications politically, and economically, only a very conditional unity. For, towards the borders it increasingly evaporates.

Popular feeling and nationalistic chauvinism are however the same thing for Coudenhove. For that reason, the secrets of this earth, as openly as they may lie, must remain hidden to the Pan-European. He does not wish to see them. The one robbed of the idea of the whole is made a fool of by his belief in the understanding. He fails before simple facts, such as those of the westerners in general.

Europe is not to be built up once again from the rubble of the destruction with construction plans out of individualistic-pacifist thought. Not the fear of Soviet Russia, but the concern about the unresolved pains of the people which break up the ground for Bolshevist seed, must be the mainspring of all work towards a new legal order. Finally: no true architect builds from outside inwards. That only those who are not experts do. Such constructions suffice for film shooting.

If the Pan-Europeans work with cosmopolitan-pacifistic means in order to give Europe a new face, Fascism does with the opposite. Already above - in the internal political part - serious doubts were brought forward, whether Fascism does not represent a culmination of nationalistic-imperialistic intellectual tradition, and therefore has remained even in that Liberalism which it allegedly strives to overcome. This book evaluates its internal political performance (deliberate economic politics, national education, constitutional reform) even as highly as its effort to set a penetrating intellectual doctrine against the western democracy. But the Fascist state centralism has, upto now, as little got round to the hurdles of the creation of a ranked society as it has not succeeded, on the other hand, to sketch a picture of the correct coming European order. The Italian politics in South Tyrol strengthens the doubt that Fascism upto now has remained in a radicalisation of the national-political idea.

This process is not new. Even the German Liberalism fell already decades ago into political-national radicalism. Every genuine revolution, however, brings not merely a change of methods but the removal of the ruling principle. Thus the individual was perhaps dethroned in Italy, but even the personality destroyed. Precisely in this way the foreign policy of the deceptive pacifism was removed, but the racial personality too was destroyed. Fascism has not yet, upto now, accomplished the turn towards organic life. The incorporation into a final unconditional worth, which the whole of life constantly offers to man, is lacking. The tendency of the West to anarchy was thereby only externally chained by Fascism, but not combatted from inside.

X

The foundations of German federal politics

The correct way is the reverse. One should begin from inside. No new construction can do without the core, which it has to let grow gradually. In this way do crystals also arise. The cell must lie in the field of the greatest difficulties, political and economic: there, where the treaties of the Paris headquarters tore up the finest interweavings, where the European peoples and states pushed against one another without natural borders, where the closed settlement territories of the peoples were recently sliced, politically, and where peoples are crowded in such a mixed situation that state borders can in general not be drawn on the basis of national segregation. The core territory, based on the needs of which the legal decrees of a union of European states must be torn apart, lies not at the border of Europe, either in the north or in the west, nor even in the extreme east, but in the centre, which has no geographically limited territory: in the territory of the settlement field of the Germans, and of the east- and south-European medium and lesser peoples, from the Baltic Sea to the Adriatic, from Finland to the Aegean and the Black Sea.

This territory is central Europe, enlarged by the near south-eastern Europe and the near eastern Europe, that which Albrecht Haushofer[146] called Inner Europe. A presentation of this territory and of the foundations of essential federal formation is given by Karl C. von Loesch.[147] Premature inclusion of the border territories of Europe makes the problem more difficult and blurs the goal.

A cell must be present to which states and peoples can be joined economically and politically. The greatest unity of this territory is the German people, the greatest of its states is the torso of the German Reich. Thence the duty and right of the Germans to the leadership in a European new formation. This conception is to be founded also economic historically, not only in remembrance of the Prussian customs-union. For, the greatest part of the territory just mentioned has received in the last 1000 years not only its intellectual but also its economic culture from Germans or through German transmission. German is there the language of trade and large communications, the work methods of the economy are German. Germans have been living there for centuries in larger and smaller islands as soil-related as the other peoples: economically a model, as a mediator unsurpassable.

The closed central European settlement territory of the Germans however reaches from the North Sea to the Baltic Sea (upto 70km. as the crow flies) almost to the Adriatic. The intermediate sector is little passable, chalk formations and foothills of the Alps fill it. Precisely there lives one of the smallest peoples of Europe. Bays of the ocean still reach even into German land. Almost all transport ways from east to west and from south to north, on land and by air, lead over the territory of the Germans: thus these are actually Europe's people of the centre. Thus, almost without natural borders or limits, Germany is politically and militarily threatened or favored: exposed to attacks and prepared for attack.

  · Italic, Italian-Germanic, Germanic, and Slavic peoples, and further a people

---

[146] September, 1926, issue of the *Volk und Reich*, Berlin.

[147] "Paneuropa - Völker und Staaten", in *Staat und Volkstum*, Berlin, Deutscher Schutzbund Verlag, [1926].

belonging to a special group, border on the German: the picture of the neighbours is therefore more mottled than anywhere else.

According to its blood mixture, the German is also in a central situation. The Nordic blood, extirpated in Russia, fully attenuated in the west and the south, predominant in the north and in the Netherlands but fully subjected to individualism in terms of the intellect and will, is still sufficiently present in Germany.

The German people must once again become legal creative, in order to find new political ideas for itself and Europe: in order to facilitate a living together of peoples on the same territory, in a painful narrowness. Beginnings towards this are already present in many fields. It is important to give them shape in order to provide, in this way, to the foreign policy of the Reich, intellectual weapons which are more effective than those upto now. Only in this way can the repeatedly characterized tendency against the European centre which leads away from the German culture be reversed into an opposite movement which leads to the collection of the people in the centre of Europe. The foundation of a universally valid European order is, accordingly, dependent on the Germans returning once again to their basic ideas of truth and justice and clothing them in modern decrees. The people which tramples underfoot the humanitarian lie of Europe and hoists the flag of true order becomes the self-active head of the new European organism. The loss of the ability "to highlight the European aspect of the German people" (Karl Anton, Prince Rohan) was responsible for the divergence of Europe from the people of the centre. The historical hour requires the full setting in of the German people for the European new formation under total affirmation and strengthening of its powers derived from the spirit of the people.

In the national political part, the picture of the coming German state was already sketched, whose forms facilitate a politics of firm federation. Since the economy, separated from the political in a certain sense, can follow its own laws, but the federation politics projected here extends the nourishment territory, the stimulus for imperialistic economic politics ceases. The same is true of the cultural life. Therewith the striven-for federation politics of the new individualistic (organic) state and of the impulse towards extension lying within it lost its threatening, or indeed hostile, aspect for the neighbouring peoples which clung inseparably to the individualistic-national state foreign politics. However, a state of the western sort, which emerged economically and culturally imperialistically, had to push the adjoining border peoples. The new Germany, however, from whose realm of influence culture and economy are derived, needs to instil no fear any longer into border peoples who rightly wish the fruits of their own work and their racial character to be untouched. Such a state exerts an attractive influence on its neighbours. For, it offers to smaller people through new federal forms the powerful attraction of being able to participate in the advantages of a superiour culture, of a developed economy, without having to give themselves up. Thus arises a healthy federal foundation while the all-consuming, all-ruling state was rejected. A state system constituted in this way can offer a secure dwelling place even to a foreign people who stand racially, geopolitically, culturally or historically close to the Germans.

Now what differentiates in the final analysis the Italian concept of the national state from the new political idea which should replace it? What makes it really capable of introducing a new European order? On the one hand, the legal idea which recognizes the rights of other peoples; on the other hand, the greater flexibility. Deep love for one's own people passes even with necessity through the knowledge that in every people a higher personality is embodied to the attention to foreign peoples and to the striving for a higher legal order among the peoples. To develop and demarcate independent laws of the racial personality with regard to the whole that is sought is a part of the new German foreign political goal. Hereby, however, it does not occur without border changes; the latter, however, have as a prerequisite a far-reaching change of the spiritual basic attitude of the Europeans, the change of the state conceptions in general. Since a new legal order has as a prerequirement the demarcation of rights, ordering principles must be set up. Karl C. von Loesch[148] has outlined them as follows:

"1. Every people should have in future the right to maintain its racial existence and to develop itself freely. The only limitation which is necessary - just as the right of the individual man in the state must be limited in favour of the maintenance of the whole - occurs to the benefit of an ordered living together of the peoples: from the "rights of the peoples" therefore follow also "duties of the peoples".

2. As political basic rights of the peoples the following are to be considered:

for the closed settlement territory of every people[149] the right to their own state.

for the sections of the people not comprehended by this, which remain outside and live in foreign states as their citizens, the right to maintenance of the intellectual and physical national cultural existence (national cultural group right).

The recognition of the right to one's own state does not naturally signify, for the peoples coming into question, the pressure towards the severing of the existing historical, territorial, and economic bonds (between peoples who live on the edge of the closed settlement territory in an interconnection of peoples or in a national cultural mixture in language islands or mixed-language territories); much less the prohibition of a far-reaching voluntary association. Pressure in no form comes into question here; it is a matter, in fact, of avoiding pressure. The will of the peoples is the decisive thing. What a people is is today, to be sure, still in no way firm; how many national cultural sections are claimed by two, indeed three, peoples

---

[148] October issue, 1928, of the *Deutsche Rundschau* [pp. 1-21, "Streben und Stil der Besiegten: Außenpolitischen Überlegungen für das deutsche Volk"].

[149] The establishment of the closed racial territory will often not be easy. Wide territories of Europe are debated. The application of mechanical principles for the establishment of the range of a nation is prohibited by itself. Popular votes do not come into consideration in all cases, often indeed the pre-war population was driven away by force.

precisely in the most dangerous storm-centres of Europe. Nevertheless, in practice, useful guidelines are easily to be found if only one avoid unfruitful historicism (historical proof) and the beloved equation of language community and membership in a national cultural group.

If, however, greater parts of national cultural bodies remain bound to foreign peoples, the degree of rights which suits them depends on the numerical relation, on the manner of settlement, on their historical and cultural significance for the whole of the state; whether they are authorized to demand recognition as a people of the state with equal rights or whether guaranteed national cultural group rights (autonomy) suffice, which also will have different scopes. Decisive are the absolute and relative number of a racial group, the density of their population, and the manner of their settlement, their social significance, their economic and communication-technological connections, their cultural development, their historical traditions, and their traditional attitude to the state-administering people. The right of free and equal use of their own language and to all possibilities which the public life offers, as well as the right to maintenance, care, and development of their own national cultural culture according to the principles of the public-legal corporate body autonomy, forms the indispensable prerequirement for each people. In any case, the ordering of this question must result in the form of constitutional determinations which cannot be changed by majority decisions".

That is, however, only one side of the problem, which requires supplementation. "Along with the right of the peoples to their own even characteristic politicality (national cultural group rights are also such partial rights which are opposed by the wrong conception of the system of the state ruling today, which does not wish to recognize the other spheres of rights) a binding link is to be set up as the fusion of the impulse to uniformity and the tendency to isolation. The consideration of one's neighbours and the closer relations produced by the neighbourliness demand an establishment of neighbourly rights and duties of the states.[150] Wars are kindled, according to experience, mostly through neighbourly friction. To avoid them is the first prerequirement for the removal of the feeling of the uncertainty under which the states suffer today. This closer binding of the neighbours forms at the same time the indispensable preliminary stage for the progressing towards the organic structure, the building up of greater economic territories which are indeed necessary if Europe wishes to maintain itself in the competition of the continent. That does not, however, mean, by far, recommending mechanical equalisation of the states and rash bindings of the states, for which the time has not yet become ripe. On the contrary! As regards neighbourly bindings of the states of the same territory, the development must rather rise gradually in organic growth from inside outwards for the formation of higher federalistic unities".

The idea of a federation, as it is expressed here, starts even from the fact that the society consists of partial realms, that it itself already separates out intellectual circles of life of a special sort and performance. Walter Heinrich[151] says on this, that the state of such a conception appears as that order (*status*) which lends to every society historical shape and form. Since every national cultural group, every national cultural fragment and every people strive to bring their life into form, within every people their life must be shaped systematically: their artistic, economic, original and familial life-expressions. "All these life-expressions must be collected in a strong protecting cover, in an order which accomplishes those foreign and internal political performances which we have characterized as state performances. There are naturally different degrees of

---

[150] The rights and duties of the peoples in the state and of the states as neighbours condition one another reciprocally. They must be built up, harmonized to and among one another. Border changes, as they are inevitable for a true satisfaction, can be carried out for themselves alone without dangerous conflicts only with difficulty. Psychological hindrances still stand against neighbourly approximation without border changes at the moment on account of the justified resentment of those who suffer injustice today. The basic agreement is still lacking from which first an European feeling can grow which is the prerequisite of lasting and stable associations. Both goals cannot be reached in one stroke. More or less numerous objective and territorial interim solutions will have to precede them.

[151] July issue of the *Europäische Revue*, 1929.

development of this politicality. Politicality is a concept of degree[152] (not only, as a typographical mistake will have it, a basic concept[153]). Not every people or indeed every national cultural group can develop its own political life which could be designated as a national cultural full state. That seems also thoroughly comprehensible. For, for an organic historical stratum, which is the true one, nowhere can an equality of peoples be established, but one observes always and everywhere the greatest inequality, in the fullness of being of the peoples as well as in their historical tasks and their historical significance. Sociological and historical research finds everywhere and always the tendency of every culture and every national cultural group to develop the politicality suited to its being. This politicality can manifest very different degrees of development and even does manifest them; this ladder proceeds from the most primitive beginnings of a kernel politicality (e.g. in the form of a hardly performed autonomy, hardly present closedness with regard to other peoples of the state, and hardly traceable bindings to other peoples, perhaps to the entire nation, of which the concerned national cultural group is a partial population or "minority") to the fully developed politicality which gets perhaps the leading role in foreign and internal politics in their state. All life in society and history strives for political forms and also develops actual politicality".

The organic state is not forced to destroy all that structure of orders which brings life with it. Rather, it may maintain, strengthen and try to develop the intermediate members of the orders. In this way also an organic European state federation can let the individual peoples live. "The more vital and genuine their own life is developed, the stronger and more powerful does the whole appear," says Walter Heinrich of the state: the same is true even of a healthy state binding. Just.as the state in reality is not based on the counting together of the wills of the individuals, not on the unorganised randomly flowing masses of state citizens, but

[152] [Gradbegriff].
[153] [Grundbegriff].

on characteristic realms of life, with regard to which it similarly embodies a closed realm of life and performance, namely as the order of politicality, as external and internal concentration, so a European state federation arches over the individual states and peoples naturally under the preservation of their rights with regard to the whole. If there is, in the organic state, already a large number of partial politicalities which are endowed with their own life and certain sovereign rights (genuine autonomy), then there arises even through the European federation one more new realm of life. Just as the autonomy of the professional realms is finally not derived (delegated) from the state, but comes also from itself, from the life and objective demands of the whole, so also the European union as a community of the Western peoples and cultures of this continent derives its justification from the living whole. Its realm of tasks is developed as a result of the new ordering of Europe also quite naturally through customs- and economic settlements to the highest development and administration of justice in this realm. It will gradually progress.

It was characteristic for the individualistic state that, as a result of the rigidity of its conceptions, it was not in a position to resolve such a simple problem as, for example, the Catalanian, in a satisfactory manner, because it just cannot acknowledge life-realms which have their own rootedness. It can make no minority forces useful for itself by building them up, because every such attempt (that is the horrible phantom of the individualistic state leaders) would immediately lead to the formation of a "state within a state", and therewith to the destruction of the idol of uniformity. The idea of the organic state, on the other hand, allows greater freedom internally and formative possibilities externally. But centralism is finally nothing but a theory. The German Reich, England, Switzerland and many other states have long demonstrated that states can be capacitated to great performances which bear a federal political or, indeed, a political federation character and thereby permit, under the guarantee of greater mobility, yet a very strict concentration through the highest authority. *Even because this system is so mobile, because it is not sworn to anything, it corresponds best to the varied facts of Europe.* What people are led in an organically built up multi-national state union is finally a historical decision; they can be diverse according to the period, just as in the multi-national states locally diverse solutions are thinkable which do not always summon the numerically greatest people to the leadership. Not every people and not every national cultural group can attain political maturity. "On this point decide their intellectual, economic, and political powers, finally their historical fate, indeed even the entire national culture to which this group of people belong" (Walter Heinrich).

Thus the German people, if it brings forward the power for the European performance, can proclaim the rule of the superiour at the same time internal- and foreign-politically. As the pioneers of a higher morality the Germans then become the prophets of a better Europe which can once again gift something to the world and which renews its intellectual predominance. The people of the highest achievement should on the basis of their achievement, under full consideration of its geopolitical central situation, be the leader in a union of free peoples. This leadership will form new spheres of power and culture.

It was a contradiction that small and medium peoples standing first on the threshold of the Western civilisation, for the most part, necessarily doing without an independent culture on account of the too small number of people, could increase the sphere of their power in the last decade under the sign of the idea of the individualistic national state, whereas, at the same time, historical peoples like the German were curtailed and enslaved. It is a sign of the downfall. Only the suppression of genuine culture and the worsip of the idol of civilisation can lead to such foolishness. For, where civilisation in its fleetingness and emptiness of content begins to displace the feeling for culture, every difference is blurred: the smallest barbaric race raises its head with civilisatory gestures and demands equal rights. But just as an organic social life is possible only when the rights of the parts, which the member proves to the whole, are ranked according to performances, so also a European order only when right and service are brought into an appropriate relation. There is no naturally given right to life of a people, but only a justification of their existence on the basis of self-felt and self-willed life obligations. The principle of equality, ruling in the self-determination rights of a Wilson, and therefore powerless for a new ordering, was responsible for Europe's anarchy. Even in the field of national relations the path towards genuine worthiness begins to become free once again only with the knowledge of the inequality of nations. For, no order is possible without a series of values, and no justice where formal equality should rule.

XI. Towards the accomplishment of the new order.
Between the west- and the east-European states. - European markets, not farmland.
- "The people without land". - Difficulties. - The new state constitution as charter
of rights for the minorities. - New war techniques.

XII

The age of the Germans

The original duties of a state, to secure peace both externally and internally, are unchangeable. Only the temporal goals are subject to change. Different ages place different chief tasks. "It is not enough that one would like to start world history where one is resentful of it on account of a lost war" (Albrecht Haushofer).[154] When the Thirty-Years war had made the German land empty of men and culture, it was the chief task of the rulers to fill it once again with men. To prescribe a normally developed child blood-forming means, just in order to attain the quantity of blood which is suitable to an adult in the conviction that then everything else will develop accordingly is foolish. Those population measures had a success not only through the increase of numbers but also as a cultural accomplishment. "Without the Thirty Years war a Goethe and a Lessing would have been impossible". We therefore affirm the belief in the final significance of history, in spite of the lost war, when we say: Without the world war there would perhaps have been no age of the Germans, to which this book is dedicated.

That success was so pervasive that, 100 years later, the population question

---

[154] [in *Volk und Reich*, Heft 4 (1929)].

became once again a concern in the reverse direction; the fear of overpopulation let the doctrine of Malthus find followers even in Germany. At first, however, there followed a wave of enormous population increase, increased hygiene decreased the mortality rate, the economic-technological upsurge offered increased bread. In this way, individualism directly increased the population numbers for the generation of the 19th century.

With the 20th century entered a turn; today, the overdeveloped individualism gradually consumes the peoples once again, it lets them grow too old. But we know that renewal is possible.

Upto today, Europe has been ruled politically by the realm of individualistic ideas of the French Revolution. But even in France powers stir to overcome it: in vain. Individualism is even the intellectual form of the peculiar blood mixture of the French, of the true heritage of late Rome. The Celtic-Germanic admixture became increasingly smaller through powerful events and slow counter-selection, coloured people penetrate daily and are unthinkingly accepted. Where once Franks, Burgundians and Goths ruled, the Eurasian-negroid future race expected by Coudenhove is already today being formed. The Italians make - apparently immaturely - similarly the tense effort to push towards the organic world-picture. The appeal to their Latinity however makes the same fears emerge as were expressed with regard to the French efforts.

The Germans, like all cultured peoples, not of one race, are better mixed: the Nordic is bound to the heritage of other European races in a much higher admixture: a fortunate sign for the future, because it promises the necessary spiritual depth.

If, in future, the German people, made truly knowledgeable and believing, economises better with its national cultural powers, in conscious defence against the false counter-selection, then it will once again grow in numbers. It can however also win wealth once again with it and become more creatively strong. In that case, the world war was not in vain. In that case, it became a turn of fate.

But the way there is long and rough. "Until one will have progressed from the plans of such goals to the recognition and finally the execution, not only much time will be lost, but also much sacrifice will be demanded: of ideas grown beloved, of flattering self-interests to which one has given oneself up. But they will be worth it, for a higher prize beckons. If the Germans succeed in ordering their continent for themselves and for the other peoples in a clever way, then they would have also founded an ordering principle which would apparently become a model, with some changes, for other continents. That requires the belief in an idea. Just as, earlier, the great transformations of the earth were called forth and borne by ideas, so will it remain in all ages".

Whether the way to German freedom goes through Europe's new formation or whether first a free Germany can build up Europe once again, nobody knows. It is doubtless, however, that first the German people must be inwardly armed: determined to establish German freedom and European new order, if necessary even with their blood. Herein lies included a moral command. To take this possibility into consideration is a duty; though it is important to avoid the mistakes of the men of 'forty-eight[155] who wished German unity without wanting also the final means. But Bismarck recognized that it must be fought for; he went to Königgrätz.[156]

The powers of the mind are strong. The weapon of a closed world of ideas is still stronger, if the will leads the arm. The highest, however, is achieved by self-sacrifice. That was always so, that is so, and that will always remain so. Should that which is thought and said here not remain a dream, but become a reality, it must be also thought of in terms of power politics. The will to power is at the same time the way of German freedom, which, in spite of all talk remains

[155] [The März Revolution of 1848 which was conducted around the two key issues of the creation of German unity and of representative government. It was defeated by a counter-revolution before the end of the year].

[156] [site in Bohemia of the chief battle between Austria and Prussia in July 1866. Prussia won the battle and began therefrom its hegemony in Europe].

a distant goal from the now almost achieved German "sovereignty". If the German mind is liberated and purified, then the highest worthiness of the German people must become the greatest concern. The purity of the soul and the sharpness of the sword belong together. The intellectual cleavage of our age gave birth to the raging lie of the opposition of mind and power. They are opposites, but only where the totality of life is denied: where mind and power, each for itself, lead a lifeless existence in isolation. Correspondingly, the German people today splits into two political camps: a power-affirming one which neglects the mind, and sees it only as an appendage of power; and then into a power-denying one which goes into raptures over a lifeless mind which hovers in the void without spiritual roots. The triumph of the new vitality establishes the whole once again: it accomplishes that synthesis of power and mind without which culture has never been.

It is important to develop the will to power, without noise, with iron logicality. The German people still has a free hand in many areas of life, preparedness to encounter the hour of destiny. The decisive determination for the great venture must be taken at any time. The first and most immediate prerequirement for foreign political action is the renewal of life, society and the state. The German man must be won for the task of throwing overboard those basic views which wish to maintain unchanged the western-financial capitalistic state form. The disintegrating rule of the inferiour calls for the establishment of a newly formed order of worth.

Already more than once the German people appeared mortally wounded, and their freedom was destroyed. Every time the German mind raised itself out of its chains and developed prophetic powers. We felt, with a feeling almost bordering on doubt, that in the present-day deep collapse self-seeking giddiness seemed to make hindsight impossible. So we looked into the depths of the German soul and created out of it the powers which extend the bow to an immeasurable width: which make the German life worth living once again. For even today what Fichte called out to the German people in the times of humiliation is valid:

"Among all young peoples it is the Germans in whom the kernel of perfection of humanity lies most decisively and to whom progress in the development of the same is entrusted".

Thought and action

... To him rose,
Steeled by the spell of the frenzied
years,
A young generation, which once
again mixed
Man and thing in true measure,
which, beautiful and serious,
Glad of its uniqueness, proud before
foreigners,
Distances itself equally from cliffs
of dark daring
And from the shallow swamp of
false brotherhood,
Which spews from itself what is
demoralized and cowardly and
indifferent,
Which, from devoted dreams, action
and endurance
Gives birth to the only man who
helps...[157]
Stefan George

The new Reich creates the creative German man. For every creation there is required a basic thought which gives him significance, a matter which may obtain form, and the power which produces the act.

---

[157] [*Das neue Reich*, 'Der Dichter in Zeiten der Wirren'].

To develop the idea of the new Reich in its manifold all-effective unity was the chief task of this work. Inner vision, unrelenting observation and scientific knowledge are the means with which it worked. The application of purely scientific methods was already not possible for the reason that the main goal of the work is not scientific but political: it does not serve merely the crystallisation of the idea, but also the elaboration of the matter in which it should obtain shape: in the living man. To him whom the longing for a higher humanity, for living reality, for form-giving morality, fills with unrest should be offered the direction of attack which upto the moment is lacking in his will ready for action.

This goal of self-consciousness and of the rousing of those who are inwardly prepared was unattainable for the author through sole application of scientific methods. Observing description of the present had to alternate with the explanation of its historical roots. Demands for the future were to be founded only on prescient insight into the conditions of the German soul. Final certainty was to be attained only from faith. Thus the splitting of the methodology became necessary. Science will call him a dilettante, the politician of the day a dreamer. And yet he is prepared to bear these objections with patience, because they confirm precisely that which had to be proved here: the breaking up of the façade and the appearance side of German life.

The friends of worn out words, the preservers of pointed pens, and the protectors of contradictory dialectics may take out stone after stone from the edifice erected here and examine individuals for their quality. Many may not yet be trimmed, in the next the necessary emphases may be missing, and again others may perhaps lack inner hardness. To these dissections at pleasure a check was placed which should also be a hindrance to their passionately conducted manual labour: the indeed moderately used, but nevertheless numerous, citations prove the timelessness of the world-view developed in this work, are evidences that even in the present day the author does not in any way stand alone in his efforts. One, however, who nevertheless does not wish to see the edifice itself, but persists captivated by individual building-blocks, does not belong to the readers whom the author wishes for himself.

There will be many who do not wish to admit the culturelessness of the civilisatory age in the present peak of its development; who, always belonging to the past, consider the 19th century as the final conclusion of wisdom; who do not recognize the mendacity of the verbal idealism sounding everywhere and intoxicate themselves with progress. They feel at ease in the world of the "professional philistine and of the thoroughly common man" (Alfred Weber). To them let their rest be granted. To those who do not wish to see, because they do not "hunt it", the author has hardly anything to say.

There are, however, also those who have already for a long time painfully felt the signs of the downfall, as this book indicates them, and therefore mourn. Woe, however, if they delight in this mourning! All too dangerous is the feeling of being better than one's surroundings. It can lead to a lifeless dreamland, but even to dimming of vision. Sunk in world-weariness, they do not see that the curtain of a new historical performance rustles open, whereas they wallow still embittered in remembrances become flaccid.

If, now, the glance of the author wanders beyond to those who should supply the real matter for the new creation, the decisive question raises itself in view of their slumbering or misled or strenuously chained powers: who among the German people is ready to go on the path to the new Reich, to dare the deed? This question must be brought to a conclusion, since political books are, to a certain extent, a makeshift, imperfect creations, a painful substitute, if they do not become the beginning of a deed. To conjure up the political powers which point to a better future means however to turn one's glance to the present situation of the German public life.

Since 1918 it has become customary to babble about the beginning of a new age. In fact, the revolution of 1918[158] only confirmed what had already

[158] [The Socialist Revolution of 1918 which overthrew the Hohenzollern monarchy and established the

been accomplished since the downfall of Bismarck: the passing over of the rule to the parties. Politicians who are used to think only in terms of parties, or in whose imagination the happiness of the German Reich coincides with the personal happiness of being a minister at one time, may feel the achievements of the revolution as the final conclusion of wisdom. They believe in the goal where in fact a new beginning just raises itself. They have "arrived" - most of them not only in the political sense but also in a very bourgeois one - and do not understand the basic dissatisfaction of larger circles. It goes well with them: therefore they consider the present order likewise as good. The formulas of the political reality are mostly much simpler than is believed.

Indeed one feels much imperfection oneself: but one reminds oneself of the haste in which the Weimar emergency structure was erected, speaks of blemishes which are easily to be wiped out. In addition, however, one talks persuasively of the famous example, it gets better and better, the age heals all wounds.

The Weimar Reich is however already burdened with desperate politics, its rulers limited in their freedom of action by enemy dictates. If the German people wish to maintain themselves, resistance forces are required which relentlessly rattle with the chains, kindle the life-will, and warningly swing the standard of freedom. A state in the situation of the German Reich requires an oppostion just as the sick man the doctor.

The dark impulse of resistance and of dissatisfaction has its causes not only in the foreign political distress of the German people. There are other torments which demand resolution. The confusion in the soul of the individual, the anarchy of society, the conflict between worth and unworthiness, have reached their high point. A comprehensive renewal movement of life goes to the battle front. The oppositional attitude grows accordingly beyond the purely political, reaches a higher level, from which the inner life of the German people can first

Weimar Republic (inaugurated on 19 January 1919)].

be newly envisioned and correctly comprehended.

The oppositional powers and groups in Germany are correspondingly manifold. In terms of parties, it is some parties of the right and some of the left which oppose the present-day political order and method of government. But whereas Communism follows a clear programme - no matter of what worth - , the right parties lack a consistency of world-view. To them belong legitimists, whose intellectual condition resembles increasingly more the royalistic movement of France in the 19th century. They feel perhaps that the dream of a great Germany scarcely agrees with the reestablishment of earlier conditions, and one also feels darkly that the purple cannot replace what the people are lacking. Even social reactionaries who cannot grasp that the patriarchical conditions belong to history find themselves isolated in those ranks. Others feel once again the threat of traditional cultural values without having the idea of a new culture of the whole; they therefore place themselves more in shelter from the cultural façade than from culture itself. Then come the pure worshippers of power, paying homage to the error that order already arises from power. Their goal is the national police-state as a substitute of the present-day system of force which is little determined in its outlines. Still others believe in the legend of the Jewish rule by conspiracy and hope all salvation from racial purity. This picture of world-view variety is basically Liberal, even if a few truly Conservative pillars rise from the radical stream. Nevertheless, this human reservoir contains the most valuable construction material. For, the feeling of the men flowing together here is pledged to value, and strives for the service of the people. Therefore even the national idea is the clasp which binds the conflicting elements.

This situation sometimes emerges as a national movement, sometimes as a party. Unfortunately, it has had a certain practical significance upto now only as a party. The form of the party is, however, difficult to manipulate for a basic opposition, indeed dangerous. For, it will always remain essential for the parliamentary system that it bind even the opposition, to a certain degree, to the existing order. Parliamentarianism demands a utilitarian opposition and not a world-view one. It is hard to combat the parties as social structures, and at the same time to affirm one's own party existence. In addition, the way to the two-party system is blocked already because there is with us a Centre party. And yet there remains nothing else for an opposition party but to take account of the system and to set itself in power. Perhaps it sacrifices itself, perhaps however it clears the path thereby to the basically oppositional movement.

Almost more important than the compulsorily chained parliamentary opposition are the resistance currents in the entire nation. Every individual one of them has arisen from a special situation, for which reason they march forward separated and could not yet think of striking in a united way. The most significant is the fact that the country people reject the present-day social and political order. The consequence of this circumstance has not yet been realized by the politicians of the present-day system, otherwise it would be hardly comprehensible that a man like Hellpach claims the peasant order as the real basis of every democracy and sets up certain hopes in view of this on the social democratic and the democratic party. The idea that the intellectual and social foundation of the present-day democracy can be false and therefore repel the country people does not come to him. He overlooks the metropolitan, bourgeois-Liberal, indeed atheistic, history of the development of democracy in Germany. In fact, country stands against state, home against asphalt, blood against abstract understanding in a battle of life and death.

The German middle class, based on the free power and the self-responsibility of the individual, belongs similarly to the step-children of this state, which would like to standardize, bureaucratize all and deprive them of independence. Even here an opposition is necessarily formed which can be buried only with the transformation of the state. In addition, there is the soil-rooted economy of an industrial sort, today crushed between the mill-stones of the trades union and the state bureaucracy. In order to rescue itself, it resorts to large economic forms, under the protection of high finance, which for its part enters into agreements with the bureaucracy and the trades unions. Even here the living personality is threatened, and only fundamental opposition can save it.

To the resistance movements of economics are added cultural ones. The Protestant Church was upto now impaired by the circumstance that its attitude of opposition was directed not only purely culturally, but also against the political form. However, after the historically traditional binding to the country-principalites has fallen, Protestantism may become aware of its cultural mission and dedicate its entire power to it. The danger exists, to be sure, that its Liberal heritage may avenge itself and not let a genuine Conservative attitude arise. This would occur more easily to Catholicism, if it were not bound to a political party whose position is to be understood only historically. In predominantly Catholic Austria, a Conservative party could develop itself from the power of a Seipel.[159] In the Reich, the Centre satisfies itself with preserving ecclesiastical interests by way of parliamentary co-operatives and making Catholic personal politics. It is becoming high time - and all signs point to this - that the truly conservative, supratemporal powers of Catholicism swing towards the front against individualistic disintegration.

Nearby stand purely intellectual powers of a national political and cultural sort. The national cultural politics whose task is the maintenance of the national cultural body, strengthening and intensifying of the national cultural feeling, culminates in the idea of a large Germany and in the idea of a great European Reich. Even it can carry out its intellectual world only in opposition against the internal and external political present. Finally, in science, philosophy, poetry and art, creative efforts are stirring which tend to a new realisation of value and, for that reason, battle vulgarisation. This is the attitude of opposition which has

---

[159] [Ignaz Seipel (1876-1932) Austrian Federal Chancellor of the coalition government, 1922-24 and leader once again in 1926. Seipel was a critic of the parliamentary democratic system and aimed at strengthening the Austrian Heimwehr].

experienced in the last years the strongest growth and the most powerful consolidation.

The social movement, insofar as it was embodied by Marxism, has in the meanwhile been wrecked. Its spring has been impaired, its leaders woo for reception into the sacrosanct circle of Republican beneficiaries, renewing strenuously from time to time the empty cannonade of revolutionary statements which should encourage the combatant in the trench of the social war. The working class, more helpless than little children without leaders, threatens to fall into petty bourgeois dullness. German Communism is the protest against this levelling out of social powers. However, ever since it has become an outpost of Russian imperialism, succumbing to a people betraying corruption, it stands almost insignificant against the well-ordered democratic Socialism with its enormous bureaucratic power and its powerful sources of support. Earlier imperceptibly, and now with contemptuous openness, German Socialism concludes its peace with high finance at the cost of the national economy. Human history never saw a more pathetic collapse of a revolutionary ideology, of a moral basic idea. One who, contented, realises the bourgeoisisation of the worker, does not see that it is indeed a matter of an incidental injury of the most valuable social powers, which should really strive against the enslavement to money. Thus the emphasis of the social attitude of resistance shifts from Socialism over to the blood-related powers of agriculture, to those of the middle class and of the culture pledged to the personality, to the national cultural personages of the national cultural politicians. But the hour is to be anticipated when the German manual worker is summoned to the reckoning. Today indeed within the fully liberalised Socialism conservative powers are stirring which sense the new front and recognize that only the organic state can incorporate the working class into the living nation.

A post-war phenomenon, especially significant for our age, is the military movement. It is the answer to the disarmament forced by external powers, but also the resistance against the internal German pacifism. Its special task within the

German opposition is the maintenance of the inner defence and of the sense of militant fatefulness. Most of the associations arisen after the war want to be understood as islands of manly virtue in the middle of the stream of the downfall. The will to truthfulness, however, is not a political programme. Because the past was military, parts of the military movement tend to want to revive it also politically. This all-too powerful sinking into the past has made the military movement incapable of collecting the people on a broader front. It has helped to maintain not only past values but also outmoded oppositions. Thus it comes about that most of the associations have become "neighbouring houses" of the great party edifices which still mark the present-day front positions like a stronghold. Neither party nor popular movement, captivated in the problematic nature of their years of development (1918-1920), they stand today on a side-track.

Thereby this situation is especially valuable in terms of power. It contains in its ranks those whom the war-experience stamped. Certainly, the war-experience is not a uniform experience; it operated differently and formed perhaps even opposed types. Its moral worth, however, it will always have as the provider of the power of the longing to advance towards a new character and genuine morality. The war gave birth to the new active man so typical of the present-day European picture. Certainly, even its worth was already prefigured; but, as everywhere, so even here the war became the trigger of an entire movement. One may think of the determined powers with which the trained volunteer youth, hardly escaped from the barrage, robbed of their shoulder pieces by mutineers, set themselves to protect the collapsing state in 1918. The state, as the form serving to national self-maintenance, stood higher to those young men than the opinions which they had on its prospects. In this way they consolidated the rule of those who were opposed to their own existence: monarchists glued the republic with their blood. At the same time, however, they pushed towards the borders which were everywhere threatened by avaricious beneficiaries of the German collapse. The will to the protection of the border had to be bullied out of the rulers; not gladly was the permission granted to be able to die for the German land. Seldom did history see such a strong acknowledgement of the idea of the state as such. To defend the state as an abstract idea with their blood, that those youth could do; to form it actually anew, to fill it with new content, was not given to them to do.

The state of Weimar did not understand how to bind those young forces, to whom the idea of service had become their life-content, to itself or indeed to enlist them for the goal of German liberation. One cannot free oneself of the painful feeling that the rulers of today have an unconscious fear of a free and powerful people. According to the famous political principle of Machiavelli, the powerless foundation of November 1918 operates disastrously in the present-day Reich. Somehow it is the powers of defeatism which bear this state along and - as contradictory as this may sound - at the same time disintegrate it. Therefore, for it, the affirmers of manly tragedy have become superfluous. Once, in 1923, it was brought into action and hoped for the collapse of the world of Versailles. From deepest need something like the will to national self-maintenance pressed to the surface. In all its levels, the German people were ready to subordinate personal destiny to the common one. The state leaders however did not dare anything. They did not tear their souls aloft from the masses; matter triumphed when the blood-battle on the Ruhr[161] became a battle for money. The figures of some martyrs rise solitarily from the ruined field of that time. With the conclusion of the Ruhr battle, the military movement lost its foreign political task; the state shook it off, denied or persecuted it. The vehmic murder trials[162] form the sad signal for the end of this development. The military movement was wrecked, no goal beckoned any more, and helplessness became its characteristic. The young

---

[161] [The Ruhr battle of 1923 was provoked by the occupation of Germany's leading mining and manufacturing territory by French and Belgian troops when Germany lagged behind in its war-reparation payments. The occupation was suspended by the Dawes Plan of 1925].

[162] [the secret tribunal instituted to judge the political assassinations conducted by Buchrucker, a retired Royal Prussian major, in Prussia between 1922 and 1923 to free Germany from its foreign oppressors and their accomplices, the Prussian police. Buchrucker was sentenced to ten years' imprisonment for high treason, but was later granted pardon by President Hindenburg].

generation perhaps thirsted for redeeming action for its people, who had grown dull. But, without intellectual help, it stood against an age which derided the longings of its blood and its dreams of a new nobility. Whose laws meant: rest and the earning of a livelihood. Then many were overcome by doubt. Simple soldierly natures who had become heroes at the head of storming-parties conducted bungling internal politics. Others withdrew disappointed in order to rescue something at least for their own future from the pacified times. Still others believed that, in order to be able to "co-operate with the state" they should adapt to the new order of the temple. Many hoped, with inward reservations, to be able to slip into this system. All too late did they recognize that it is a machine which crushes everyone who approaches it. The catchphrase of co-operation with the state revealed itself as a clumsy decoy; for, what was meant was the train-bearer service in the party.

In this way it could not fail to appear what the destiny of those activistic youth would be: the old in spirit, become quiet in 1918, once again raised their heads and bound anew to themselves those disappointed by the Weimar state, through an appeal to their national feeling. The most valuable powers were thus consolidated, old enthusiasts of the military and young ones enthusiastic of success sank into a fruitless denial. A good part, however, threw themselves into the arms of radicalism. Not on account of their ideas and on account of their goals, which mostly were lacking; but only out of a protest against the inactivity and the dullness of the bourgeois politicians. The right radicalism displayed a chain of misfortunes which it owed not to superiour opponents but to their own incompetence. But nevertheless its activity drew the youth magnetically to itself, defying all the laws of political reason. One should have become clear in Germany on the fact that here the essential characteristic of the 20th century comes to expression: the active, ready for action, prepared for sacrifice, man enters in place of the indifferent, ballot-bearer of weak character, who has remained as the last remnant of the formal democratic age. Activism against quietism, vitality against dullness, is the battle cry of a new age which is moved more by feeling than it is ruled by deliberation. If the champions of a clear, reasonable, national politics persist in a quietistic attitude, the feeling-impelled activism will, even if its goals may appear so unreasonable, tread over it. It is the tragedy of 1930 that in Germany there is only an activism without clear guiding principles, but no objective reasonable politics of an active stamp. The destiny of the German people will depend on the fact that reason and feeling contract no weakening compromise with each other, but an honour which increases in effectiveness.

Beginnings to such a development are present. A great part of the activistic youth have drawn their lessons from the experiences of the last decade. They are indeed ready to defend the state at any time with their body, but now under other conditions: with their own responsibility and with their own political will. The merely activistic persons have, in the meanwhile, become political men, their mobility of feeling became an impulse to intellectual striving for renewal. These youth felt the pulse of a coming age and wanted to remove with their hands the veil of their future history. They do not love the state of Weimar, but defend themselves against the falsifying interpretation of this attitude. One can however love the state, insofar as this is, in general, thinkable, without affirming its present form. Out of a love for the state one can indeed combat a certain form with all one's power, if it does not represent the pure embodiment of the spirit of the people. This fact must be set against the present-day propaganda. It is dishonorable to brand as hostile to the state everyone who does not wish to be a tiny hair in the blanket of interests which calls itself the present-day German state.

Thus arose a situation, in no way organized, of thinking people who sought to recognize the last causes of the downfall and pondered over new forms with a burning heart and a cool head. The work of the thinking persons from the war-generation encountered the understanding of people of the same mind from the older generation. Both worked together, acting in their own way, while the foolhardy came to a standstill. The quiet combatants recognized that we do not live in an age of the unconditional; that their power can be made useful only when that which ferments in them in their blood has won a purposeful clarity and shape through the intellectual work of those who can sift the problems. Therewith that gap began to close which was responsible for the impairing of the German opposition: the lack of intellectual leadership.

The powerful work of raising the present-day Germany from its brittle world-view pivots can succeed only if a new idea works in a significant manner, and the new world-view is formed. Upto now only beginnings were present towards this, valuable partial work was performed in all fields. It was the task of this work to produce a uniform framework which can take up all the individual work and partial performance into itself. With its help, uncertain ideas should be solidified into clear outlines. The hour of the quiet combatant has come, resistance turns from denial to steadfastness of purpose. The moment all scattered opposition powers find themselves together under a higher leadership the destiny of the present-day society and of state order is decided. With stormy steps - what do a few years mean here? - we approach the turning point. A new leadership, whose lack since Bismarck's downfall was the tragic fate of the German people, is in the process of becoming. It will first of all have to be carried out within the resistance movement. A stubborn battle between the old in spirit who defend their oppositional partial field with senile doggedness and the young bearers of a new feeling of the whole, which makes possible the overview of the arrangement of powers in the German people, will flare up. It will be so much more quickly decided, the more eagerly the present-day leaders go down. The hour will strike at one time when even the patient German remarks that there is no more serious offence than the incompetence of leaders. Among the leaders of second rank are many willing ones who wait for only that person who orders their partial striving into a greater combination with the whole. The intellectual powers must therefore enter more strongly into the foreground than upto now and, to a certain degree, set forth openly its competence for leadership.

Opposition means not denial, but affirmation and the establishment of that which should enter in place of the thing combatted. Opposition is the gleaming standard of a new idea which should lead out of the desert into a fruitful land. Opposition at this hour is not a mere "will to rule oneself" but a striving for power for the sake of a clear goal. Would the position of the German people be basically improved if men assumed the leadership of them who were different from the state leaders upto now perhaps only in the fact that they sing a strophe of a national song instead of the morning litany? This erroneous belief which rules the nationalistic camp today cannot be destroyed ruthlessly enough. The establishment of the true community of the people is not possible by way of a compromise between the parties either; the people are not the sum of the parliamentary factions. But also not by way of the seizure of power and of an educational dictatorship by "nationalistic" men. Both ideas betray a captivation in mechanistic thought. The first ended with that politics of the Centre (towed along by Socialism) which does not in general give evidence of a will to leadership any longer, but is a mixture of bad administration, thoughtless continuance of work and well-calculated distribution of sinecures. The laws were directed against this conception of the community of the people. But not in order to oppose to it the correct ones: one wished to advance to the community of the people from the right precisely in the same way as the others from the centre. It was perhaps correctly recognized that wrong internal boundary demarcations had to be removed, that the powers tending naturally to state maintenance were to be made serviceable once again to the political life. But, in practice, the politicians fell constantly back into the party political position. One could not deny one's starting point, one spoke of the people and meant the party. Thus the powers of the resistance were uselessly squandered, indeed supplied in effect to the opponents. The much attacked foreign minister Stresemann lived in truth on the incompetence of his political antagonists. The only platform which remains for the reestablishment of the inner unity of the German people is of another sort: it consists in the birth of a new myth of nationality, leadership and service; in the consciousness of having to increase a cultural heritage; in the historical feeling of being able to gift Europe a new justice. Only on a higher plane which leaves behind it the current crowding of world-view remnants, doctrines and illusions, can the powers of the German national soul form a new reality. The lever must be set up from outside. For the renewer of German life the current party differences do not exist. He knows only German men who follow false words and must be brought under a standard of the people, no matter which army leader they have hitherto listened to. But precisely for this reason the renewer is the opposite of the compromiser. He introduces rather the true division of minds in order to mercilessly destroy the madness. But he sees the latter everywhere, not just, as the present-day parties do, outside one's own party. He will never believe in the victory of a party, never consider as possible the breakthrough to an organic world-picture from a limited angle. One who is of good will, one who does not cling to the outmoded, one who presses towards worth and order, one who longs for new morality, belongs in the camp of German renewal, no matter where he comes from. In this way does the new community of the people represent itself: not as a middle line of the falsely arranged political powers but as the penetration of all Germans with the idea of a new valuableness.

But what do the present-day masters of Germany think of the ever increasing waves of resistance? At first they actually wanted to be convinced of defending the new state against revolutionaries and reactionaries. They lived still in the long overcome idea of the battle for the form of the state. They did not remark that the republic in Germany is uncontested, that it is only a question of its mind and its content. They misunderstood all opposition currents because they could not observe anything else through their spectacles of resentment, without which they did not, their whole life long, take a glimpse at German politics. Now, after the crisis of German political life has become apparent, even they, to be sure, raise their voices and praise German renewal. But the observant audience of this sonorous renewal music hears the false undertones and feels that it is an empty demonstration for the appeasement of the public. In order to overcome those who proceed earnestly to reforms, our masters have passed over to methods which would do honour to the Inquisition, which Metternich would scorn as mindless. Their tense flight into the arms of force typifies inner uncertainty. One has not yet noted the change of roles: the standard of freedom is today borne by the opposition, the police state, the semi-Socialistic state of Weimar, is reduced to reaction and force. In comfortable times even the weakling wants to "rule". But the times begin to become uncomfortable. Too difficult are the tasks to be resolved, the cry for leadership too common. One knows in the German nation that it indeed has many ministers, but it has seldom been so leaderless in its history. The prescient knowledge of this situation completely impairs the otherwise weak will to lead of the rulers. Thus we approach the juncture which stormily demands solutions.

Every revolution is dependent in its success on the fact that not only the attackers possess power but also that the garrison of the stronghold is impaired in its will to power. All revolutions begin from above: with the rulers' prohibition of shooting. Nothing injures the will to maintenance of the current power-holders more than the self-felt incapacity of becoming the master of the situation. The crisis itself can be of an internal- and foreign political sort. The economic and social difficulties have already today grown over the heads of the present rulers. They must let themselves be told by foreign countries, that Germany must be reformed, and do not have the power to carry out this work against the parties. But the present-day system is not even equal to foreign political disturbances. One who has observed carefully the current attitude of the Weimar politicians in military questions must come to the conclusion that the case of the war requires the removal of the present-day method of government, if the German people should not be exterminated from the earth. There remains therefore only one way out of encountering powerful conflicts: by approaching the inner renewal at the right time, and energetically. Whether the decisive revolution happens gradually and peacefully or volcanically depends less on the attackers than on the rulers. In their hand lies immediately the destiny of the German people. Seldom in history has a method of government found so little affirmation in the people as the present one. If the leadership nevertheless opposes the cry for reform and can afford to persist in reactionary ossification, then this is so only due to the intellectual inadequacy of the opponents. The restructure of the social and political forms will become possible - apparently peacefully - the moment that the clenched power of a new intellectual world and of a resolute will challenges the swaying instability of today to a decision. The pacifists of life believe in self-active development. They forget that there may be such a thing in spiritual matters, that it must however be followed in the field of the social by the seizure of power and formation, if a dying principle should be replaced by a new one. With Lasalle we call this process revolution. Whether thereby a wrong development is interrupted, whether the oppositions will be fought out in an intellectual or in a blood battle, whether the people rebel against their weak leader, or whether the leadership itself puts its shoulder to the wheel of history, all these are subordinate questions. The force of the revolutionary thought alone settles the matter. Men who have comprehended the significance of the turning point can support themselves on the longing for redemption of the people and their own vocation, and will remove the decomposing leadership. The more unreasonably and violently the power-holders shut themselves off from the demands of a new age, the harder will the fate of the necessary purification burden German life. Instead of breaking out in laments on childish Putsch-ists, the rulers of today should have become clear on the fact that it is their inadequacy which produces hard decisions.

If a government which feels itself responsible only for the German people and the hour is formed without consideration of the party wishes, if it is endowed with the necessary total power, then it would have the people on its side. If the Parliament opposed their work of reform, then it could be attempted to make government elections. The people would hail the one who had the courage to drive out the spectre of the party with a hard hand. This development preserving the forces of the German people can only be wished for in its interest.

Much valued is another possibility of bringing in the revolution: the young forces should penetrate into the parties and conquer them. Experiences upto now and the insight into the inner nature of the party state make this way appear as almost without prospect. A variety of such a reflection is the idea of founding a new party. If this is considered as a goal in itself, it would incorporate itself into the general party system, then this would mean wanting to drive out the Devil with Beelzebub. More useful is the plan of a party of orders which aims only at conquest and renewal of the state. It requires political impetus, great mobility, basic community of character, and skilled leadership, to attain the goal with the help of such a party. It would, with regard to the people, be burdened with the fact of the new party formation, beset by the hostility of all the remaining parties.

Thus there still remains the extra-parliamentary popular movement, a way which different associations have set out on. Their procedure is different from the Austrian militia in a double aspect. First, in that they have not succeeded in becoming a broadly established popular movement. Somehow they still remain bound, sometimes with ropes, sometimes with silk threads, to the party grouping of the German people. In addition, there is the differently disposed political situation in Austria: there one brings in now what was already forestalled in the Reich in 1919, the conflict with radical Marxism. In Austria, the conflict can be a basic one, since the division there between Communism and Socialism has not yet taken place. With us, it was a result of only the radical side, while the sneaking Marxism became the ruling component of politics.

There is no popular movement corresponding to the intellectual situation of the German people around 1930. What was attempted upto now from the right by way of advances had to fail because the necessary breadth was lacking. By that the numerical majority should not in any way be understood; that would mean paying homage to a materialism of numbers which would be inwardly opposed to the new world-view of superior worth. Only a minority can transform what moves us into political forms. But this minority must cleave the current world-view and party situation, must go through it entirely, must draw its power from all strata and orders. Its virtues and its readiness for action are what guarantee victory, not the number of hangers-on. This knowledge is lacking upto the moment in the German right-wingers. Why does it not sharpen the bright sword of the mind, instead of counting votes and windproof jackets? It is bitter to have to establish that intellectual accomplishment is so gladly scorned by nobody so much as by the politicians of the right. Here lies the reason why they - in foreign policy, without justification - have arrived at the summons of empty worshippers of force. The pressure of the party programme, of social advantages, of intellectual formulas, is impressive precisely in the right. With that one would be in the position of setting all the powers of personality and of intellectual freedom against the backward rule of force of the left-wingers. Unfortunately, the right gives up this fortunate opportunity and treats the few who work for a new world of ideas for the people and the state in principle badly. In the youth it sees only zealous young men whom one pats on the shoulder with superiour goodwill and to whom one holds out the prospect of entering the Parliament as grandfathers. It of course takes into account the development of a new world, but only for matters of the party or association. The most dangerous deviation from their own basic ideas remained reserved to the military associations: they, who however only wanted to operate through manliness and selection, seize the ballot as an emergency weapon, that dagger of the unheroic which does not have the courage to hold high its world-view in the flood of inferiority. But the hour seems to come closer when the insight won in bitter defeat grows; when there is space for a new mind and new men. For it is not that the war-generation sleeps or rejects its leadership task. It has become thoughtful and waits until the time is ripe.

The most important instrument of the public opinion, the press, is not, to be sure, at its disposal. It was therefore impossible for it upto now to form that focus of oppositional forces around which these could have grouped. What is the use, however, of all intellectual prepatory work if their effectiveness is limited to the publicistic aspect? The power-holders of the press are unfortunately no believers in the mind. They refuse their trust to the same youth who entrusted their entire existence to it on the battle field and in the civil war. Especially the situation of the economy is of a disturbing lack of belief in the power of the spiritual. Credulous, on the other hand, is one with regard to the person who conjures up organisatory Potemkin-like villages. Nothing is more beloved than the question of what "stands" behind a politician. The ambitious reply that they are sketching a scintillating backdrop. On that then a dubious undertaking is built up which, after a short while, is wrecked. The association swindle is a dangerous sickness of our age. But the credulity of leading men is moving. They look less at the head and heart of the person standing before them than at his mouth. And the swindling of political naïvety repeatedly succeeds. Thus there is, in the camp of the right and the associations, masters of direction who do nothing else but regroup once again the same patient national masses. The building of formations has become a favorite game of organisers without an occupation. In spite of all bad experience, the insight has steadily prevailed that a head with one idea is worth more than hundred consecrations of flags. But, nevertheless, one organises once again diligently. If the small organisation stands, then there comes the breaking of heads over the political programme. So that the organised masses do not disperse, an "action" is decided on. As if horse movements were the chief task of the cavalry! One fills revolutionary heat to a certain degree into thermos flasks; if one opens them they are empty. But where did organising ever precede the idea? The idea always lives first and then creates for itself, in goal-conscious action, the marching troop.

The associations which owe their existence to the political camp of the immediate post-war years are today to be valued still only as material, no longer as the bearer of a new German destiny. They have fulfilled their mission, are heralds of a deeper, greater coming popular movement. The new age demands new ideas and new methods. The future belongs to the few who bear in their heart and brain the guarantee of a revolution to the better. One who devotes himself to the mastery of superiority, must foster faith in the victory of the mind; must bear solitude and be able to wait for the historic hour; must touch the feeling of the people and sense when it is ready to perform its adherence. If the time is ripe, the redeeming formulas are easily coined. In the first assault then succeeds what gossiping popular assemblies could not the whole year long. It would be useless to want to break the bitter resistance of all the beneficiaries of the present-day conditions by persuasion. For, all who feared the renewer draw together in quiet, tenacious defence. All means of power are set up against him. The law of numbers, the majority stands against him. And yet, capacity and purity of will will force the people once the age is ripe for men.

On nobody did an age place more demands than on its overcomer. Renunciation and pride are the only attitude which guarantees success. But history is an undeceiving proof of the correctness of the way which we traverse. Even if we succumb to the tragedy of the pioneer, if the glimpse into the extolled land is prohibited to us, still there remains for us the inner certainty that the power of the facts will at one time vindicate us. Swaying between wish and goal, we will perhaps never participate in fulfilment. It may be that the division of the age may become the divison of our political life, that we may remain to our death "wanderers between two worlds". But do we not ourselves teach the tragic as the basis of all existence? Who then gives us the right to cast it away from our petty life?

To those however who prejudge that such personal sacrifice is useless, that we squander our forces instead of adapting ourselves intellectually to our age, to those we young people oppose the simple answer: we cannot do anything else. For what drives us to our position lies outside our reckoning. The powers which move us lead an incomprehensible and, for that reason, so much more real life. As they command, so must we fulfil ourselves.

Perhaps the turn will only succeed when tragedy once again is held up as a model. If the German people see that, among them, combatants still live, then they become aware also of combat as the highest form of existence. The German destiny calls for men who master it. For, world-history makes the man. The formative impulse streaming from the suprasensual realms works through itself; so much the more, the more formless an age is. If it remains undisturbedly fixed on the high goal of a higher humanity, then will the hour strike also for the German people in which we believe with highest and desperate zeal. And only to this zeal are the gates to the new Reich opened.

BIBLIOGRAPHY

I. Edgar Julius Jung[1]

Die geistige Krise des jungen Deutschland. Rede vor der Studentenschaft der Universität München, Berlin, Verlag Der Student - Deutsche Akademische Stimmen, 1926.

Die Herrschaft der Minderwertigen. Ihr Zerfall und ihre Ablösung. Berlin, Verlag Deutsche Rundschau, 1927.

Die Herrschaft der Minderwertigen. Ihr Zerfall und ihre Ablösung. Berlin, Verlag Deutsche Rundschau, 1929/30.

Föderalismus aus Weltanschauung, Berlin und Leipzig, J. Schweitzer Verlag, 1931.

(ed.) *Deutsche über Deutschland. Die Stimme des unbekannten Politikers*, München, Albert Langen-Georg Müller Verlag, 1932.

Sinndeutung der deutschen Revolution, Oldenburg, Gerhard Stalling, 1933.

The speech that Jung wrote for Papen is available, as 'Marburger Rede Papens v. 17. Juni 1934', in *Der Prozeß gegen die Hauptkriegsverbrecher vor dem Internationalem Militärgerichtshof, Nürnberg 14. Nov. 1945 bis 1. Okt. 1946.* Amtlicher Text. Deutsche Ausgabe, Bd.XL Nürnberg 1949, Dokument Papen, pp. 543-58. It is also printed in E. Forschbach, *Edgar J. Jung: ein konservativer Revolutionär 30. Juni 1934*, Pfullingen, 1984, pp.154-174. An English translation of the same is to be found in O. Dutch, *The Errant Diplomat: The life of Franz von Papen*, London, 1940, pp.191-209.

---

[1] This list includes only Jung's books and not his several articles. For a complete bibliography of the latter see B. Jenschke, *Zur Kritik der konservativ-revolutionären Ideologie in der Weimarer Republik: Weltanschauung und Politik bei Edgar Julius Jung*, München, 1971.

II. Intellectual Relations

Aeroboe, Friedrich *Agrarpolitik*, Berlin, 1928.

Aust, Oskar *Die Reform der öffentlichen Verwaltung in Deutschland*, Berlin, 1928.

Balzac, Honoré de *Scènes de la vie de campagne*, Paris, 1845.

Bente, Hermann *Organisierte Unwirtschaftlichkeit*, Jena, 1929.

Benz, Richard *Die Stunde der deutschen Musik*, Jena, 1927.

Berdiaiev, Nikolai, *La philosophie de l'inégalité, lettres aux adversaires en philosophie sociale* (in Russian), Berlin, 1923.
Das neue Mittelalter, Darmstadt, 1927.
Le nouveau Moyen Âge, Lausanne, 1985.
Christianity and Anti-Semitism, N.Y., 1954.
The Destiny of Man, London, 1959.
Freedom and the Spirit, N.Y., 1935.
The Meaning of History, Cleveland, 1962.
Solitude and Society, London, 1938.
Spirit and Reality, London, 1946.
The realm of the spirit and the realm of Caesar, N.Y., 1952.

Bie, Richard *Revolution und Karl Marx*, Leipzig, 1929.

Bismarck, Otto von *Gedanken und Erinnerungen*, 2 vols., Stuttgart, 1828.

Blüher, Hans *Die Theorie der Religionen und ihres Untergangs*, Berlin-Tempelhof, 1912.
Der Geist der Weltrevolution, Prien, 1920.

Böhmer, Rudolf *Das Erbe der Enterbten*, München, 1928.

Bott-Bodenhausen, Manfred *Formatives und funktionales Recht in der gegenwärtigen Kulturkrise*, Berlin, 1926.

Brauweiler, Heinz *Berufstand und Staat: Betrachtungen über eine neuständische Verfassung des deutschen Staates*, Berlin, 1925.

Brunner, Emil "Die Krisis im Protestantismus", *Süddeutsche Monatshefte*, Bd.25,ii (1928), pp.638-42.

Brunstäd, Friedrich *Die Idee der Religion: Principien der Religionsphilosophie*, Halle, 1922.

Bryce, James, Viscount *Modern Democracies*, 2 vols., London, 1921.

Cassel, Gustav *Theoretische Sozialökonomie*, Leipzig, 1921.

Chamberlain, H.S. *Politische Ideale*, München, 1915.

Coudenhove-Kalergi, Richard Graf von *Paneuropa*, Wien, 1926.
Paneuropa, 1922 bis 1966, Wien, 1966.
History of the Paneuropean movement, Basle, 1962.

Diesel, Eugen *Der Weg durch das Wirrsal*, Stuttgart, 1926.

Dingler, Hugo *Der Zusammenbruch der Wissenschaft und der Primat der Philosophie*, München, 1926.

Dostoievski, F. *The Brothers Karamazov*, tr. C. Garnett, London, 1912.

Fahsel, Kaplan *Ehe, Liebe und Sexualproblem*, Freiburg, 1928.

Fehr, Hans *Recht und Wirklichkeit: Einblick in Werden und Vergehen der Rechtsformen*, Zürich, 1928.
"Krisis der Justiz", *Süddeutsche Monatshefte*, Heft 4 (1929).

Fichte, J.G. *Reden an die deutsche Nation*, Hamburg, 1955.

Flügge, Ludwig "Die rassenbiologische Bedeutung des Adels und das Prinzip der Immunisierung", *Süddeutsche Monatshefte*, Bd.23,i (1925/26), pp.403-9.

Ford, Henry *My Life and Work*, Garden City, N.Y., 1922.

Frantz, Constantin *Kritik aller Parteien*, Berlin, 1862.
Die Widerherstellung Deutschlands, Berlin, 1865.
Die Naturlehre des Staates als Grundlage aller Staatswischenschaften, Leipzig, 1870.
Das neue Deutschland, Berlin, 1871.

Freyer, Hans *Revolution von rechts*, Jena, 1931.

Gattineau, Heinrich *Verstädterung und Arbeiterherrschaft*, Berlin, 1929.

George, Stefan, *Gesamtausgabe der Werke*, 18 vols., Berlin, 1927-34.
  Poems, tr. C.N. Valhope and E. Morwitz, N.Y., 1943.

Giese, Fritz *Die Frau als Atmosphärenwert*, München, 1926.

Gleichen, Heinrich von "Opposition und Nation", *Der Ring*, 1928.

Gneist, Rudolf von *Das heutige englische Verfassungs- und Verwaltungsrecht*, Berlin, 1857.

Göring, Helmut *Tocqueville und die Demokratie*, München, 1928.

Haller, Karl Ludwig von *Restauration der Staatswissenschaft oder Theorie des natürlichen Zustandes, der Chimäre des künstlich-bürgerlichen entgegengesetzt*, 6 Bde., 1816-34.

Haushofer, Albrecht "Paneuropa - Völker und Staaten", *Staat und Volkstum*, Berlin, 1926.

Heller, Hermann *Europa und der Faschismus*, Berlin, 1929.

Hellpach, Willy *Politische Prognose für Deutschland*, Berlin, 1928.

Herder, J.G. *Werke*, ed. B. Suphan, Berlin, 1877-1913.

Herrfahrdt, Heinrich *Das Problem der berufsständischen Vertretung von der Französischen Revolution bis zur Gegenwart*, Stuttgart, 1921.

Hitler, Adolf *Mein Kampf*, München, 1925.
  Mein Kampf, N.Y., 1939.
  Reden und Proklamationen 1932-1945, 2 Bde., ed. M. Domarus, Würzburg, 1962.
  Speeches and Proclamations, tr. M.F. Gilbert, London, 1990.

Horneffer, Ernst *Die große Wunde*, München, 1922.

Hübscher, Arthur "Lagarde über Neugestaltung des Adels", *Süddeutsche Monatshefte*, Bd.23,i (1925/26), pp.410-13.

Humboldt, Wilhelm von *Ideen zu einem Versuch die Grenzen der Wirksamkeit des Staates zu bestimmen*, Breslau, 1851.

Ihering, Rudolf von *Der Geist des römischen Rechts auf den verschiedenen Stufen seiner Entwicklung*, 3 Bde., Leipzig, 1852-58.
    Der Kampf ums Recht, Wien, 1872.
    Der Zweck im Recht, 2 Bde., Leipzig, 1877-83.

Jacobsen, Jens Peter *Niels Lyhne*, Copehnagen, 1880.

Jünger, Ernst *Der Kampf als inneres Erlebnis, Berlin, 1922.*
    Feuer und Blut. Ein kleiner Ausschnitt aus einer großen Schlacht, Hamburg, 1926.
    Der Arbeiter. Herrschaft und Gestalt, Heidelberg, 1932.

Kayserling, Hermann Graf von   "Das richtig gestellte Eheproblem", in *Das Ehebuch: eine neue Sinngebung im Zusammenklang der Stimmen führender Zeitgenossen,*

Kelsen, Hans *Vom Wesen und Wert der Demokratie*, Tübingen, 1929.

Kjellén, Rudolf *Der Staat als Lebensform*, Leipzig, 1917.

Kitson, Arthur *Unemployment: The cause and a remedy*, London, 1921.

Klages, Ludwig *Der Geist als Widersacher der Seele*, Leipzig, 1929-33.

Köhler, J.P. *Die Hindenburg-Linie und die Herrschaft der Mitte*, Leipzig, 1928.

Kretschmer, Ernst   *Körperbau und Charakter: Untersuchungen zum Konstitutionsproblem und zur Lehre von den Temperamenten*, Berlin, 1921.

Krieck, Ernst *Der Staat des deutschen Menschen*, Berlin, 1927.

Lagarde, Paul de *Deutsche Schriften*, Göttingen, 1886.

Leontiev, Constantin *Against the current: Selections from the novels, essays, notes and letters of Konstantin Leontiev*, ed. G. Ivask, tr. G. Reavey, N.Y., 1969.

List,   Friedrich   *Das   Wesen   und   der   Wert   einer   nationalen Gewerbsproduktivkraft*, Berlin, 1839.
    Das nationale System der politischen Ökonomie, Stuttgart, 1841.

Loesch, Karl Christian von   "Streben und Stil der Besiegten", *Deutsche Rundschau*, Okt. 1928, pp.1-21.

Lorenz, Ottokar "Karl Marx als Schrittmacher des Kapitalismus", *Süddeutsche Monatshefte*, Bd.25,i, (1927/28), pp.314-33.

Lubosch, W. "Der Spießburger und der Philister", *Süddeutsche Monatshefte*, Bd.24,ii (1927), pp.435-43.

Lüddecke, Theodor "Der Einfluss der Reklame auf das Antlitz der Kultur", *Deutsche Rundschau*, Oct. 1929.

Luther, Hans *Von Deutschlands eigener Kraft: Versuch einer gemeinverständlicher Darstellung unserer Lage in der Weltwirtschaft*, Berlin, 1928.

Mahraun, Arthur *Das Jungdeutsche Manifest. Volk gegen Kaste und Geld. Sicherung des Friedens durch Neubau der Staaten*, Berlin, 1927.

Marr, Heinz "Großstadt und politisches Lebensform. Ein Beitrag zur Soziologie des heutigen deutschen Parteiensystems" in *Großstadt und Volkstum. Vorträge d. 3. Tagung für Nationalerziehung von der Fichtegesellschaft veranstaltet vom 6.-9. März, 1927*, Hamburg, 1927, pp.75-152.
Klasse und Partei in der modernen Demokratie, Frankfurt a.M., 1925.
Proletarisches Verlangen: ein Beitrag zur Psychologie der Massen, Jena, 1921.

Marx, Karl; Engels, Friedrich *Gesamtausgabe*, Berlin, 1929ff.

Michels, Robert *Zur Soziologie des Parteiwesens*, Leipzig, 1925.

Moeller van den Bruck, Arthur *Das dritte Reich*, Hamburg, 1923.
Germany's Third Empire, tr. E.O. Lorimer, London, 1934.
Das Recht der jungen Völker, München, 1919.

Müller, Georg *Das neue Rechtsbuch der katholischen Kirche*, Langensalza, 1928.

Nietzsche, F. *Werke und Briefe*, München, 1933-42.
Complete Works, ed. O. Levy, London,

Pareto, Vilfredo *Trattato di sociologia generale, Firenze, 1916.*
The Mind and Society, New York, 1935.

Quabbe, George *Tar-a-Ri. Variationen über ein konservatives Thema*, Berlin, 1927.

Rabbethge, E. *Verfall oder Rettung?*, Magdeburg, 1923.

Radbruch, Gustav *Grundzüge der Rechtsphilosophie*, Leipzig, 1914.

Rathenau, Walter *Gesammelte Schriften*, 6 Bde., 1925-29.

Riehl, W.H. *Naturgeschichte des Volkes als Grundlage einer deutschen Socialpolitik*,
The Natural History of the German People, tr. D.J. Diephouse, Lewiston, 1990.

Rosenberg, Alfred *Der Mythus des 20. Jahrhunderts*, München, 1930.
Wesen, Grundsätze und Ziele der Nationalsozialistischen deutschen Arbeiterpartei, München, 1934.
Blut und Ehre: Ein Kampf für deutsche Wiedergeburt. Reden und Aufsätzen 1919-1933, ed. T. von Trotha, München, 1934.
Gestaltung der Idee. Blut und Ehre II. Band. Reden und Aufsätze von 1933-1935, ed. T. von Trotha, München, 1936.
Kampf um die Macht. Aufsätze von 1921-1932, ed. T. von Trotha, 1937.
Tradition und Gegenwart. Reden und Aufsätze 1936-1940. (Blut und Ehre IV. Band), ed. T. von Trotha, München, 1941.

Scheffen-Döring, Luise *Frauen von heute*, Leipzig, 1931.

Schiffer, Eugen *Die deutsche Justiz: Grundzüge einer durchgreifenden Reform*, Berlin, 1928.

Schwabach, E.E. *Revolutionierung der Frau*, Leipzig, 1928.

Schlung, P.E. "Krisis im Katholizismus"?, *Süddeutsche Monatshefte*, Bd.25,ii (1928), pp.633-38.

Schmitt, Carl *Politische Romantik*, München, 1919.
Political Romanticism, tr. G. Oakes, Cambridge, Mass., 1986.
Die geistesgeschichtliche Lage des heutigen Parlamentarismus, München, 1923.
The crisis of parliamentary democracy, tr. E. Kennedy, Cambridge, Mass., 1985.
Der Begriff des Politischen, Hamburg, 1927.
Verfassungslehre, München, 1928.

Sokolowski, Paul von *Die Versandung Europas: eine andere grosse russische Gefahr*, Berlin, 1929.

Sombart, Werner *Die Juden und das Wirtschaftsleben*, Leipzig, 1911.
  The Jews and modern capitalism, tr. M. Epstein, N.Y., 1962.
  Der Bourgeois. Zur Geistesgeschichte des modernen Wirtschaftsmenschen, München, 1913.
  Die Ordnung des Wirtschaftslebens, Enzyklopädie der Rechts- und Staatswissenschaft, Berlin, 1925.
  Deutscher Sozialismus, Charlottenburg, 1934.
  A new social philosophy, tr. K.F. Geiser, Princeton, N.J., 1937.

Sorel, George *Reflexions sur la violence*, Paris, 1908.

Spann, Othmar *Der wahre Staat. Vorlesungen über Abbruch und Neubau der Gesellschaft*, Leipzig, 1921.
  Fundament der Volkswirtschaftslehre, Jena, 1923.

Spengler, Oswald *Der Untergang des Abendlandes. Umrisse der Morphologie einer Weltgeschichte*, München, 1918-23.
  Preußentum und Sozialismus, München, 1920.
  Neubau des Reiches, München, 1924.
  Politische Schriften, München, 1932.
  Jahre der Entscheidung, I. Teil: Deutschland und die weltgeschichtliche Entwicklung, München, 1933.

Spranger, Eduard *Die Verschulung Deutschlands*, Leipzig,

Stapel, Wilhelm *Antisemitismus und Antigermanismus. Uber das seelische Problem der Symbiose des deutschen und des jüdischen Volkes*, Hamburg, 1928.
  Der christliche Staatsmann. Eine Theologie des Nationalismus, Hamburg, 1932.

Stegemann, Hermann *Das Trugbild von Versailles: weltgeschichtliche Zusammenhänge und strategische Perspektiven*, Stuttgart, 1926.

Steinhausen, Georg *Der politische Niedergang Deutschlands*, Osterwieck, 1927.

Stolper, Gustav *Das deutsche Wirtschaftsproblem*, Berlin, 1928.
  Ein Finanzplan: Vorschlag zur deutschen Finanzreform, Berlin, 1929.

Tocqueville, Alexis de *La démocratie en Amérique*, Paris, 1836.

Tönnies, Ferdinand *Gemeinschaft und Gesellschaft. Grundbegriffe der reinen Soziologie*, Berlin, 1926.

Turner, Jr., H.A. "Hitler's secret pamphlet for industrialists, 1927", *Journal of Modern History*, 40 (1968), pp.348-74.

Unamuno, Miguel de *L'agonía del Cristianismo*, Madrid, n.d.
Die Agonie des Christentums, München, 1928.

Weber, Max *Wirtschaft und Gesellschaft*, Tübingen, 1925.
Die protestantische Ethik und der Geist des Kapitalismus, Tübingen, n.d.
The Protestant ethic and the spirit of capitalism, tr. T. Parsons, London, 1930.
Gesammelte Politische Schriften, München, 1921.

Wiese, L. von "Liberalismus und Demokratie in ihren Zusammenhängen und Gegensätzen, *Zeitschrift für Politik*, Bd.9.

Winnig, August *Der englische Wirtschaftskrieg und das werktätige Volk Deutschlands*, Berlin, 1917.
Das Reich als Republik, 1918-1928, Berlin, 1928.

Ziegler, Leopold *Der europäische Geist*, Darmstadt, 1929.

III. Secondary Sources

Bergmann, W., Dittmar, W., etc. (ed.) *Soziologie im Faschismus, 1933-1945*, Köln, 1981.

Braatz, W.E. "Two neo-conservative myths in Germany 1919-1932: The 'Third Reich' and the 'New State'", *Journal of the History of Ideas*, 32 (1971), pp.569-84.

Dupeux, L. (ed.) *La Révolution conservatrice allemande sous la république de Weimar*, Paris, 1992.

Favrat, Jean *La pensée de Paul de Lagarde (1827-1891): Contribution à l'étude des rapports de la réligion et de la politique dans le nationalisme et le conservatisme allemande au XIXème siècle*, Paris, 1979.

Forschbach, Edmund *Edgar J. Jung: ein konservativer Revolutionär, 30. Juni 1934*, Pfullingen, 1984

Gerstenberger, H. *Der revolutionäre Konservatismus: Ein Beitrag zur Analyse des Liberalismus*, Berlin, 1969.

Grass, Friedrich "Der Politiker Edgar Julius Jung. Zum 25. Jahrestag seiner Ermordung - Ein Beitrag zur zeitgenössichen Geschichte", *Pfälzische Heimatblätter*, 6 (Juni 1959), 41-42.
"Edgar Julius Jung (1894-1934), *Pfälzische Heimatblätter*, 8, 63-64.

Herf, Jeffrey *Reactionary Modernism: Technology, culture, and politics in Weimar and the Third Reich*, Cambridge, 1984.

Jenschke, Bernhard *Zur Kritik der konservative-revolutionären Ideologie in der Weimarer Republik. Weltanschauung und Politik bei Edgar Julius Jung*, München, 1971.

Jones, Larry Eugene "Edgar Julius Jung: The conservative revolution in theory and practice", *Central European History*, 21 (1988), 142-174
"The limits of collaboration: Edgar Jung, Herbert von Bose, and the origins of the conservative resistance to Hitler, 1933-34", in *Between Reform, Reaction, and Resistance: Studies in the history of German conservatism from 1789 to 1945*, Oxford and Providence, R.I., 1993, 465-501.

Jones, L.E. and Retallack (ed.), *Between Reform, Reaction, and Resistance:*

Studies in the History of German Conservatism from 1789 to 1945, Oxford and Providence, R.I., 1993.

Klemperer, Klemens von *Germany's Conservatism. Its History and Dilemma in the Twentieth Century*, Princeton, NJ, 1957.
"Der deutsche Widerstand gegen den Nationalismus im Lichte der konservativen Tradition", in *Demokratie und Diktatur*, ed. M. Funke, H.-A. Jacobsen, H.-H.Knütter, H.-H. Schwarz, Düsseldorf, 1987, 266-284.

Koehl, Robert   "Feudal Aspects of National Socialism", *American Political Science Review*, 54 (1960), pp.921-33.

Knoll, J.H.   "Konservatives Krisenbewußtsein am Ende der Weimarer Republik. Edgar Julius Jung - Ein geistesgeschichtliches Porträt", *Deutsche Rundschau*, 1961, pp.930-40.

Kolb, Eberhard   *Die Weimarer Republik*, München, 1984.
The Weimar Republik, tr. P.S. Falla, London, 1988.

Kruse, Christina   *Die Volkswirtschaftslehre im Nationalsozialismus*, Freiburg im Breisgau, 1988.

Lebovics, Herman   *Social Conservatism and the Middle Classes in Germany, 1914-1933*, Princeton, NJ, 1969

Lukashevich, S.   *Konstantin Leontev 1831-1891: A Study in Russian 'Heroic Vitalism'*, N.Y., 1967.

Markovic, Marko   *La philosophie de l'inégalité et les idées politiques de Nicolas Berdiaev*, Paris, 1978.

Merlio, Gilbert   *Oswald Spengler: Témoin de son temps*, 2 vols., Stuttgart, 1982.

Möller, Horst   "Parlamentarismus-Diskussion in der Weimarer Republik: Die Frage des 'besonderen' Weges zum parlamentarischen Regierungssystem", in *Demokratie und Diktatur*, ed. M. Funke et al, 140-157.

Mohler, Armin   *Konservative Revolution in Deutschland, 1918-1932, Grundriß ihrer Weltanschauungen*, Stuttgart, 1950.

Mommsen, Hans   *Beamtentum im dritten Reich*, Stuttgart, 1966.

Mosse, G.L.   *The Nationalization of the Masses: Political symbolism and mass*

movements in Germany from the Napoleonic Wars through the Third Reich, N.Y., 1975.
"Der erste Weltkrieg und die Brutalisierung der Politik: Betrachtungen über die politische Rechte, den Rassismus und den deutschen Sonderweg", in M. Funke et al (ed.), *Demokratie und Diktatur*, 127-139.

Neuhrohr, Jean   *Der Mythos vom Dritten Reich. Zur Geistsgeschichte des Nationalsozialismus*, Stuttgart, 1959.

Noakes, Jeremy   "German conservatives and the Third Reich: an ambiguous relationship", in *The radical right and the establishment in twentieth-century Europe*, ed. M. Blinkhorn, London, 1990, pp.71-97.

Nolte, Ernst   "Konservatismus und Nationalsozialismus", *Zeitschrift für Politik*, Jg.11, Heft I (1964), pp.3-20.

Petzold, Joachim *Wegbereiter des deutschen Faschismus: Die Jungkonservativen in der Weimarer Republik*, Köln, 1978.

Phelan, Anthony (ed.)   *The Weimar Dilemma: Intellectuals in the Weimar Republic*, Manchester, 1985.

Raphaël, Freddy *Judaïsme et capitalisme. Essai sur la controverse entre Max Weber et Werner Sombart*, Paris, 1982.

Romoser, George   "The crisis of political direction in the German resistance to Nazism" (doct. diss., Univ. of Chicago, 1958).
"The politics of uncertainty", *Social Research*, 31 (1964), pp.73-93.

Schneller, Martin   *Zwischen Romantik und Faschismus: Der Beitrag Othmar Spanns zum Konservatismus in der Weimarer Republik*, Stuttgart, 1970.

See, Klaus von *Die Ideen von 1789 und die Ideen von 1914: Völkisches Denken in Deutschland zwischen französischer Revolution und erstem Weltkrieg*, Frankfurt am Main, 1975.

Sontheimer, Kurt   *Antidemokratisches Denken in der Weimarer Republik. Die politischen Ideen des deutschen Nationalismus zwischen 1918 und 1933*, München, 1962.
"Die Idee des Reiches im politischen Denken der Weimarer Republik", *Geschichte in Wissenschaft und Unterricht*, Jg.13 (1962), pp.205ff.
"Nationale und konservative Revolution", *Der Monat*, Jg.14 (1962/63), Heft 168, pp.22-32.

"Der 'Deutsche Geist' als Ideologie: Ein Beitrag zur Theorie vom deutschen Sonderbewußtsein", in M. Funke, et al (ed.), *Demokratie und Diktatur*, 35-45.

Stirk, S.D. *The Prussian Spirit: A Survey of German Literature and Politics*, 1914-1940, London, 1941.

Struve, Walter *Elites against Democracy. Leadership ideals in bourgeois political thought in Germany, 1890-1933*, Princeton, NJ, 1973.

Tschirschky, F.G. von *Erinnerungen eines Hochverräters*, Stuttgart, 1972.

Woods, Roger "The radical right: the conservative revolution in Germany", in *The nature of the Right: European and American politics and political thought since 1789*, ed. R. Eatwell and N. O'Sullivan, London, 1989, pp.124-145.

STUDIES IN GERMAN THOUGHT AND HISTORY

DATE DUE
